STANDING ON GUARD FOR THEE

THE PAST,
PRESENT AND
FUTURE OF
CANADA'S
CHRISTIAN RIGHT

MICHAEL WAGNER

Copyright © Freedom Press Canada Inc, 2012
All rights reserved
No part of this publication may be reproduced or transmitted in any form or by any means, graphic, electronic or mechanical, including photocopying, recording, or any information storage and retrieval system, without permission in writing from the publisher. Requests for photocopying of any part of this book shall be directed in writing to

Freedom Press Canada Inc.
12-111 Fourth Ave. , Suite 185
St. Catharines, ON L2S 3P5

Printed in the United States of America

Standing On Guard For Thee: The Past, Present and Future of Canada's Christian Right
ISBN 978-0-9812767-3-1
Second Edition (Revised)

Cover: Toronto Marriage Rally, May 23, 2005.
Photo by Kevan Ashworth

Standing on Guard for Thee is a ground breaking history of the Christian Right in Canada. Many Canadians, including Christians, are under the false impression that the Christian Right is an American import. Nothing could be further from the truth, and historian Michael Wagner proves this point beyond a reasonable doubt in this excellent new book.

How many times have you heard Christian-baiters say: "Stop imposing your morality on Canadians?" Michael Wagner's ground breaking history of the Christian Right in Canada is the answer to that question. Wagner's thorough and engaging book demonstrates that Christianity was here first.

For anyone interested in an accurate history of Canada's Christian Right, this is it. Wagner tells the story from the beginning of social conservative thought in the early days of our great country, right through to the marriage wars of 2003-2005.

This revised edition of *Standing on Guard for Thee* now includes a chapter covering the years from 2005 to the first months of 2012, bringing the reader updates on the important issues.

This book is the antidote to the secular-humanists who are imposing their foreign morality on everyone else. It makes good reading for the layman, yet it could also be used as a classroom textbook, and would be superior to just about any other comparable book being used today.

Michael Wagner is a freelance writer and home schooling father. He has written articles for a number of publications, including the Byfield-era *Report* newsmagazine(s) and *The Alberta Journal of Educational Research*. Most of his recent writing has been for *Reformed Perspective* magazine. Wagner has a BA (Honours) and MA in Political Science from the University of Calgary and a PhD in Political Science from the University of Alberta. He lives in Edmonton with his wife and nine children.

WHAT PEOPLE ARE SAYING...

Canadians owe Mr. Michael Wagner a debt of gratitude. This book is an accurate assessment of Canada's history because it includes the right events, the right places, and the right people. Michael's approach differs markedly from the post-modern kill-joy relativists who pass as historians today; he outclasses them in every way. This book is the most important historical thesis on Canada's Religious Right to date, because it asserts what few historians are saying: that far from being an American import, the Christian religion and its influence on Canadian politics and sociology has been an intrinsic part of the country's fabric from the very beginning.
Tristan Emmanuel, *Former President*
Equipping Christian for the Public Square
www.ecpcentre.org

In this very readable book, Michael Wagner has done three things well. He has assembled the remarkable history of many Canadian conservative pioneers whose labours might otherwise have been lost and forgotten. He has chronicled what worked and what didn't in the social upheavals of the last
half-century. And most importantly, he has shown why – hard though it so often is to see – we are actually winning the battle.
Link Byfield, *Chairman*
Citizens Centre for Freedom and Democracy
www.ccfd.ca

This book tells the story of the pro-life pro-family cause in Canada that needed to be told. The media and various governments have done everything to ignore the voice of those resisting their anti-life, anti-family policies. The book stands as a monument to those who strenuously resisted such policies. It is a thoroughly researched, well-written, and fascinating account of the true story behind the headlines.
C. Gwendolyn Landolt, *National Vice President*
REAL Women of Canada
www.realwomenca.com

When I was first asked to proof this manuscript, my initial reaction was "Oh no! A history book!" But Wagner has succeeded in making

the players in Canada's Social Conservative movement come alive in this engaging, detailed, and incredibly well-researched work. As someone who has spent 30 years in Canadian media, reporting on many of the events outlined here, I was impressed with the way Michael has pulled so many threads together into a seamless and well-written tapestry of history and conflicting worldviews – the conflicts sometimes even extended to within the movement itself. This book shows how social conservatism in Canada has survived in spite of internal struggles and external opposition, and also clearly puts the lie to the notion that somehow the "Christian Right" in Canada is some kind of late 20th century American import.
Al Siebring, *Host*
"No Apologies" News
www.noapologies.ca

If this was fiction it might be classified as a horror story... with a happy ending. It is a gore-filled account of Canada's spiritual decline, but also a heroic tale of giants like Ted Byfield, Ken Campbell, and Gwen Landolt who have fought against the growing darkness. These giants may have lost more battles than they'll ever win, but Wagner leaves no doubt about who will ultimately triumph.
Jon Dykstra, *Editor*
Reformed Perspective Magazine
www.reformedperspective.ca

Michael Wagner presents a detailed, thorough and interesting history of conservative Christian political activism in Canada. While noting this movement's significant setbacks and defeats, Dr. Wagner points to the likelihood that traditional values will eventually triumph in the public square.
John Carpay, *Executive Director*
Canadian Constitution Foundation
www.canadianconstitutionfoundation.ca

To Léo Gaumont,
prophet of home education
and man of action.

TABLE OF CONTENTS

Time Line Of Important Events	i
Foreword	vii
Preface	xi
Chapter 1 Introduction	1
Chapter 2 Before the Christian Right	7

- Ralph Connor's Vision for Canada
  Black Rock: A Tale of the Selkirks
  The Sky Pilot: A Tale of the Foothills
  The Foreigner: A Tale of Saskatchewan
- Connor proves the point
- Precursors to the Christian Right? Social Credit Party Leaders in Western Canada
- William Aberhart
- Ernest Manning
- Alberta Social Credit in the 1960's
- Robert Thompson as a Precursor to the Christian Right
- Conclusion

Chapter 3 The Rise of the Christian Right in the 1970s	31

- The Early Years of the Pro-Life Movement
- Ken Campbell and the Birth of the Christian Right in Canada
- The First Step
- Formation of Renaissance
- Anita Bryant Rallies

- *The Body Politic*
- Toronto Election Impact
- Ken Campbell and Jerry Falwell
- Ted Byfield's Contribution to the Christian Right
- Bernice Gerard and the Christian Right
- David Mainse
- Censorship Issues
- Conclusion

Chapter 4 The First Part of the 1980s: The Volcano Begins to Erupt 71

- The Pro-Life Movement Enters the 1980s
- The Canadian Christian Right and the Constitutional Reference to God
- *The United Church Observer* on the New Right
- Evangelical Fellowship of Canada
- AFWUF
- REAL Women of Canada
- Borowski
- Henry Morgentaler vs. Ken Campbell
- Conclusion

Chapter 5 The Latter Half of the 1980s: Trying Harder, but Losing Bigger 123

- Attempts to Restrict Pornography
- The Equality Reports of 1985 and 1986
- Conservative Christian Responses
- Bill 7 in Ontario
- Christian Heritage Party
- Focus on the Family
- George Parkin Grant and the Christian Right
- George Parkin Grant on Abortion
- The Morgentaler Decision

- Aftermath of the Morgentaler Decision
- Bob Birch
- Conclusion

**Chapter 6 The Struggle Against Homosexual
Rights Takes Center Stage   175**

- Abortion Legislation
- The War Against the Family
- The Reform Party of Canada and
  the Christian Right
- Attacks Against Alberta Report
- Intervening in Important Court Cases
- The Mossop Case
- Bill 167 in Ontario
- Hate Crimes and Human Rights Act Amendment Bill C-33 (1996)
- Origin of CFAC 1997
- The Vriend Case
- Conclusion

**Chapter 7 The End of Traditional Marriage
and the Growing Attack Against Christians   215**

- Stockwell Day
- Larry Spencer
- Ken Campbell Before the
  Human Rights Commissions
- Bill C-250
- Tristan Emmanuel
- Same-Sex Marriage
- The 2004 Federal Election
- Gay Marriage Battle Resumes
- Results of the Same-Sex Marriage Fight
- American Influence on the
  Same-Sex Marriage Debate

- The Growing Number of "Human Rights" Cases
- Conclusion

Chapter 8 Human Flourishing Through Traditional Family Life   **257**

- The Sexual Revolution
- Marriage
- Effects on Children
- Cohabitation
- Effects of Divorce
- Effects of Daycare
- Homosexuality
- Reasons for Optimism

Chapter 9 Conclusion   **273**

Chapter 10 Afterword   **277**

TIME LINE OF IMPORTANT EVENTS

May 1969	The House of Commons passes the Omnibus Reform Bill decriminalizing homosexuality and liberalizing abortion restrictions.
November 1973	Ted Byfield's *Saint John's Edmonton Report* begins publication.
March 1974	The Renaissance organization is formed by Ken Campbell.
January 1978	Anita Bryant makes the first appearance of her Canadian tour on behalf of Ken Campbell's Renaissance.
February 1978	Campaign Life is formed.
September 1978	Joe Borowski begins a court challenge of Canada's abortion law.
November 1980	Ken Campbell leads a successful campaign to unseat Toronto mayor John Sewell.
January 1981	Gwen Landolt warns the country of the consequences of adopting the Charter of Rights and Freedoms.
April 1982	The Charter of Rights and Freedoms officially becomes part of Canada's Constitution.
November 1982	The Alberta Federation of Women United for Families (AFWUF) holds its first convention.
May 1983	Joe Borowski's case against the abortion law is finally heard by the Saskatchewan Court of Queen's Bench.
June 1983	Henry Morgentaler opens the first elective abortion clinic in English-speaking Canada in Toronto.

July 1983	Morgentaler's Toronto clinic is raided by police leading to criminal charges.
October 1983	Saskatchewan Court of Queen's Bench rules against Joe Borowski.
February 1984	The formation of REAL Women of Canada is formally announced.
September 1984	Brian Mulroney and his Progressive Conservative Party win the federal election.
November 1984	Henry Morgentaler is acquitted.
December 1984	Ken Campbell forms Choose Life Canada.
October 1985	Henry Morgentaler's acquittal is set aside.
February 1986	The federal government of Brian Mulroney officially endorses homosexual rights.
April 1986	The Christian Heritage Party of Canada is officially registered.
June 1986	Justice Minister John Crosbie introduces Bill C-114, a tough anti-pornography bill.
October 1986	The Supreme Court of Canada hears Morgentaler's appeal.
December 1986	Ontario adds sexual orientation to its Human Rights Code.
May 1987	Justice Minister Ray Hnatyshyn introduces Bill C-54, an anti-pornography bill.
November 1987	The Christian Heritage Party of Canada holds its founding convention.
January 1988	Henry Morgentaler wins his case at the Supreme Court of Canada, and the country's abortion restrictions are struck down.
October 1988	The Supreme Court of Canada hears Joe Borowski's appeal.

November 1988	Brian Mulroney's government is re-elected.
March 1989	The Supreme Court of Canada declares Joe Borowski's case against the abortion law to be moot.
August 1989	The Supreme Court of Canada strikes down an injunction preventing Chantal Daigle from obtaining an abortion.
May 1990	New abortion legislation, Bill C-43, passes the House of Commons.
January 1991	Bill C-43 is defeated in the Senate.
October 1993	Jean Chretien and his Liberal Party win the federal election.
June 1994	Bill 167 extending benefits to same-sex couples is defeated in the Ontario Legislature.
May 1996	Bill C-33 adding sexual orientation to the Canadian Human Rights Act is passed by the House of Commons.
March 1997	The Canada Family Action Coalition (CFAC) is officially formed.
April 1998	The Supreme Court of Canada adds sexual orientation to Alberta's human rights legislation in the *Vriend* decision.
May 1999	The Supreme Court of Canada extends benefits to same-sex couples in Ontario in the *M. v. H.* decision.
July 2000	Stockwell Day becomes leader of the Canadian Alliance.
November 2000	Jean Chretien and his Liberals are re-elected in the federal election.
July 2001	Stockwell Day resigns as leader of the Canadian Alliance.

March 2002	Stephen Harper is elected leader of the Canadian Alliance.
June 2003	The Ontario Court of Appeal strikes down the traditional definition of marriage in the *Halpern* decision.
September 2003	Bill C-250 adding sexual orientation to the hate crimes provisions of Canada's Criminal Code is passed by the House of Commons.
April 2004	Bill C-250 is passed by the Senate.
June 2004	Paul Martin and his Liberals win a minority government in the federal election.
February 2005	The federal government introduces Bill C-38 to legalize same-sex marriage.
April 2005	A massive pro-marriage rally is held on Parliament Hill.
June 2005	The House of Commons passes Bill C-38.
July 2005	The Senate passes Bill C-38.
January 2006	Stephen Harper and the Conservative Party win a minority government in the federal election.
December 2006	A government motion to re-open the same-sex marriage debate is defeated on a free vote in the House of Commons.

FOREWORD

I've never been particularly fond of genealogies. As a child, I used to dread it whenever my pastor read a chapter out of the Old Testament book of Numbers, especially if it was one of those chapters with the long list of ancient Hebraic names. How boring was that? It was hard not to fall asleep during those genealogies. What kept me awake as a child was listening to what I imagined were cuss-words in a foreign language, and watching the shower of spittle literally descending in a fine mist on the unfortunates who had chosen to site in the front pews. The regular members learned never to sit there if we knew there was an Old Testament sermon series underway.

And I could never quite understand why the biblical accounts included a roll call of a people that I neither knew nor cared much about. I mean, what relevance did Elizur the son of Shedeur, or Shelumiel the son of Zurishaddai, or Nahshon the son of Amminadab have in my life, in 1960's Canadian society?
Well, several decades have passed since then. And wisdom – not to mention an earned post graduate degree in Church history – has come with age. I now see the relevance behind those genealogies. It's interesting that you won't find mention of them in Egyptian histories. The Greeks and Persians didn't care much

about them either. And the Romans didn't have much time for the itemization of the names of "ordinary people". Their rulers and their Caesars, perhaps, but for the most part, people in the ancient worlds didn't think much of each other. And certainly the chroniclers of ancient history didn't care much for the places, events and peoples that preoccupied the comings and goings of the land of Canaan. But – in those days much like today – most historians weren't too shy about their preconceived prejudices.

This may sound xenophobic in the context of post-modern theories about the study of the ancient world, but I have come to see that in the grand scheme of things, those genealogies are actually records of the most important players in human history. And that is because they are part of redemptive history – the driving impetus behind all human history. In other words, one could say that even though the "world" didn't think so, and still doesn't, the people in these genealogies were the important players – they were an integral part of the redemptive process that led to the birth of Christ; and that's why they are worth itemizing and knowing.

As I said, post-modern historians would probably want to quibble with me about that bold assertion, and probably call me a racist and a bigot as well. But the fact is, some cultures and peoples really do matter. And the experts, for a multiplicity of reasons, have purposefully avoided that fact.

Not surprisingly, these experts generally don't think much of the real players in modern history either. And this comes out in their writings. Whether they are chronicling ancient peoples, the Medieval era, the Reformation, or the Enlightenment; or whether they are writing about people like Genghis Khan, Julius Caesar, Plato, or Alexander the Great, postmodern historians refuse to give sufficient weight to the real people who were the driving impetus behind human history.

And that is because these experts begin with a false set of assumptions about history. To write history well, one needs to ask the right questions, look for the right context, and most importantly focus on the right people.

Perhaps because I don't accept a chaotic theory of history, and because I refuse to succumb to the influence social-Darwinism has had on the study of history, it is hard for me to understand the relativistic myopia of the "experts". I believe the study of our past must begin with the fundamental assumption that history has a purpose; that it has a projected trajectory which includes a beginning, a middle, and a predetermined end-point.

I assume from the very outset that there are important events, times, places, movements and people in this trajectory. And because they reject the fundamental notion behind this model of the study of the past, most of the "experts" have got it all wrong.

The cynical, humanist-centered study of history is wrong. Like Michael Wagner, I do not believe that history is relative. And I disagree with Winston Churchill, who wrote that "history is written by the victors". Perhaps he was right in the military sense; it certainly helps to be in the driver's seat, but as Wagner argues, the important players in Canada's history are rarely if ever associated with victory. In fact, to listen to the so-called experts on Canadian political and cultural affairs you would hear some very unflattering denunciations of the religious right. And that is because these "experts" have a skewered view of who the important people really are.

That is why I believe Canadians owe Mr. Michael Wagner a debt of gratitude. In this book, he has undertaken a profoundly important task. He has sought to accurately assess Canada's history and include the right events, the right places, and the right people.

And that is why the book you are holding in your hands is so important. Michael's approach not only differs from the post-modern kill-joy mentality of the relativists who pass as historians today; he outclasses them in every way. As a trained historian and expert political analyst, Wagner has written the most important historical thesis on Canada's Religious Right to date. He not only deals with the people, but he asserts what few historians are saying: that far from being an American import, the Christian religion and its influence on Canadian politics and sociology has been an intrinsic part of the country's fabric from the very beginning. And the players in this movement – notwithstanding what the naysayers think – have accomplished incredible feats and left an indelible stamp on the fabric of Canadian society.

But Wagner even goes one better. Not only does he rebut the critics and their false caricatures, he gives us hope. He asserts that the Christian Right is ultimately the people who will make all the difference in Canada's future. They are the people who – not because of their own powers, but because of Supreme Providence – have an appointment with destiny. They will rise to take Canada back. And the influences of social-Darwinism and the relativistic meaninglessness of what passes for modern historical scholarship won't be able to do a thing about it. That is why this book is so important. It is not only a well written historical account. It is much more. It's a history book with hope.

Right on, Michael, Right on! Finally, someone has told the truth about Canada's religious right. Finally, a history we can be proud of.

Tristan Emmanuel,
Publisher, Freedom Press.

PREFACE

Some elements of the media like to portray the Christian Right as a bunch of inarticulate Bible-thumpers who are trying to impose their morality on everyone else. Canada is a secular society, we are told, and these awful people are trying to mix politics and religion, violating the sacred "separation of church and state."

Baloney.

Conservative Christian activism, embodied in the Christian Right, is a response to the advance of secularism and the cultural and political implications of that advance. Christianity was here first. There was a general Christian ethos to Canadian society, at least until the 1960s. It was only when the secularists began to achieve many of their cultural and political goals that conservative Christians felt obliged to push back. The Christian Right is a defensive movement, trying to preserve what is best in our traditional Western culture. This has nothing to do with violating any supposed "separation of church and state."

This book attempts to provide an historical sketch of the Christian Right in Canada from a sympathetic perspective. Some of the people discussed in this book are my friends and acquaintances, while others are people I admire from afar. Their stories deserve to be told in a way that highlights their virtues as concerned citizens and the intellectual strength of their positions. The goal of this book is to help make you, the reader, appreciate to a greater degree the significant contributions of those Canadians who have courageously defended traditional morality in the face of bitter opposition from the political, judicial, academic, and media establishments.

Besides the historical account, I offer evidence that optimism is in order for social conservatives. God created human beings with a particular nature, and His rules for living are the surest guide for promoting human well-being. People who live according to God's stipulations will follow "lifestyles" more suited to the thriving of the human condition than those lifestyles advocated by the social Left. Social science is increasingly rediscovering the superiority of socially conservative ways of life. As this becomes more generally known, it will become harder to justify "alternative lifestyles" and mock traditional morality. These factors all bode well for the future of the Christian Right.

I originally conceived the idea for writing this book more than five years ago. I managed to get bits of work done on it here and there, but the end was nowhere in sight. That all changed when Tristan Emmanuel phoned me late one afternoon to ask me to get this book written. So one phone call—and one year—later, voila!

This is my tribute to the leaders and foot soldiers of Canada's Christian Right. We have a great country, one worth fighting for.

Michael Wagner,
Edmonton, Alberta
November 2007

CHAPTER 1 | INTRODUCTION

The Christian Right in Canada is a collection of people, organizations, and publications which, because of their conservative Christian principles, are determined to oppose the effects of the Sexual Revolution. Many of these people, organizations and publications are evangelicals in their outlook and theology, but others are not. Thus, the Christian Right in Canada should not be confused with the broader evangelical Christian community. Certainly many conservative evangelicals can be considered to fall within my definition of Christian Right, but many conservative Roman Catholics and some conservative Eastern Orthodox adherents would also fit.

Interestingly, of the three people I consider to be most important in the history of Canada's Christian Right, Rev. Ken Campbell, lawyer Gwen Landolt, and publisher Ted Byfield, the first is an evangelical, the second a Roman Catholic, and the third Eastern Orthodox (although he had been some sort of Anglican for much of the period considered in this book). Thus for the purpose of the book, the Christian Right will include all politically active conservative Christians, not just evangelicals.

Furthermore, within this broad definition there is considerable overlap of terms such as the "pro-family movement" and "social conservatism." It would be rather difficult to distinguish the Christian Right, the pro-family movement, and social conservatism from one another in Canada. There seems to be no point in doing so. Thus, for the purposes of this book these three terms will basically be used interchangeably.

It's also important to note that the focus of this book is only on English-speaking Canada. Notwithstanding the failure of Brian Mulroney's "Meech Lake Accord", Quebec does constitute a "distinct society" within Canada when it comes to its social and religious fabric, and the politics of that province are considerably different from those in the rest of the country.

The Sexual Revolution brought many changes to Canada, as it did to most of the rest of "the West" in the 1960's. These changes included a number of political ramifications, the most prominent of which were the legalization of abortion and the extension of homosexual rights. Since the early 1970s there has been consistent activity by conservative Christians in Canada to oppose both abortion and homosexual rights. Other issues such as pornography and the use of adult literature in public schools have also entered the picture from time to time, but the only constant struggles, from a political perspective, have been over abortion and homosexual rights. Thus for this book the main focus will be on conservative Christian activism in opposition to those two features of modern society.

This book is primarily a history of the Christian Right in Canada. Its object is to demonstrate that Canada has long had such a movement, that it is indigenous to the country, and that its long-term future is bright.

The debate over same-sex marriage during 2005 awakened the media to the presence of a Christian Right in Canada. Many saw the Christian Right as a new phenomenon here. Even worse, it was alleged by some to be an American import, infusing American values into Canadian politics.

But, in fact, the Christian Right in Canada is neither new nor American-inspired. Home-grown Canadian activists have been involved at least since the early 1970s, and in some cases their efforts received national attention during that decade. While the Canadian Christian Right has at times looked to its American counterparts for advice and support, the same can also be said of the "pro-choice" and homosexual rights movements in Canada. The social Left also looks to its counterparts in the United States.

I argue that the perspective of traditional morality and heterosexual family life advocated by the Christian Right will make a comeback. Heterosexual monogamy, with parents raising their own children, is a way of life that maximizes the flourishing of human culture and society. This view has been increasingly supported by social science research over the last 30 years. The supposed "liberators" responsible for the Sexual Revolution have brought bondage and misery to many people in the name of freedom. The lifestyles they represent minimize health and reproduction, ensuring that their cause will flounder at some point. A form of natural selection will favour people with socially conservative lifestyles, leading to the ultimate success of social conservatism generally.

The historical part of the book begins with precursors to the Christian Right in Canada. The focus here is largely on three Social Credit leaders, William Aberhart, Ernest Manning, and Robert Thompson. Then the focus shifts to what is commonly recognized as the contemporary Christian Right, with the emergence of pro-life activism and organized opposition to the homosexual rights movement in the 1970s. Gwen Landolt was an early leader of the pro-life movement, Rev. Ken Campbell was the first leader of an organization opposing homosexual rights, and Ted Byfield began publishing the magazine that would become *Alberta Report*. His magazine stood foursquare against the Sexual Revolution and its consequences.

Gwen Landolt became even more prominent in the 1980s due to the formation of REAL Women of Canada and the key role it would play on many issues. The election of the Progressive Conservatives under Brian Mulroney in 1984 may have raised the hopes among conservative Christians that Canada was about to experience positive political change, but those hopes were quickly dashed. Although Mulroney's government would sponsor tough anti-pornography legislation (which was never passed), it strongly supported the feminist movement and publicly backed homosexual rights. In response, some Christians formed the Christian Heritage Party of Canada. Social conservative despair may also have contributed to the rapid rise of the new Reform Party of Canada in the West.

The pro-life cause met its Waterloo with the Supreme Court of Canada's *Morgentaler* decision of 1988. There were a few subsequent court cases of considerable significance on the abortion issue in the next couple of years, but they turned out to be just mop-up operations for abortion advocates, as the Supreme Court always favoured the "pro-choice" position. Further, the Mulroney government's proposed abortion legislation of the early 1990s was too liberal for most pro-lifers to stomach.

It was during the 1990s that the homosexual rights movement's long march through the courts began to bear fruit, with case after case decided in favour of homosexual rights by the Supreme Court. The *Vriend* decision of 1998 and the *Halpern* decision of 2003 were both knock-out blows. The Charter of Rights and Freedoms, adopted in 1982, proved to be a boon to homosexual rights activists, as it had for those clamouring for abortion rights. During the 1990s the gay rights movement was on a roll, and the Canada Family Action Coalition (CFAC) was formed in response to that.

The early years of the new millennium witnessed increased use of government power to limit opposition to the homosexual rights movement through "human rights" commissions and the courts. Finally, the gay rights movement achieved its ultimate political goal—the legalization of same-sex marriage. While this was a stinging defeat for the Christian Right, the controversy over the issue led to an increased political mobilization of conservative Christians in Canada. That mobilization, if it can be sustained, holds the potential to change the country's political landscape.

Perhaps more important than any political movements though, was the growing evidence of harm to human beings resulting from the lifestyles favoured by proponents of the Sexual Revolution. Sexual promiscuity, whether heterosexual or homosexual, is harmful to its practitioners. Sex is a powerful force for good within marriage, but a very destructive force outside of marriage. Chapter 8 summarizes some of the social science findings demonstrating that, generally speaking, the well-being of humans is promoted by traditional morality and the traditional family. As this becomes increasingly hard to ignore, there may be a cultural shift in favour of traditional morality. Reality cannot be ignored forever. And this provides hope for the future for the Christian Right in Canada.

CHAPTER 2 | BEFORE THE CHRISTIAN RIGHT

The easiest way to dispel the notions that the Christian Right is "new" or an "American import" is simply to look at Canada's history. Conservative Christianity, and conservative evangelicalism in particular, has long had a significant presence in Canada, and conservative evangelicals have at times made noteworthy political contributions.

This chapter will review some of the conservative evangelical political activities in Canada from the 1930s through the 1960s; activities which can reasonably be argued to, in some sense, foreshadow the development of the Christian Right. These precursors are largely associated with the Social Credit Party.
Before looking at those politically-specific issues, it may be helpful to take note of the significance of evangelical Protestantism in Canada earlier in the twentieth century. I propose to do this in a very unorthodox way, by looking at a best-selling Canadian novelist of the early 1900s, Ralph Connor. I am not arguing that Connor was necessarily a precursor to the Christian Right. However, the popularity of his early books demonstrates the widespread appeal of evangelical Christianity in English-speak-

ing Canada, proving that evangelicalism does not represent any kind of externally imposed American cultural invasion.

RALPH CONNOR'S CHRISTIAN VISION FOR CANADA: "IT IS A RIGHTEOUS CANADA THAT WILL ENDURE, AND NO OTHER"

In the early 1900s one of the biggest selling novelists in the world was a Canadian missionary and pastor. Charles W. Gordon, a minister in the Presbyterian Church of Canada, first served as a missionary in southern Alberta in the 1890s and subsequently became pastor of a church in Winnipeg. He began writing under the name of Ralph Connor in the 1890s to generate support for Presbyterian mission work in western Canada. His writing was so popular that his first three novels sold a combined total of more than five million copies. President Woodrow Wilson of the United States was a prominent fan of Connor's novels, as was Henry Ford. Connor was famous throughout the English-speaking world, especially in Canada and the USA. The sales of his books made Connor a major literary figure in the early twentieth century. While he is no longer well-known among most contemporary Christians, his popularity decades ago seems to indicate that Canadian culture was at one time very receptive to the perspective of evangelical Christianity.

Many of Connor's earliest novels had a strong evangelical Protestant punch. The heroes tend to be Presbyterian ministers. While later in life his focus appears to have changed somewhat (perhaps reflecting a shift towards more liberal theology), his earlier period (before World War One) shows a deep concern for evangelization. In an address to a meeting of the Presbyterian Church of Canada in 1913, Gordon stated,

> ...if Canada is ever going to be great and become one of the world powers, and is to bring light and leading to the

nations, it will not be because of her great wheatfields, or her marvelous resources, but because of the character of the people, because of our relation to Almighty God. It is a righteous Canada that will endure, and no other (Layton 2001, 3).

Gordon used his writing as Ralph Connor to promote his Christian vision for Canada. It was a distinctively evangelical vision in the sense that he was calling people to a personal commitment to Christ, to reading the Bible and to prayer. This comes across most clearly in some of his earliest and most popular novels. Among these are *Black Rock*, *The Sky Pilot*, and *The Foreigner*.

BLACK ROCK: A TALE OF THE SELKIRKS

Black Rock is written from the first person perspective of Ralph Connor, in this case an artist working as "an illustrator and designer for railway and like publications" (Connor 1901, 157). Black Rock is the name of a fictitious town in the Selkirk Mountains of western Canada, a focal point for the forestry and mining industries in the region. The miners and lumbermen spend their free time and their money in Black Rock on rest and recreation--mostly vice, especially drinking at the saloon.

Within this environment labors a Presbyterian minister, Mr. Craig, intent on turning the men from their hard-drinking ways and to Jesus Christ. He manages to organize an Abstinence League among some of the men. But many are lured back to a night of drunken revelry by a clever saloon keeper and his anti-abstinence cohorts. The death of one of the revelers, who had violated his own abstinence pledge, then leads to a reconstitution of the League on a stronger basis than before. And when the saloon keeper's infant dies, he too turns his back on alcohol.

A major theme within the book is the struggle within men to overcome their temptation to do what feels good rather than to do what is right. The miners and lumbermen spend countless hours at work to earn their wages, but when they are given time off, they feel an uncontrollable urge to go to town and get drunk, spending their hard-earned dollars on temporary pleasure. Then they go back to work and start all over again. Craig thus refers to Black Rock as "this devil's camp-ground, where a man's lust is his only law, and when, from sheer monotony, a man must betake himself to the only excitement of the place—that offered by the saloon" (Connor 1901, 86-87).

In this kind of situation only God's divine help can enable men to resist such temptation and live clean. Only those who turn to Christ will succeed and get ahead. The explicitly Christian and evangelistic theme of the book is unmistakable. Early in the book, for example, Craig gives his own testimony of personal salvation. Old man Nelson turns to Christ, and later he also gives his personal testimony: "The old man's voice steadied as he went on, and he grew eager as he told how he had been helped, and how the world was all different, and his heart seemed new. He spoke of his Friend [Jesus Christ] as if He were someone that could be seen out at camp, that he knew well, and met every day" (Connor 1901, 152). After his conversion Nelson is one of the most stalwart abstinence supporters. And he presents his testimony just before one of the major events of the book, namely the formation of Black Rock Presbyterian Church.

Craig is concerned about more than just his local congregation, however. He is concerned for western Canada as the railway arrives and opens up the region. "With the eye of a general he surveyed the country, fixed the strategic points which the Church must seize upon.... 'The Church must be in with the railway; she must have a hand in the shaping of the country. If society crystallises without her influence, the country is lost, and British Columbia will be another trap-door to the bottomless pit" (Connor 1901, 132).

One of the final chapters, entitled "Graeme's New Birth," focuses on the spiritual awakening of one of the book's main characters. Graeme returns to his parents' house in Ontario. His father was apparently a Presbyterian minister. Connor writes, "I saw Graeme as a new man the night he talked theology with his father. The old minister was a splendid Calvinist, of heroic type, and as he discoursed of God's sovereignty and election, his face glowed and his voice rang out" (Connor 1901, 284-285).
Graeme would subsequently have opportunity to testify to his faith in Christ while in conversation with some old friends. One of the old friends, Rattray, takes the Lord's name in vain, and Graeme quickly rebukes him for doing so. At that point another fellow, Beetles, replies that "no one takes seriously any longer the Christ myth." Graeme responds, "I fooled with that for some time, Beetles, but it won't do. You can't build a religion that will take the devil out of a man on a myth. That won't do the trick. I don't want to argue about it, but I am quite convinced the myth theory is not reasonable, and besides, it won't work" (Connor 1901, 292). Then after discussing some of the events that occurred in Black Rock, and on his trip back to Ontario, he says, "That's why I believe in Jesus Christ, and that's why I think it a crime to fling His name about!" (Connor 1901, 293).

There was much evangelistic work yet to be done as western Canada was being developed and filled with settlers, but Craig and his fellow-laborers were rising to the task.

THE SKY PILOT: A TALE OF THE FOOTHILLS

Like *Black Rock*, *The Sky Pilot* is written from the first person perspective of Ralph Connor. In this instance Connor is a college student who comes to visit a cousin on his ranch in the foothills of southern Alberta. After his arrival, he becomes the schoolmaster of the local town, Swan Creek.

As schoolmaster Connor receives a note from a missionary who wants to come out to Swan Creek to plant a church. The news that a missionary is coming was welcomed by the few young families in the region, but resented by many of the single men. They saw "the establishment of a church institution" as "an objectionable and impertinent as well as unnecessary proceeding" (Connor 1900, 39). One long-time resident of the area (known only as the "Old Timer") who was particularly negative towards the arrival of a missionary, nick-named him "The Sky Pilot," and the term stuck.

Connor does not state the denominational affiliation of the missionary, whose name is Arthur Wellington Moore. However, when Moore demonstrates his proficiency at playing baseball, he is asked where he learned to play so well, and he replies, "Oh! I used to play in Princeton a little" (Connor 1900, 71). That comment is significant because Princeton Seminary was a prominent bastion of orthodox Calvinism during the late 1800s and early 1900s. It was a leading seminary of the Presbyterian Church (U.S.A.), and had an international reputation for its defense of historic Protestantism against the cancerous inroads of theological liberalism. As such, it is reasonable to conclude that Moore was a conservative Presbyterian of sorts.

Before the baseball episode, a number of local ranchmen give Moore a hard time at his inaugural Sunday service. Moore realizes that things went poorly for him, yet resolves, "But I am right! It's true! I feel it's true! Men can't live without Him, and be men!" (Connor 1900, 64). Shortly thereafter Moore is called upon to fill in for a fellow who was to be playing baseball, and when the ranch men see his tremendous skill at the game, he is hailed as a hero and the resentment towards him quickly dissipates.

With his newfound status, Moore continues regular services, now with much more success. "The preaching was always of the simplest kind, abstract questions being avoided and the concrete in those wonderful Bible tales, dressed in modern and in western garb, set forth" (Connor 1900, 75).

One of the ranchers, Bruce, begins to drink his life away. He no longer takes care of his cattle, his home or himself. Moore asks why no one helps Bruce, but is told that "a man ought to look after himself." Moore agrees but states that a man should also look after his brother a little. "You all do just what pleases you regardless of any other, and so you help one another down" (Connor 1900, 80). People are, to some degree, responsible for each other. "This was certainly a new doctrine for the West; an uncomfortable doctrine to practice, interfering seriously with personal liberty, but in The Pilot's way of viewing things difficult to escape" (Connor 1900, 81).

The Old Timer is a widower with a teenage daughter named Gwen. Gwen's mother died when she was quite young, so she was raised by her father with the help of some Indian companions. Gwen emerges as a talented cowgirl, and is admired by the ranchers who know her. Moore introduces her to Christianity and Bible stories, which she eagerly receives.

> And, as more and more it grew upon The Pilot that the story he was reading, so old to him and to all he had ever met, was new to one in that listening group, his face began to glow and his eyes to blaze, and he saw and showed me things that night I had never seen before, nor have I seen them since. The great figure of the Gospels lived, moved before our eyes. We saw Him bend to touch the blind, we heard Him speak His marvelous teaching, we felt the throbbing excitement of the crowds that pressed against Him (Connor 1900, 133).

Gwen is especially delighted to find out that her mother was a Christian and is therefore in Heaven with Christ. Noting that Gwen's mother sees Him all the time, Moore goes on to say that "He sees us, too, and hears us speak, and knows our thoughts." Gwen's introduction to the Bible and its message changed her. "The experiences of the evening had made the world new to her. It could never be the same to her again" (Connor 1900, 134).

Moore and Gwen become close companions, and he reads to her frequently from the Bible and also John Bunyan's *Pilgrim's Progress*. However, Gwen's new faith is sorely tried when she has a ranching accident and loses the use of her legs. She becomes quite angry at God. Moore is able to comfort her, though, by making an analogy between her situation and the growth of flowers in a nearby canyon, both of which are very dear to Gwen. The canyon is like a large wound in the prairie, and within it grows the most beautiful flowers. In the same way, the "fruits of the Spirit," the most beautiful character traits, will take root within Gwen due to the trial of her handicap. As Moore puts it, "The fruits—I'll read 'flowers'—of the Spirit are love, joy, peace, long-suffering, gentleness, goodness, faith, meekness, self-control, and some of these grow only in the canyon" (Connor 1900, 178). Gwen was tremendously encouraged by this teaching.

Moore wants to erect a church building in Swan Creek, but even some of his parishioners oppose the idea because they think it would be too expensive. When Gwen hears of this she uses her influence among some of the ranchers to help raise the funding necessary for the task. Thus Moore triumphs as his church is built. However, he soon falls seriously ill, and is unable to lead the first service in the new church building. Shortly thereafter he dies.

Moore's burial service is conducted by his "chief," probably a denominational superintendent. This man had been a pioneer missionary himself. "But out of his kindly blue eye looked the heart of a hero, and as he spoke to us we felt the prophet's touch and caught a gleam of the prophet's fire" (Connor 1900, 294). The hero of the book was dead, but not before endearing himself to all the people of the region, pointing many to the Savior, helping the ranchers to be better men, and especially encouraging Gwen through her trials.

THE FOREIGNER: A TALE OF SASKATCHEWAN

Unlike *Black Rock* and *The Sky Pilot*, *The Foreigner* is written from the third person perspective. This book focuses on eastern European, especially Russian, immigrants to western Canada in the late 1800s. As a group, these people are often referred to as "Galicians." The central figure of the story is Kalman Kalmar, the son of a Russian "Nihilist" (revolutionary). Kalman and his sister Irma live with their step-mother in an immigrant ghetto in Winnipeg. Their birth mother had been killed by the Russian authorities, and their father has dedicated his life to avenging her death on an ex-Nihilist, Rosenblatt, whose betrayal of the Nihilist cause led to her death.

Michael Kalmar, Kalman's father, comes to Winnipeg where Rosenblatt has become a successful businessman among the immigrants. He attempts to kill Rosenblatt, but fails and is sent to prison. Later, Kalman himself (who is only thirteen years old) tries to kill Rosenblatt in a fight, but Rosenblatt gets the best of him and Kalman barely survives with his life. In order to improve the boy's life prospects, a lady friend of the Kalmar family, Margaret, sends Kalman to live with her brother-in-law, Jack French, on a ranch in Saskatchewan. It is there that Kalman develops into a man, and learns to farm and ranch.

Toward the end of the book, Kalman accidentally discovers a coal deposit, and with the help of Jack French and some other friends, is able to develop a coal mine. This puts him on a clear path towards financial success. And to top it all off, he becomes engaged to Marjorie Menzies, the daughter of a venture capitalist who has helped to finance the development of the coal mine. A happy ending, indeed.

But one other very important fact about Kalman needs to be noted. After coming to Saskatchewan he and Jack French befriend Dr. Brown, a Presbyterian missionary. Brown's mission activity consists primarily of providing medical and educational services to a settlement of Galician immigrants in that region of Saskatchewan. Brown is a hardworking man of integrity who is liked by all except for a Polish priest among the immigrants, Klazowski, who fears Brown's Protestant influence. When Jack and Kalman first encounter Brown and ask if he's a preacher, Brown briefly describes his efforts among the immigrants and then says, "in short, do anything to make them good Christians and good Canadians, which is the same thing" (Connor 1909, 165-166).

During their first encounter, the three men, Jack French, Kalman, and Brown, spend some time singing hymns and praying together. It is at this time that Kalman first truly turns to God. "Through all his after years Kalman would look back to that night as the night on which God first became to him something other than a name" (Connor 1909, 173).

Shortly thereafter, Kalman writes a letter to his sister in Winnipeg describing his life in Saskatchewan and his new friends. He says to her, "I like it best on Sunday afternoons, for then we sing, Brown and Jack and the Galician children, and then Brown reads the Bible and prays. It is not like church at all. There is no crucifix, no candles, no pictures. It is too much like every day to be like church, but Brown says that is the best kind, a religion for every day" (Connor 1909, 175).

The immigrants, of course, brought with them their religion, either Roman Catholic or Greek Orthodox. These forms of religion contrast sharply with the Protestantism of Dr. Brown. When, towards the end of the book, a Roman Catholic priest, Father Garneau, asks Kalman for a confession, Kalman politely refuses. He tells the priest, "I have for some years been reading my Bible, and I have lived beside a good man [i.e. Brown] who has taught me to know God and our Lord and Saviour Jesus Christ. I seek to follow Him as Peter and the others did. But I am no longer of the Galician way of religion, neither Greek nor

Roman" (Connor 1909, 221). When the priest replies by asking if he has denied the faith, Kalman responds, "No, I have not. I try to please Christ" (Connor 1909, 222).

Nevertheless, this book is less evangelistic than *Black Rock* or *The Sky Pilot*. Like those other two books, one hero in this story is a Presbyterian missionary, Dr. Brown. And an important secondary theme of this book is the evangelical conversion of at least one main character. But as a proportion of the whole, the explicitly Christian component is smaller than the previous two. But this book does make it clear that in Ralph Connor's view, "good Christians and good Canadians" are "the same thing."

CONNOR PROVES THE POINT

The culture of the English-speaking world in the early twentieth century was much more conservative and Christian than it is now. The popular literature of the time reflected this fact. By today's standards Ralph Connor's novels would be seen as backward or even intolerant because evangelical Protestantism triumphs over other influences. But his novels express the sincere sentiments of many people in an earlier period of Canadian history. And the fact that Connor's works sold more than five million copies – especially in a time when the population figures were much lower than they are today, is further testimony that Evangelical Christianity was most certainly alive and well in Canada in that day, and that it is not a late 20th century American import. Indeed, a century ago, it was a major influence among the English-speaking people of the country, proven in part by the fact that there was a ready market for Ralph Connor novels.

A revival of the reading of these novels would not only familiarize people with an important aspect of Canadian literary history, but also expose them to the kind of Christian mindset that pervaded much of the English-speaking world a hundred years ago.

PRECURSORS TO THE CHRISTIAN RIGHT?
SOCIAL CREDIT PARTY LEADERS IN WESTERN CANADA

Imagine a popular radio evangelist using his radio audience as the foundation for a political movement that would make him premier of a province. It's unthinkable today, but it was the political reality in Alberta in 1935. As a matter of fact, Alberta had two radio-evangelists as premier; the first until 1943, and his successor until 1969.

WILLIAM ABERHART

In 1935 William "Bible Bill" Aberhart became premier as the result of the Social Credit Party's provincial election victory, a victory that was in no small part secured by Aberhart's stature as a radio evangelist.

Aberhart had been a Calgary public school principal but was also an evangelical religious entrepreneur. He led Bible studies that became so popular he decided to found a Bible school, the Calgary Prophetic Bible Institute, which officially opened in 1927. The guest speaker for the opening ceremony was William Bell Riley, one of the best-known American fundamentalist leaders of the time. Previously, late in 1925, Aberhart had begun broadcasting a radio program called the "Back-to-the-Bible Broadcast". This was a decisive new initiative contributing to Aberhart's religious influence and political success. "The radio had not only increased Aberhart's audience but also widened the financial base from which he could draw funds for his new Bible Institute. His radio audience proved to be more important to his religious career than his local supporters, who were always embroiled in church politics" (Elliott and Miller 1987, 75).

Due to the onset of the Great Depression, and the suffering he viewed all around, Aberhart was drawn to the economic theory of Social Credit, which considered the Depression to be a consequence of private control of credit. It advocated government-controlled credit rather than bank-created credit as the solution to all economic problems. Aberhart used his radio broadcasts to promote this view to Albertans, many of whom came to adopt Social Credit ideas. Ultimately, the supporters of Social Credit formed a provincial political party with Aberhart as its leader, and this party won a landslide election victory in 1935. Aberhart's popularity as a fundamentalist religious leader was a major factor in propelling him into political power. And he remained in power until his death in 1943.

At least until the 1980s, the standard academic view was that Aberhart and his Social Credit Party were decidedly right-wing. For example, John Irving wrote in 1959 that "Aberhart was an arch-conservative in education, religion and politics." As he saw it, "Social Credit has constantly reaffirmed the ideal values of Christian capitalistic society" (Irving 1959, 345). C. B. Macpherson (1962) similarly saw Social Credit as inherently pro-capitalist. Recent scholarship, however, has pointed to the radical and left-wing implications of Aberhart's Social Credit Party. Elliott and Miller argue strongly for this view. As they put it, "Aberhart may have been the first active fundamentalist to have organized a political movement with a 'socialistic' character" (1987, 119). Yet as another proponent of this view argues, Aberhart was nevertheless shifting to the political right in the last years of his life (Finkel 1989, 83).

It seems to me that the recent scholarship brings compelling evidence for the view that in its earliest formulations in Alberta, Social Credit had socialistic tendencies. I think it's reasonable to see Aberhart as politically confused. He was looking for solutions to the problem of the Depression, and Social Credit (a confusing theory to begin with) suited his purpose. Although Social Credit did have socialistic aspects, it does not appear that Aberhart considered himself a socialist. Perhaps more important, however, is the fact that with Aberhart's death and Ernest Manning's rise to the leadership of Alberta's government, the Social Credit Party took a more explicitly pro-free enterprise and anti-socialist position.

ERNEST MANNING

Ernest Manning was born in Saskatchewan in 1908. In 1925 he began listening to William Aberhart's radio broadcast and was converted to fundamentalist Christianity as a result. He moved to Calgary in 1927 to enroll in the Calgary Prophetic Bible Institute. Manning excelled in his studies and caught the attention of Aberhart himself. "Aberhart saw in the young man a person who could greatly assist him. Aberhart became Manning's mentor, and Manning, in turn, emerged as Aberhart's trusted assistant" (Mackey 1997, 20).

With the election of 1935, Manning was made provincial secretary. And when Aberhart died in 1943, Manning was selected by the Social Credit caucus to be the new premier. After noting that the only competition for that position was from a cabinet minister, Solon Low, who happened to be a Mormon, journalist Lloyd Mackey writes, "It would have been unthinkable, at the time, for Mormons or evangelical Christians to rise to the top of the political heap in other parts of Canada. ...But in Alberta, those otherwise relegated by the establishment to religious oddballery were in the ascendancy" (1997, 30).

Manning not only replaced Aberhart in the political sphere but also in the religious sphere. He became the head of the remaining religious organizations created by Aberhart. Thus Manning became the preacher for Canada's National Back to the Bible Hour, and as it was later known, Canada's National Bible Hour. So during his tenure as premier of Alberta (and afterwards for more than 20 years), Canadians could hear Manning preaching the Gospel over the radio. It's virtually inconceivable that a radio evangelist, especially one presenting a conservative evangelical perspective, could simultaneously be a premier in today's Canada. And as Mackey notes, the Christian institutions Manning took control of could all "be described as belonging to evangelical Christianity's fundamentalist wing" (1997, 126).

While there is some scholarly debate as to whether or not Aberhart's Social Credit measures should be considered left-wing or right-wing, there is a consensus that under Manning the Alberta Social Credit government was decidedly right-wing. Macpherson writes that "Manning's social credit was no menace to private enterprise but the best protection against the growing strength of the socialist C.C.F. The menace of socialism became and remained the staple of the official Alberta social credit propaganda" (1962, 206).

ALBERTA SOCIAL CREDIT IN THE 1960S

During the 1960s at least some people considered Alberta to be ruled by right-wing Christians. This is apparent from a journal called *Edge* which was published by a University of Alberta (and later Concordia University, Montreal) professor of English from 1963 to 1969. It only published nine issues during that period, but it made somewhat of a splash. At least one issue of *Edge* contained poetry by Margaret Atwood (Spring 1965).

In 1964 *Edge* published an article arguing that Alberta was ruled by a theocracy.

> To speak of 'politics' in Alberta is almost a misnomer. There is little serious opposition to the Social Crediters who, for all the 'loyal oppositionist' attacks, are entrenched in a monolithic system of theocracy. Because this writer has no direct access to the facts and figures linking Alberta's oil, wheat,

and cattle interest with Social Credit, the degree to which this theocracy is also fascistic and capitalistic remains an open question (Sperber 1964, 52).

The article then goes on to compare the Alberta Social Credit regime with the early Puritan settlements of New England.

> *Theocracy* is the maintenance of political authority according to religious values and interests. The justification for demanding obedience to its politics is that (a) the policies are divinely inspired, (b) the policy makers are divinely ordained, and (c) disobedience will result in eternal damnation. The differences between Alberta today and the Calvinist theocracies in early American history are not easily discerned (Sperber 1964, 52)

This is a very extreme view and many people would likely just dismiss it. But it does convey some sense of how Manning's government was perceived by certain opponents on the left.

Besides broad-brushing Alberta as a theocracy, this article gives purported examples of the repression and ignorance encouraged by the Social Credit regime. It's alleged that Alberta's "Minister of Education is obliged to give reassurances both to the legislature and the general public that Darwin's theory of evolution is *not* part of public school education" (Sperber 1964, 47). Anything to do with sexuality is censored or suppressed.

> One need not be surprised to observe that abortion and divorce are the two most illegal and immoral acts a citizen can ordinarily commit (except for condemning Social Credit) in Alberta, that the individual who suffers as a consequence of Alberta's 'righteousness' is legally and morally required to endure these grievances for life, that such endurance is righteously justified as the 'bearing of responsibility for heinous sins' (Sperber 1964, 45).

No doubt these statements are highly exaggerated, but they still give a taste of how some people perceived Manning's government. And they resemble the kind of criticisms leveled at the contemporary Christian Right, namely, the suppression of sexuality, moral self-righteousness, etc.

ROBERT THOMPSON AS A PRECURSOR TO THE CHRISTIAN RIGHT

Robert Thompson was the leader of the federal Social Credit Party from 1961 to 1967. That party had 30 MPs elected to the House of Commons in the 1962 election, 24 MPs in the 1963 election, and 5 in the 1965 election. Although the numbers were relatively small, the minority government situation of the Canadian Parliament in the early to mid-1960s gave them a surprising degree of potential influence. Thompson was a well-known Canadian political leader of the 1960s and a prominent conservative evangelical.

Thompson grew up in rural central Alberta, and his father was a devoted listener to William Aberhart's radio program. Thompson himself took to Aberhart and became a Social Credit speaker and organizer. Aberhart saw Thompson's potential and invited him to attend his weekly class in Calgary for prospective Social Credit speakers. Thompson readily agreed, and later noted that "those three months under the tutelage of William Aberhart were more influential upon my understanding of economics and political and social responsibility than any course I was to take in formal university studies" (Thompson 1990, 13).

Thompson goes on to state that upon attending those meetings, "William Aberhart immediately became my political mentor" (Thompson 1990, 24). Furthermore, "He also was my role model as teacher and administrator. I admired his Christian convictions and compassionate motivation, and even his more rigid Presbyterian and Baptist perspectives. To me, he was a Christian layman who personified faith and works in their proper relationship" (Thompson 1990, 24).

Thompson wanted to be a candidate for the 1935 Alberta election, but the party disqualified him because he was only 20 years old. He then tried to get a Social Credit nomination for the 1935 federal election, but narrowly lost to another candidate. He subsequently returned to teaching, although he spent some time as a Social Credit organizer in Manitoba. He then went to a chiropractic college in Iowa, returning to Red Deer in 1939. In 1940 he joined the Army, and then transferred to the Royal Canadian Air Force. In 1943 he was sent to Ethiopia with two other Canadians to help in the East African campaign against the Italians. He remained in Ethiopia for a few years after the war, working in the Ethiopian civil service, and becoming personal friends with the country's emperor, Haile Selassie. In 1951 he left the Ethiopian civil service to work for an evangelical missions agency, Sudan Interior Mission. When that came to an end in 1958, Thompson moved back to Alberta.

Upon his return, Thompson embarked on a North American lecture tour on African affairs. Premier Ernest Manning of Alberta, who had been an old friend since his Social Credit days, recruited Thompson to assess his national popularity, ostensibly to see if it might be feasible for the premier to switch to the federal political arena. Another old friend, Roger Kirk, strongly encouraged Thompson to become involved in national politics himself. Kirk told Thompson of a particular interpretation of Psalm 33:12.

> The verse would mean that the blessing of God would come to Canada through those people who respected the laws of God and would influence their Parliament. If there were no practicing Christians in Parliament, how could Canada's

laws reflect our Christian heritage. Without any question, he felt I ought to be in politics, and he was so insistent that he even promised to do something about the interim financial support I might require (Thompson 1990, 66).

Premier Manning encouraged Thompson to seek the leadership of the federal Social Credit Party shortly thereafter, and this gave him the confidence to do so. Thompson later discussed the matter with BC Premier W.A.C. Bennett, who gave Thompson the impression that he was in support as well. Thompson subsequently became leader of the party in 1961, and was one of the 30 Social Credit MPs elected in 1962.

Shortly after being elected, Thompson and one other fellow initiated a weekly Parliamentary Prayer Breakfast. The people involved in that group decided to hold a National Prayer Breakfast in 1964, and these prayer breakfasts were also held in subsequent years. As Thompson puts it, "Since 1964, the annual *National Prayer Breakfast* has sought to provide an opportunity for leaders, regardless of political or religious affiliation, to gather in the spirit of Christ to express their spiritual values and reflect on the spiritual heritage of Canada" (Thompson 1990, 124).

With Canada celebrating its centennial in 1967, Thompson delivered a speech focusing on the Fathers of Confederation. One of the major themes of this speech was that the

> "Fathers of Confederation were, above all, convinced that as the new nation of Canada emerged in the northern half of North America, it would be a nation under God. At the Quebec conference in 1864, Sir Leonard Tilley, the governor of New Brunswick, proposed that Canada should have as its motto the words of Psalm 72: 'He shall have dominion from sea to sea.' This motion which recognized God's dominion and sovereignty over Canada was unanimously accepted by the founding Fathers. Today, that motto is inscribed on

the arch above the Peace Tower entrance to the Parliament Buildings, and is included in the seal of Canada. May it always remain so!" (Thompson 1990, 150-151).

As leader of the federal Social Credit Party, Thompson gave speeches across the country outlining his views. By 1964 he "was recognized as a popular spokesman of conservative issues rather than just Social Credit issues" (Thompson 1990, 137). In 1965 a number of these speeches were compiled as a book entitled *Commonsense for Canadians* which sold over 40,000 copies. One of the speeches was delivered to the Ontario Sunday School Association and strongly encourages "commitment to Christ, commitment to the Scriptures, commitment to the spreading of the Gospel" (Thompson 1965, 129). Thompson also indicated he hoped Canada would experience an evangelical Christian awakening: "Canada needs a Wesley—urgently so. Canadian Christians desperately need a wave of spiritual revival" (Thompson 1965, 128). The other speeches in the book are largely defenses of conservatism, free enterprise, and Social Credit, in the context of the issues of the 1960s.

Thompson served his final term as an MP, 1968-1972, as a member of the Progressive Conservative Party. In 1972 he became professor of political science at Trinity Western College (later Trinity Western University). In 1979 Trinity College Press published his book *From the Marketplace* which sets forth his political and economic views. It seems reasonable to conclude from passages in this book that had he been politically involved in the 1980s, his perspective would have reflected that of the Christian Right.

For example, Thompson saw a close connection between individual morality and the law. As he sees it, although law cannot force people to be good,

> Individual morality is, and must be, closely related to public

morals and to legal responsibility. When personal morality has a public consequence, the law must assume a definite responsibility. It follows that it is the responsibility of government to legislate concerning the public and legal aspects of moral behavior. It is necessary for government to enact divorce laws, although it is not possible for government to legislate a happy marriage (Thompson 1979, 77).

Thompson was decidedly pro-life: "I believe it is a scientific fact that life begins at conception" (Thompson 1979, 78). He opposed abortion even when pregnancy resulted from rape and incest.

Pregnancy in young girls, whether by seduction or through high school promiscuity, is increasingly being recommended as a justifiable reason for abortion. However, the evil or tragic aspect is the seduction or the deterioration of morals, not the baby the girl bears. The situation caused by rape and incest is difficult; yet, here too divine norms must speak clearly. The unborn child, in spite of the tragic circumstances, is entitled to life, to protection and to care (Thompson 1979, 79).

Thompson's views on homosexuality were also very conservative. In his view, "Homosexuality has always had a debasing effect on morals and on personality" (Thompson 1979, 81). It appears that he even may have wanted laws against homosexuality. "The full weight of the Christian view of man and of society opposes the legalization of homosexuality. Moral force rooted in the Christian ethic is the only instrument that can effectively regulate human conduct" (1979, 81).

Robert Thompson's many years of political activity took place largely before the major social issues roused by the Sexual Revolution came to prominence. Those issues were just beginning to arise in Canadian politics as he served his last term in Parliament, and he seemed preoccupied with other matters. However, it's clear from his later writing that he strongly opposed both abortion and homosexuality, the two main targets of the Christian Right.

CONCLUSION

Long before anyone ever heard of a "Christian Right," evangelical Christians had a major presence in English-Canadian society. They certainly weren't seen as being American invaders. One of Canada's most beloved novelists of the early twentieth century used his narrative skills to promote evangelical Christianity, even while weaving together interesting tales. And evangelicals (some would prefer the term "fundamentalists") played a significant role in politics through the Social Credit Party, especially in Alberta.

REFERENCES

Connor, Ralph. 1901. *Black Rock: A Tale of the Selkirks*. Kessinger Publishing facsimile reprint.

Connor, Ralph. 1900. *The Sky Pilot: A Tale of the Foothills*. Kessinger Publishing facsimile reprint.

Connor, Ralph. 1909. *The Foreigner: A Tale of Saskatchewan*. Kessinger Publishing reprint.

Elliott, David R., and Iris Miller. 1987. *Bible Bill: A Biography of William Aberhart*. Edmonton: Reidmore Books.

Finkel, Alvin. 1989. *The Social Credit Phenomenon in Alberta*. Toronto: University of Toronto Press.

Hamilton, Jacques. 1977. *Our Alberta Heritage*. Calgary Power Ltd.

Irving, John A. 1959. *The Social Credit Movement in Alberta*. Toronto: University of Toronto Press.

Layton, Kirk H. 2001. *Charles W. Gordon/Ralph Connor: From Black Rock to Regina Trench*. Trafford Publishing.

Lennox, John. 1987. *Charles W. Gordon ["Ralph Connor"] and His Works*. ECW Press.

Mackey, Lloyd. 1997. *Like Father, Like Son: Ernest Manning and Preston Manning*. Toronto: ECW Press.

Macpherson, C. B. 1962. *Democracy in Alberta: Social Credit and the Party System*. Second edition. Toronto: University of Toronto Press.

Sperber, Irwin. 1964. "Sociological and Ethical Dimensions of Alberta, Part One." *Edge*. No. 3, Autumn 1964, 40-53.

Thompson, Robert N. 1965. *Commonsense for Canadians: A Selection of Speeches Analysing Today's Opportunities and Problems*. Toronto: McClelland and Stewart Limited.

Thompson, Robert N. 1979. *From the Marketplace*. Langley, BC:

Trinity College Press.

Thompson, Robert N. 1990. *A House of Minorities: The Political Memoirs of Robert N. Thompson*. Burlington, ON: Welch Publishing Company Inc.

CHAPTER 3 | THE RISE OF THE CHRISTIAN RIGHT IN THE 1970s

There have been three central figures in Canada's Christian Right, Ken Campbell, Ted Byfield, and Gwen Landolt. All three of them were involved as the movement began to emerge in the 1970s. Ken Campbell became a crusading political activist in 1974 and founded the first organization that can be considered as part of Canada's Christian Right in the strictest sense, Renaissance International. Ted Byfield began publishing a weekly newsmagazine in 1973 that would grow into *Alberta Report*. This magazine would be the most significant print media voice for the social conservative perspective in Canada for many years. Gwen Landolt founded and was the first president of the Toronto Right to Life Association and was one of the founders of Campaign Life Coalition. However, her emergence as a major national leader of the Christian Right would take place in the 1980s and will be covered in the next chapter.

Needless to say, there were also other concerned Christians who did what they could to resist the consequences of the Sexual Revolution, including abortion, homosexual rights, pornography, public nudity, and immoral literature in public schools.

Bernice Gerard and David Mainse were two evangelical leaders who also contributed to the Christian resistance against these trends.

THE EARLY YEARS OF THE PRO-LIFE MOVEMENT

It can be reasonably argued that the legislative spark that would ultimately lead to the rise of a Christian Right in Canada was the Omnibus Criminal Code Reform Bill introduced by then Justice Minister Pierre Trudeau on December 21, 1967. The changes to the Criminal Code that were envisioned by this bill included the decriminalization of homosexual acts and a liberalization of restrictions on abortion. In October of that year a House of Commons committee had already begun hearings on abortion law reform, receiving briefs and presentations from interested parties, mostly favoring liberalization of the law. But the Omnibus Reform Bill was introduced months before the abortion reform committee had a chance to finish its work.

Pierre Trudeau was very clever in the manner and timing of his changes to the law regarding abortion and homosexuality. The changes were buried among numerous unrelated Criminal Code reforms, giving those more controversial aspects less prominence in the overall bill. As well, by introducing the bill just before Christmas, the opposition was caught off guard.

> Still more skillful was Trudeau's handling of the bill before the press and the public. The homosexuality and, by extension, the abortion provisions were justified in what turned out to be a rhetorical masterstroke. "The state," Trudeau quipped to reporters, "has no business in the bedrooms of the nation." This offhand, almost flippant remark would subsequently permeate the consciousness and political vocabulary of the entire society. It seemed to justify in a single sentence the new sexual freedom of the sixties, the ultimate

rejoinder to any attempt by society to control the sexual behaviour of its citizens. Pierre Trudeau was obviously a man in tune with the spirit of the times (Morton 1992, 23).

Before the bill could be passed, however, Prime Minister Lester Pearson resigned. This led to a campaign to select a new leader of the Liberal Party. Trudeau won that leadership, and was subsequently elected Prime Minister in a general election that followed. The omnibus bill was then reintroduced, and serious parliamentary debate started on it early in 1969.

The New Democratic Party strongly supported the bill. Both the Liberals and Progressive Conservatives were divided over it, although most Liberals would support it and most PCs would vote "no."

> The most cohesive and outspoken opposition to the abortion bill came from the fourteen remaining members of the Ralliement Creditiste in Parliament. All French, all Catholic, and all representing rural Quebec ridings, the Creditistes attacked the bill on many fronts—medical, legal, religious, and philosophical. Defending the right to life of the unborn, the Creditistes argued that the bill violated not just Catholic teaching but such secular norms as the Canadian Bill of Rights (Morton 1992, 25).

But the Liberals used their parliamentary majority to pass the bill on May 14, 1969.

Although the bill's reforms did not completely decriminalize abortion, they did make the procedure more readily available. A hospital's therapeutic abortion committee (TAC) could approve an abortion after three doctors confirmed that a pregnancy would likely endanger the life or health of a particular woman. Women seeking abortions were normally approved for the procedure.

Professor Michael Cuneo writes that "The Canadian pro-life movement originated in response to the 1969 abortion legislation" (1989, 5). He notes, however, that a group of Catholic laypeople submitted a brief to the parliamentary committee on abortion reform. This group would evolve into Canada's first pro-life organization, Alliance for Life, in 1968.

> The Alliance for Life was for several years the principal organizational force of the Canadian movement. As the national umbrella for all right-to-life groups, the Alliance was responsible for conducting research, disseminating educational materials, formulating political strategy, and in general coordinating the varied activities of the movement's scattered troops. The organization adopted a rotating provincial office system, and was administered nationally by an elected board and a skeletal office staff located in Ottawa, the Alliance's first national seat, and subsequently in Toronto and then Winnipeg. Throughout its checkered history, the Alliance has been funded entirely by affiliation fees and private donations. An Annual General Meeting has provided delegates from right-to-life groups across the country with an opportunity to overview the organization's performance as well as to plot its future course. Pro-Life News Canada, a low-key journal still published six times annually by the Alliance, was for several years the movement's most important informational organ (Cuneo 1989, 9).

The Alliance for Life was basically educational in function. After the 1972 federal election, the Alliance decided to create another organization which would focus on political activities. "Thus, in 1973 the Coalition for Life (in 1978 renamed Coalition for the Protection of Human Life) was formed to undertake explicitly political functions such as lobbying, canvassing of politicians, and designing election strategies" (Cuneo 1989, 1). Many Coalition activists were in fact NDP supporters, but by 1986 all had resigned their NDP memberships due to that party's determined support for abortion on demand (Cuneo 1989, 10-11).

Writing in the summer of 1974, one of Canada's foremost pro-life thinkers described the apparent growth of the country's pro-life movement.

> The Right-to-Life groups concentrate on the educational and political aspects of the abortion issue. They have spread to cities and towns throughout English-speaking Canada, numbering approximately 75 groups. Recently they have also entered Quebec. They are federated nationally in the Alliance for Life whose headquarters in Toronto sponsors a publication which appears 5 times a year and which has a circulation of 10,000. Its very active president, Dr. Heather Morris, has appeared several times on national television and has addressed numerous meetings and spoken on many local radio shows throughout Canada. As an indication of the interest these groups have aroused it may be noted that last year Right-to-Life groups, mostly in English-speaking Canada, garnered 352,000 signatures for a petition which was handed to Prime Minister Trudeau requesting a stricter law and safeguards against abuse of the existing law. Presently, they are conducting a campaign for a petition bearing one million signatures (de Valk 1974, 9-10).

In some instances the pro-life groups experienced significant opposition. At the time, Saskatoon had two pro-life groups, one for the city and one at the University of Saskatchewan.

> The university group, centering around one strong personality has been active to such an extent that it incurred the ire of pro-abortion students represented by such groups as the Women's Directorate, the Committee for the Repeal of the Abortion Law and others, who succeeded in having the Students' Union rescind its status as a university campus club. It

is only a small incident but, nevertheless, indicative of strong currents of hostility (de Valk 1974, 10).

The Canadian pro-life movement became increasingly divided by the mid-1970s. The division was between the movement's "professional elite who preferred to address the abortion issue within a strictly civil rights frame of reference, and its flourishing grass roots supporters for whom anti-abortionism was inextricably a crusade against feminism, secularism, and the rise of moral permissiveness in Canadian society" (Cuneo 1989, 11).

According to Cuneo,

> 1975 represented a high-water mark of organization for the movement. Buoyed by the success of a 1973 campaign, in which 350,000 signatures were collected on a petition of protest against legalized abortion, the Alliance organized the Petition of One Million campaign which garnered 1,017,000 signatures. These, along with the brief entitled "Stop the Killing", were presented to the federal government by MP Ursula Appolloni following a mass rally on Parliament Hill (1989, 12).

In 1975 the federal government established a committee to study the operation of the 1969 abortion law. In 1977 this committee released its findings, commonly referred to as the Badgley Report.

> While this study supported the contention of pro-choice advocates that there existed an inequable access to abortion across Canada, it also confirmed several perennial grievances of pro-life activists: first, that a majority of the therapeutic abortions reported by Statistics Canada were justified for vague and mostly dubious reasons of mental health; second, that therapeutic abortion committees in Ontario were in the habit of giving blanket approval to abortion applications; and

third, that a minority of hospitals continued to discriminate against medical personnel who had moral qualms about participating in abortion procedures (Cuneo 1989, 15).

Later in 1977 the leadership of Coalition for Life prepared a brief that was to be presented to the Ontario Legislature in October. It contained four recommendations, two of which aroused considerable controversy among pro-lifers. The first recommendation was to clarify the guidelines that should be followed to justify therapeutic abortions. Many activists saw this as a compromised position. The other controversial recommendation called for expansion of government aid to low income women, such as low-rental housing and increased access to day care. The Coalition amended the brief in an attempt to mollify the criticism, but that didn't work (Cuneo 1989, 15-17).

There was a fundamental division in the ranks of the pro-life movement. The leadership of the Coalition for Life came from one side, and its critics came from the other. Basically, the Coalition leadership figures were to the Left of many activists. The grassroots activists were committed to a broader social conservative position characterized by more than just opposition to abortion.

This division would be institutionalized with the creation of Campaign Life in Toronto on February 26, 1978.

> The establishment of Campaign Life gave solid organizational shape to the movement's ideological dichotomy. It also meant that the Coalition, divested of much of its former influence, would be consigned a spectator role as the movement plunged more deeply into a one-dimensional conservatism. In both its understanding of the abortion issue and its modus operandi, Campaign Life was the antithesis of the Coalition: confrontational, politically absolutist, and unrepentantly hostile to post-1950s Canadian culture.

Considered self-condemned by the 1977 brief, the Coalition lost over the next few years the support of many right-to-life groups, including Canada's flagship pro-life group in Toronto which elected in March 1978 to align itself with the proven orthodoxy of Campaign Life. Relations between the representative executives of the Coalition and the Alliance for Life, the national umbrella for right-to-life groups, systematically deteriorated to the point where the latter decided in April 1978 to completely dissociate from the Coalition and to ban Coalitionists from the Alliance's Toronto headquarters (Cuneo 1989, 21-22).

The following year another organizational split occurred. Moderates on the board of the Alliance for Life ousted its conservative president. Some local groups then broke from the Alliance.

The powerful Toronto right-to-life group, as well as neighbouring groups in Halton, Barrie, and elsewhere, seceded from the Alliance in a demonstration of allegiance to the deposed president and her right-wing policies. Thus, by the end of 1979 the balkanized movement consisted of the following configurations: a quasi-national educational organization enervated by three years of internal jousting (the Alliance); a dispirited political organization in process of relocating its national office from Toronto to Ottawa (the Coalition); and a maverick Toronto right-to-life group which, together with its affiliated groups and the fiercely energetic Campaign Life, would effectively set the tone of the movement for the next seven years (Cuneo 1989, 23-24).

The Alliance national office was moved to Winnipeg in 1979, explicitly to break the hold of the embroiled Toronto executive. The move was also an attempt by moderates in the Alliance to stem the reactionary tide in Toronto that threatened to engulf the organization. In deserting the media centre and cultural capital of English Canada, however, the Alliance would lose much of its former dynamism and become reduced to basically a regional organization. More significantly, the removal of the Alliance and Coalition national offices from Toronto—the epicenter of anti-abortionism in Canada—meant that

Campaign Life would have the field to itself as the temperature of the abortion debate rose dramatically in the 1980s. The separatism of the Toronto right-to-life group, as well as the rise to dominance of Campaign Life, was like a bisection of the movement's brain into right and left hemispheres. On the one side were Coalition for Life people and moderates within the Alliance, sensitive, bright, nuanced, but with limited will and drive; on the other were the activists represented by Toronto right-to-life and Campaign Life, mountains of will and drive, but unsophisticated, obstinate, and inflexible (Cuneo 1989, 24).

The pro-life movement in Canada has been predominantly Roman Catholic. This was especially true during its first ten years or so. However, by the late 1970s evangelicals became increasingly involved. Ken Campbell, for instance, was the most prominent conservative evangelical political activist of the 1970s, but he did not become significantly involved in the pro-life cause until about 1984. At that point he started to emerge as one of the most controversial and news-worthy pro-life leaders. However, Campbell got his start in political activism opposing the homosexual rights movement.

KEN CAMPBELL AND THE BIRTH OF THE CHRISTIAN RIGHT IN CANADA

For those who see the Christian Right as an exclusively evangelical phenomenon, Canada's Christian Right can be said to have been born on February 16, 1974. It was on that day that Ken

Campbell, a Baptist evangelist from Ontario, decided to take action against immoral activities that had taken place in the public school his children were attending. His protest against immoral literature, homosexual activism, and sex education helped galvanize considerable public support for his views and led to the creation of a committee that would grow into a national organization. Campbell would be the leading figure in Canada's Christian Right in the 1970s and into the early 1980s.

Ken Campbell was born in Hartford, Ontario, in 1934. His father was a Baptist pastor. After high school Campbell attended a Bible college in the US and subsequently became a Baptist pastor himself, with the Fellowship of Evangelical Baptist Churches in Canada. He also ministered as a popular traveling evangelist. "For seventeen years during the 1960s and early 70s, Ken carried out 'a crusade ministry of global evangelism,' spending one-third of his time away from Ontario on the Canadian prairies and in the U.S." (Petrasek 1991, 32). But in the 1970s, his evangelistic crusades began to give way to political activism.

There were basically two main issues that triggered Campbell's jump into political activism. The first was his discovery that the recommended reading list of the English department at his children's high school included immoral materials. Shortly after this discovery he had to travel to western Canada on one of his evangelistic trips. While in Saskatoon to speak at a men's breakfast, his conscience forced him to face his personal responsibilities.

As he saw it, for an evangelist "to evade the social implications of the Gospel which he preaches as they relate to his parental and citizen responsibilities, is to deny the Gospel which he preaches" (Campbell 1975, 13). And this applied directly to himself: "I have no business preaching to anyone anywhere if I am unwilling to be all that a Christian father and citizen ought to be in his home and community" (Campbell 1975, 13). Campbell therefore vowed to God that he would deal with the "educational crisis" facing his family upon returning to Ontario.

THE FIRST STEP

Shortly after returning home Campbell phoned the principal of the school to discuss the English department's recommended reading list. The children had the option of making selections from the list, but were not being forced to read the more scandalous books. Campbell didn't think that the immoral materials should even be an option for the students, but he couldn't make any headway with the principal.

The following evening Campbell learned that there had been a presentation by four members of a gay liberation movement organization at the school. This was "the last straw."

He contacted a student who had seen the presentation to find out what happened. The presentation took place in a twelfth grade health and physical education class, but no advance notice had been given. Campbell asked the student about the nature of the presentation. The student replied that it was "To lead us to accept the Gay lifestyle as normal for many people living in our society—a perfectly socially acceptable lifestyle" (Campbell 1975, 24).

As he analyzed the situation, Campbell came to three basic conclusions. First, that the incidents involving immoral literature and homosexual rights were symptoms of a larger problem. Secondly, that the larger problem is the underlying secular humanist philosophy dominating the public education system. And thirdly, that his only "leverage" over the public education system was the property taxes he paid to support the system. He therefore decided to withhold the educational portion of his property taxes until his grievances were dealt with.

FORMATION OF RENAISSANCE

Campbell's tax protest elicited considerable controversy in the media, with public education officials openly opposing Campbell's views and charges concerning the system. Campbell was able to meet with some education officials, but still his concerns were not addressed. He therefore determined to organize his supporters into a group "seeking the improvement of the public educational system" (Campbell 1975, 72). On March 14, 1974, a steering committee was created for the formation of the Halton Renaissance Committee.

With Campbell as the Chairman of the Committee, a public meeting was held on March 28 at the Milton District High School. Over 600 people attended to hear speakers address concerns regarding the state of public education. "By the close of the evening Renaissance was enthusiastically launched with over 300 members" (Campbell 1975, 88). Local newspapers carried major stories about this meeting the next day. A short time later, in the middle of the night, a rock was thrown through Campbell's daughters' bedroom window. Attached was a note containing an obscene message.

Renaissance continued to hold meetings through the spring and summer. By August it had approximately 600 members. On August 22 a delegation from the Committee presented a detailed brief to the Halton Board of Education on its views regarding the improvement of the education system. The presentation focused on the need for the system to be more responsive to parents. About 150 spectators were present, "the largest number ever to attend a Board of Education meeting" (Campbell 1975, 118).

Campbell was pleased by the reception given to the presentation by the Board trustees. The Board created an ad hoc committee to study the Renaissance brief, and on October 10 this committee recommended accepting many of the brief's suggestions. Impressed by the responsiveness of the trustees, Campbell decided to pay the taxes he had previously withheld.

Nevertheless, the Renaissance Committee soldiered on. It expressed concerns about psychological testing of students as well as some of the books included on a list to be used in Halton's public schools. However, the salient issue at this point was sex education. In February, 1975, Renaissance arranged for a film being used in Grade Twelve family life courses, "Sexuality and Communication," to be shown to concerned parents. About 150 people attended the meeting, and most of them subsequently supported a resolution to the Ontario government asking that sex education be optional. Renaissance also began a campaign for a more pluralistic education system, such as a voucher system whereby parents can decide which school to send their children to. And Campbell pulled his five children out of the public schools and sent them to private Christian schools.

The activity of the Renaissance Committee caught the attention of people across Canada and even in the United States. The Committee received donations from other parts of Canada as well as the U.S., and decided to expand into a national organization with provincial affiliates. "In order to cope with the demands of Renaissance growth, in mid-May [1975], the Halton Renaissance Committee established itself as the steering committee for Renaissance Ontario and Renaissance Canada, with Ken Campbell appointed as chairman" (Campbell 1975, 244-245). By this point there were Renaissance members in every province except Prince Edward Island. Thus Ken Campbell's forays into activism at a municipal level led to his launch into broader political activism.

ANITA BRYANT RALLIES

In 1978 Renaissance sponsored a cross-country speaking tour by Anita Bryant. Bryant was an American celebrity who had become prominent in conservative Christian circles by actively opposing the homosexual rights movement in the USA. Campbell was impressed by her willingness to stand up for her Christian beliefs despite jeopardizing her career.

Although Bryant was American, and her activism involved leading a successful referendum campaign to overturn a gay rights ordinance in Florida, she was a lightning rod for anger from Canada's homosexuals. Canada's main homosexual publication of the time, *The Body Politic*, followed her activities closely and featured news of her prominently in 1977 and 1978. One important article about her 1977 Florida victory began,

> On June 7th in Dade County, Florida, the United States gay movement lost its first major battle in the struggle for gay civil rights. Unlike previous court rulings either pro- or anti-gay which had occurred over the post-Stonewall (1969) period, the Anita Bryant vs. the gays controversy had captured the attention of the American public, and particularly in Florida, brought the discussion of homosexuality, if not the gay people themselves, out of the closet (Hamburg 1977, 1).

Many Canadian homosexuals reacted angrily to Bryant's triumph. They organized and protested.

> Canadian gays followed the Dade County struggle closely, alerted to its progress by unprecedented coverage in the media. The Toronto community took the most definite steps with the formation of a representative Coalition to Stop Anita Bryant. It generated two spontaneous and highly visible evening demonstrations along Yonge Street in June and July [1977]. Bryant was burned in effigy at the first march… and the July 22 demo, with over 500 people, was the largest in Canada to that date (*The Body Politic* 1978a, 13).

The first Anita Bryant rally was held at the People's Church in Toronto on January 15, 1978. Campbell believes about 4,000 people turned out that Sunday night, and that there were 25 policemen in the audience due to fears generated by the controversy. More than 500 protestors demonstrated in front of the church. The pastor of the church, Paul Smith, was hit by a pie thrown by a lesbian. The CBC had to interview Bryant at a police station due to security concerns. According to Campbell, her news conference the next morning was the largest news conference ever held in Toronto to that point.

One of the protest leaders was Linda Jain, a lesbian activist with the group Women Against Violence Against Women. As quoted in *The Body Politic*, she clearly enumerated the problems the Canadian Left had with Bryant's positions on moral issues:

> Anita Bryant is against everything that feminists stand for: day care, abortion, equal pay and, more recently, control over our own sexuality. She is not alone. There are many right-wing forces which support her in the U.S. and we are seeing more clearly that these same forces exist everywhere. The Renaissance group which invited her to Canada is not alone in its fight against women and gay people. They know that both movements are a real threat to the status quo. All of these right-wing groups have connections to the conservative element in political parties and the power of these political groups is enormous (Leslie 1978, 7).

After the Toronto rally, Campbell organized Anita Bryant rallies in Peterborough (April 28), Edmonton (April 29), Winnipeg (April 30), Moose Jaw (July 1), and London, Ontario (September 10). Campbell said that they were well-attended, with 2000-3000 in Peterborough, 6000 in Edmonton, and 3000 in Moose Jaw. Press reports from the time give somewhat lower figures. Each rally also attracted anti-Bryant protestors.

St. John's Edmonton Report gave considerable attention to Bryant's Edmonton appearance, even putting her picture on the cover of the April 21, 1978 issue. There were two local co-hosts of the Edmonton event. One was Rev. Gordon Quantz of the Edmonton Missionary Church, a personal friend of Ken Campbell and an organizer for Campbell's Renaissance organization in Alberta. The other co-host was Orvis Kennedy, a very prominent Alberta Social Credit organizer and close associate of Ernest Manning (*St. John's Edmonton Report* 1978a, 24).

Although Ken Campbell estimated the turnout in Edmonton to be 6000, even the sympathetic *St. John's Edmonton Report* gave it a much lower number. It stated that

> the concert-cum-Christian rally did seem to achieve its avowed purpose of bringing some Edmonton Christians "out of the closet," at least as far as the Coliseum. Although the turnout was disappointing to some—the 3,700-odd patrons giving the Coliseum a vacuous look—the response to both Miss Bryant's singing and Mr. Campbell's preaching was enthusiastic (*St. John's Edmonton Report* 1978b, 36).

In the midst of the Bryant controversy, *The Body Politic* described Ken Campbell's Renaissance International as "the heart of the Canadian anti-gay movement." The same article noted that the head of Renaissance's BC chapter was Robert Thompson, the former leader of the federal Social Credit Party (*The Body Politic* 1978b, 1).

Left-wing protestors appeared at each of Bryant's rallies. During her rally at the London Gardens in London, Ontario, a bomb threat was phoned in and the building was evacuated. Shortly after the London event,

> Bryant appeared at the Queensway Cathedral in Etobicoke, a suburban borough of Toronto. Bryant supporters were greeted by a spirited picket line of about 125 anti-Bryant

people. A majority of lesbians, along with a number of gay men, straight supporters and a large showing from the Revolutionary Workers League and the International Socialists, made the late, wet Sunday night picket an especially militant and boisterous event. A number of lesbians linked arms and tried to enter the church to hear Bryant, but were threatened with arrest by Metro Toronto police, who had also prohibited the use of loud-hailers by the gay demonstrators (Trollope 1978, 12).

According to Campbell, the Bryant meetings "had a great impact on the nation." However, many evangelicals criticized him for bringing her to Canada, and few evangelical ministers were willing to join him on the platform at the rallies. He was becoming too controversial for many. "I knew I was burning bridges," he said (Campbell 2005).

Sadly, within two years Anita Bryant had let down her supporters. She separated from her husband and filed for divorce. This was likely due to her relationship with another man. Ken Campbell was outspoken about his disappointment with her. "The fact is, she has violated the Christian conscience of every person who supported her," he said (*Alberta Report* 1980, 47).

THE BODY POLITIC

Shortly before Bryant's appearance in Toronto, in December, 1977, the offices of the homosexual periodical, *The Body Politic*, were raided by Toronto police. Three officials of the periodical were charged with using the mail to distribute "immoral, indecent, and scurrilous" material due to an article it carried entitled "Men Loving Boys Loving Men." As one might gather from the title, it was believed the article encouraged pedophilia.

Eventually, after two trials, both of which resulted in acquittals, the case was dropped. However, in the first trial, which took place early in January, 1979, Ken Campbell appeared as a Crown witness. This was due to his high public profile on the homosexual rights issue.

Rallies in support of *The Body Politic* were held across Canada as well as in Boston, New York and San Francisco. On January 3, 1979, Toronto Mayor John Sewell spoke at one of the rallies in support of the paper. This became a major news story and was carried throughout the country. The following day, Toronto City Hall received hundreds of angry calls in opposition to Sewell's public support for *The Body Politic*.

> It became clear later in the day, however, that the response was scarcely spontaneous—most calls came after right-wing Evangelist Ken Campbell had appeared on the religious programme *100 Huntley Street* and broken down in tears as he related his experience as a witness for the Crown in *The Body Politic* trial. During the programme, the telephone number of the mayor's office was flashed regularly across the screen (Hannon 1979, 9).

Campbell and David Mainse of *100 Huntley Street* also held a "Faith, Freedom and the Family" rally at Toronto City Hall in response to Sewell's support for *The Body Politic*.

On April 11, 1980, the Coalition for Gay Rights in Ontario (CGRO) filed a letter of complaint with Revenue Canada against Renaissance International. CGRO alleged that Renaissance had violated the conditions of its charitable status by indulging in political activities (Wells 1980, 14).

TORONTO ELECTION IMPACT

In the 1980 Toronto municipal election campaign, Mayor Sewell endorsed the candidacy of George Hislop, a prominent gay activist, for a seat on city council. Gay rights became a major component of the election, and both Sewell and Hislop were defeated.

Sewell's main competitor for the mayoralty was Art Eggleton who publicly spoke out against the spectre of "gay power politics." As Eggleton put it, "Homosexuals are a power group in Toronto and I don't believe any mayor should align himself with any power group. People are well aware of what has happened in San Francisco with the gays, and they are genuinely concerned the same thing will happen in Toronto" (Jackson 1980, 14).

Conservative Christians, most notably Ken Campbell himself, played a leading role in this election campaign.

> Renaissance International alone distributed 100,000 copies of a tabloid, urging the defeat of Sewell and other municipal election candidates seen as being supportive of gay and lesbian rights. The day before the election, Renaissance published a two-page advertisement in the *Toronto Sun* attacking the gay community and calling for a vote for Toronto the Good. Another group formed by fundamentalist Christians, calling itself Metro's Moral Majority, distributed a Homosexuality Fact Sheet door-to-door. One of its purported facts was that '1 out of 3 sexual assaults on children are committed by homosexuals.' Positive Parents, billing itself as a 'pro-family crusade against the radical homosexual lobby,' held a two-hundred-person 'decency' rally at City Hall, attended by Campbell, Salvation Army officers, and an allegedly reformed homosexual (Warner 2002, 139).

According to Campbell, Sewell publicly acknowledged the Renaissance tabloid's role in his defeat. It was commonly reported at the time that the "gay issue" sunk Sewell's campaign (Strauss 1980, 5).

George Hislop, the prominent gay activist who failed to win a seat on Toronto city council, lashed out at Renaissance in his post-election speech to his campaign workers.

> He questioned the legality of Renaissance International's charitable status, flaunted in a tax deduction registration number which appeared in the previous day's two-page spread in the Sunday Sun calling for a defeat of candidates supporting gay rights. "It's a political movement masquerading as a religious organization," he charged (Jackson 1981, 9).

Ten days after the election, "Campbell received a letter from Revenue Canada which proposed that the government take away Renaissance's religious tax status" (Haiven 1984, 154). In November, 1982, after a legal fight that cost $20,000, "the federal court of appeal restored Renaissance's charity status on the grounds that Campbell had been denied the natural justice of a proper hearing" (Haiven 1984, 156).

KEN CAMPBELL AND JERRY FALWELL

Beginning in the late 1970s, Rev. Jerry Falwell became increasingly prominent as a leader and spokesman for conservative Christians in the USA. He remained well-known in this role up until his death in the summer of 2007. Ken Campbell is perhaps the closest thing that Canada has ever had to a Jerry Falwell figure. Indeed, the two men were friends. Campbell brought Falwell to Toronto and Edmonton to speak in 1982. At the Edmonton meeting, Falwell told the crowd of almost 2000 that "the Moral Majority and the whole fundamentalist 'tidal wave,' were winning. The 1980s were to be 'a decade of revival'" (Weatherbe and Regaly 1982, 40).

Campbell wrote a book in 1980 entitled *No Small Stir* in which Falwell wrote the Foreword. Falwell noted that "Ken Campbell has been my friend for years" (Campbell 1980, 14) and that Campbell "wants to do for Canada what Moral Majority is beginning to do for America—call the nation back to God" (Campbell 1980, 13).

In that book Campbell identifies himself with Falwell's efforts. He writes, "as 'the voice of Canada's Moral Majority,' Renaissance is now associated with Dr. Jerry Falwell's parallel crusade throughout the United States—for breaking the grip on the controls of our society held by a handful of radical secularists" (Campbell 1980, 189). Earlier in the book Campbell had spoken in glowing terms of the impact of the Moral Majority on American politics. He recounted watching the 1980 Republican Party convention on TV.

> At the convention there were repeated references by political analysts as to the impact of Dr. Jerry Falwell and 'Moral Majority' in rousing the sleeping giant of Bible-believing Christianity from its irrelevancy. This could mean ten million fundamentalist Christian voters registered to vote who have not voted before. And there are heartening evidences of a parallel, though in typically conservative Canadian fashion, less spectacular awakening to righteousness in Canadian public life"(Campbell 1980, 120).

It seems reasonable to conclude that Ken Campbell was the first prominent Canadian leader of the movement that would come to be known as the "Christian Right." This movement has never become as large or as influential as its American counterpart, but it has had a presence in Canada in one form or another at least since the mid-1970s. The Canadian Christian Right is certainly not an American import. Ken Campbell's political activism and leadership began as a direct result of issues he faced in his own locale, not due to any American influences. Although Campbell subsequently embraced American Christian figures such as Anita Bryant and Jerry Falwell, he had already been involved in activism for a number of years before he looked to them for support in his endeavors.

TED BYFIELD'S CONTRIBUTION TO THE CHRISTIAN RIGHT

In a book against the Reform Party and Canadian Alliance, political scientist David Laycock refers to "the far-right, fundamentalist Christian *Alberta Report* and *BC Report* magazines" (2002, 15). That's putting too fine a point on it, but nevertheless, the *Report* family of magazines was undoubtedly written from a generally conservative Christian perspective. The magazines covered the issues that were important to conservative Christians, and they did so from a consciously conservative perspective.

Another academic, sociologist Trevor Harrison, basically gets it right in his brief description of *Alberta Report*:

> In articles and, more especially, editorials and columns (written by Ted and, in recent years, his son Link and other guest writers), the magazine has stood firmly for corporal and capital punishment, the teaching of fundamentalist Christian religion in schools, the rights of the family (that is, the parents), and free enterprise, while espousing an often virulent hatred of metrification, pro-choice advocates, feminism in general, public school curriculum and methods of discipline, divorce, human rights commissions, 'mainstream' Christianity, homosexuality, penal reform, sex education, unions, public ownership, teachers' associations, and rock music (1995, 51).

Basically, *Alberta Report* and in later years its sister publications, *Western Report* and *BC Report*, was the closest thing the Christian Right in Canada ever had to a full-fledged magazine.

The founder of *Alberta Report*, its precursors and sister publications, was Ted Byfield. Ted Byfield was born in Toronto in 1928. When he was 17 he entered George Washington University in Washington, DC, but quit shortly thereafter to work for the *Washington Post* as a copy boy. Eighteen months later he moved back to Ontario and became a reporter for the *Ottawa Journal*. Following that, he did some reporting and editing for papers in Timmins and Sudbury, after which he was involved in a failed attempt at starting a weekly newspaper. In 1952 he moved to Winnipeg to work for the *Winnipeg Free Press*, and he even won the National Newspaper Award for political reporting in 1957 for his coverage of that year's federal election.

While in Winnipeg Byfield was evangelized by some Anglicans and he became a dedicated conservative Christian. Together with his wife and his new Anglican friends, he:

> founded the Company of the Cross, an organization committed to spreading Christianity through schools and the media. The group built a boarding school 25 miles north of Winnipeg in 1962, St. John's Cathedral Boys' School. A second St. John's School was founded west of Edmonton in 1966. Five years later the Company of the Cross established *St. John's Edmonton Report*. A *Calgary Report* followed in 1978. The two united into *Alberta Report* as of 1980 (M. Byfield 1983, xii).

The Company of the Cross was not for slackers. Members worked long hours, and were required to commit to daily private prayer and Bible reading, to attend daily religious services and to partake of Communion twice a week. (M. Byfield 1983, xii). By the late 1970s, however, the magazine was forced to hire staff rather than rely on Company of the Cross members.

In 1962 Byfield left his newspaper job to teach at the St. John's School in Selkirk, Manitoba. While still a teacher there, he wrote a book responding to Pierre Berton's best-selling critique of the Anglican Church, *The Comfortable Pew*. Byfield's book, Just *Think, Mr. Berton* (*A Little Harder*), describes his own conversion to Christianity, and in doing so offers a strong apologetic for Christianity and the church.

In many respects this book foreshadows the kind of writing that would drive *Alberta Report*. One can already see the central themes of Byfield's perspective. For one thing, the then-current sexual revolution was described as an attack on Western civilization.

> The Christian rule on sex has never, of course, been popular. It has been flouted to varying degrees ever since it was proclaimed by both Christian and secular societies. Neither are sexual revolutions particularly novel. Third and fourth century Rome witnessed a 'sexual revolution,' but historians are not inclined to look upon the period as a broadening or awakening of the human spirit. They are more apt to say, instead, that the popular rejection of moral principle inevitably precedes and contributes to the fall of a civilization (Byfield 1965, 72).

In Byfield's view, Pierre Berton was attacking the idea of moral absolutes and promoting relativism as a form of "liberation." People would be freed from the traditional morality that historically underlies Western societies. But the supposed new freedom was really an escape from the rules necessary for civilization. "Throughout every faction of society, we find evidence of the same 'liberation.' Homes break up and the divorce rate rises because people have been liberated from the grandiose pretension that marriage was for better or for worse" (Byfield 1965, 139).

Ultimately, Western civilization is based upon certain principles, and the relativism promoted by Berton and his ilk undermine those principles. "When the principles collapse, the civilization collapses. In this, more than in atomic bombs, or racial discrimination, or social welfare programmes, lies the root problem of our times" (Byfield 1965, 140). This was fundamentally the same drum that he would beat throughout the life of *Alberta Report*.

As noted previously, Byfield subsequently left the Manitoba school to work at the Alberta school. Once there Byfield decided to start a magazine which would ultimately debut in 1973. The goal was

> not an overtly religious publication but a magazine called *Saint John's Edmonton Report*, which so far as anyone knows was the first newsmagazine anywhere to be founded on a purely local basis. It would be read, its founders hoped, by religious and irreligious alike, though it would not strive for 'objectivity.' The latter, said publisher Byfield, is an impossibility anyway. Every news judgement involved a value judgement. So *Saint John's Edmonton Report* would be candidly Christian (Hedlin 1983, 23).

By 1980 *Saint John's Edmonton Report* had become *Alberta Report*. Then in 1986 "an identical but renamed version of *Alberta Report*, the *Western Report*, was produced for sale in the three remaining western provinces. This was followed, in 1989, by the creation of a somewhat distinctive version, *BC Report*" (Harrison 1995, 51). In June 1991, *Alberta Report*'s paid circulation was about 40,000, *BC Report*'s about 21,000, and *Western Report*'s about 1500.

Alberta Report struggled with a declining base of subscribers throughout the 1990s. In 1999 all three of the sister magazines were consolidated into a single, national *Report* magazine. Unfortunately, the magazine ultimately folded in June 2003.

Nevertheless, there can be no question that *Alberta Report* was influential on certain issues. For example, it has widely been seen as having been a central factor in the creation and rise of the Reform Party.

This may seem like a bit of an aside, but I just want to provide evidence to support the assertion that *Alberta Report* was influential on some issues, especially in Alberta. Private education was a controversial issue in the province for much of the 1980s, largely due to the Christian school movement. In 1988 the Progressive Conservative government introduced and passed a new School Act, one that was widely perceived as favouring private education.

Because Byfield was a leading proponent of private education, and *Alberta Report* strongly advocated this view, his name was brought up a number of times in the Legislature during debates about private schools and the new School Act. On June 8, 1988, when Calgary Liberal MLA Sheldon Chumir was making the point to Education Minister Nancy Betkowski that the new School Act would encourage the creation of new private schools (which she disputed) he said, "Well, Ted Byfield thinks they're encouraged" (*Alberta Hansard* 1988, 1581). Five days later, when he was making the point that the new School Act was a boon to private schools, Chumir mentioned that "Mr. Byfield, who is a great and untiring advocate of private religious schools, has expressed ecstasy with respect to the changes in the Act" (*Alberta Hansard* 1988, 1672). On June 17, NDP leader Ray Martin was very concerned that the new Act posed a threat to public education, and again invoked Byfield's name in defense of his concerns: "Now, the minister [of Education] has her ally Mr. Ted Byfield who thinks this is a great thing because it's the end of public education and the start of private education" (*Alberta Hansard* 1988, 1823). On June 28 Chumir once referred to Ted Byfield to justify an interpretation of a particular part of the new Act, saying that "while we disagree very, very strongly with respect to the direction schooling should take, let there be no mistake that (Byfield is) a very perceptive observer of what is going on in the world of education" (*Alberta Hansard* 1988, 2118).

Thus it is clear that Ted Byfield was the leading public voice for conservative Christians in Alberta on this issue at that time; hence the frequent invocations of his name in the Alberta Legislature. But he was also a leading public voice for conservative Christians on other issues. Although he was widely known as a spokesman for causes such as provincial rights and Senate reform, his impact as a conservative Christian journalist is unmistakable.

BERNICE GERARD AND THE CHRISTIAN RIGHT

Bernice Gerard was a Pentecostal preacher and radio broadcaster in Vancouver. In the mid-1970s she also became a Vancouver city alderman. She consciously wanted to maintain the Judeo-Christian basis of law and saw that as part of her task.

One incident she was most noted for was a protest against the increasing nudism at some Vancouver area beaches in 1977. She had been unable to get the city to do anything about the nudism. "Since we could not rouse City Hall either to show concern or take action, our Citizens for Integrity committee, which included Pastors Robert Birch and Allen Hornby, and Alderman Stella Jo Dean of North Vancouver, decided that we would conduct a silent protest by going for a walk on the beach Sunday afternoon" (Gerard 1988, 190-191).

The media had a field day mocking Gerard and her associates as "Victorian prudes" who "were intruding needlessly on the idyllic innocence of the young and the beautiful" (Gerard 1988, 193). But the real issue at stake was what kind of community Vancouver would be. As Gerard puts it, "We were doing our symbolic trek to draw attention to the fact that a long stretch of easily accessible public space was being used as an unregulated nudist camp. Nudism is not legal at any beach, but it takes the B.C. Attorney General to act for law enforcement" (Gerard 1988, 195).

Indeed, Gerard saw this episode as part of the larger culture war that is currently underway:

> The problem we face is not about people dressed or undressed; rather, we are in a social war to determine what foundations will guide our society. Most of my really nasty mail came from militant homosexuals who evidently had staked out their territory on the beach, and saw our protest as directed against them. During that turbulent time the secretaries at City Hall never knew what they would find in my fan mail. The greater part was supportive, but I remember letters with pictures of the male anatomy plus crude remarks (Gerard 1988, 196).

There was even a bomb threat at the radio station where she broadcast, intending to keep her off the air. It didn't work.

Gerard also had face-to-face incidents with people who opposed her Christian stand.

> One crisp November evening, unexpectedly released from a City Hall meeting, I decided to attend the *100 Huntley Street* rally with Rev. David Mainse at the Orpheum Theatre. From a distance I could see a crowd filling the sidewalk in front of the Orpheum; then at the entrance, I found myself in a marching crowd of about two hundred people, mostly young, carrying placards and chanting in unison, "Down

with born-again hate! Down with born-again hate!" Just as I was adjusting to the scene, a young woman with a placard came alongside and shouted amid the din, "Are you Bernice Gerard?" I nodded, "Yes." With that she spat full in my face, her saliva streaking down the upper front of my jet black fur coat. In the crush of things, all I thought to say to her in reply was, "And what's your name?" At which point she gave me another mouthful (Gerard 1988, 196-197).

As it turned out, the protest had resulted from a false rumor that Anita Bryant was to appear at the rally. She wasn't there. Gerard states, "My public profile as an active community-minded Christian made some of the gays try to cast me in an Anita Bryant role" (Gerard 1988, 197).

Gerard was also noted for her opposition to pornography. She explains that:

> In 1977, as a city alderman, I had tried to persuade City Council to cancel the stage play *O Calcutta!* which had been scheduled by the theater management to run in Vancouver's own civic theater, the Queen Elizabeth, even though *O Calcutta!* was a focus of obscenity trials in several parts of the world. I argued unsuccessfully that it was foolish for the city to allow its tax-subsidized theatres to be rented to just any theatrical group. "If *O Calcutta!*, with its group masturbation, mass copulation and bondage sex is welcome in the theater, then anything would be welcome," said I (1988, 198-199).

Similarly, in 1981, with the help of Citizens for Integrity, she protested against the movie *Caligula*, a hard-core pornographic movie. "We did everything we could to draw the attention of our busy elected officials to the fact that the first hard-core pornography was running in a Vancouver commercial theater" (Gerard 1988, 200).

Unable to get any action from government officials, Gerard and her associates decided to picket the movie. "The first week of the picket line I received a telephoned death threat, and several obscene phone calls. Frank Dorst, leading the group of picketers, was physically assaulted so that he was bruised and his clothes torn" (Gerard 1988, 201). Unfortunately, opposition to Caligula only seemed to increase its popularity.

Besides her opposition to pornography, Gerard was also active in opposing abortion.

> She first got involved in the formal pro-life movement when Dr. Heather Morris, president of the Alliance for Life of Canada, called to invite me to speak at the Festival for Life in Ottawa, in November 1973. The Alliance, which had affiliates across Canada, was presenting a petition on behalf of protection for unborn children. When we were all together in Ottawa, the speakers at the conference addressed the question of how best to persuade the country to reject abortion and other anti-life practices. British author-journalist Malcolm Muggeridge drew a standing ovation from the overflow crowd packed into the Ottawa Technical School's eleven-hundred-seat auditorium for his remarks in defense of the unborn child's right to live (Gerard 1988, 209).

After meeting Muggeridge through this pro-life activism, Gerard developed a friendship with him and his wife Kitty. They appeared on Gerard's radio program, and exchanged personal letters. Gerard would later visit the Muggeridges in their Sussex home in 1985 (Gerard 1988, 172).

It would be wrong to suggest that Bernice Gerard has been a major figure in Canada's Christian Right, but it would also be wrong to ignore her contribution. She used her influence as an elected official to oppose social decline, and she used her public platforms to promote Christian morality.

DAVID MAINSE

One of the significant features of American society that is widely seen as a contributing force to the strength of the Christian Right in the US is the prevalence of Christian television. In the late 1970s and at least until the televangelist scandals of 1987-1988, televangelism was seen as fueling the Christian Right.

Canada's situation is quite different, thanks to the CRTC. Until relatively recently, the only notable Christian television program in Canada has been *100 Huntley Street*. The moving force behind that program has been Pentecostal minister David Mainse. Mainse debuted on television in 1962, but began working in television full-time in 1970, and took his show to prime time and national attention in 1972.

In June 1981 *100 Huntley Street* used a mobile TV studio to travel across Canada and broadcast live from 25 different cities. This effort was called the "Salute to Canada." Writing shortly after the event, Mainse stated that "Salute was apolitical. Even so, some of the secular media were already trying to equate it with the Moral Majority movement in the States" (1981, 9). He was adamant that the Salute to Canada was not political.

Nevertheless, on the second day of the Salute, Mainse and his co-host Bernice Gerard discussed the abortion issue. Gerard stated that, "If Canada doesn't begin to take account of their stewardship of the innocent unborn, I think we are going to experience the judgment of God, so I feel very deeply about this." Mainse quickly agreed, commenting, "I sometimes wonder what is in the heart of God, concerning our society? Abortion must be an absolutely heinous stench in His nostrils" (Mainse 1981, 42-43).

The claim to be apolitical and the strong comments against abortion may seem to be paradoxical. Mainse explained the paradox this way: "Well, we said we weren't going to be political, but that did not mean we weren't going to speak God's truth, as He gave it to be spoken" (Mainse 1981, 43).

This same paradox appeared again. When the Salute entered Montreal, Mainse was interviewed on a radio program. Apparently the host wanted to make his program provocative by asking controversial questions. Mainse was forced to state, "No, we were in no way connected with the Moral Majority." Subsequently, he went further saying, "we are not being drawn into any political discussion" (Mainse 1981, 161).

The radio host then brought up the abortion issue asking, "Do you have the right to impose your own moral viewpoint? What if a person does not believe that life begins at the moment of conception ... is abortion then wrong for them?" Mainse answered, "A country has to establish its standards. I think that where abortion is wide open, infanticide is the very next step, which we can see in other civilizations. And euthanasia is the next step. And then, of course, it becomes a wide-open thing, where life itself is held to be cheap" (Mainse 1981, 162).

In an interview with Judith Haiven, Mainse again stated strong pro-life views while also disclaiming any political involvement. After being pushed on the abortion issue in the interview, and defending the unborn, he said, "I will never get involved in something like a Moral Majority. But I will seek to see that the lives of doctors who perform abortions, politicians or judges, have their lives redirected in the faith of God (Haiven 1984, 80).

On other occasions, Mainse seemed less reluctant to express politically-relevant views. Certainly some leftists considered him to be political to one degree or another. At one rally held by *100 Huntley Street* in Vancouver, 300 to 400 protestors arrived carrying placards and chanting slogans. Mainse attributed the protest to his political views:

We had been outspoken lately on a number of issues that were close to my heart: the plight of the unborn, with abortions now numbering three for every birth; the need to strengthen family relationships and the bonds of Christian marriage in the face of an epidemic of divorce; and for young marrieds, an emphasis on a wholesome, heterosexual lifestyle. But those days, when you spoke out for old-fashioned Christian principles and did so on national commercial network stations for ninety minutes every day, you were going to make enemies, no matter how positively you presented it (Mainse 1983, 16).

David Mainse should not be considered a leader of the Canadian Christian Right as such. But he did use his influence at times to support social conservative political causes such as opposition to abortion and opposition to homosexual rights. This contribution deserves to be recognized.

CENSORSHIP ISSUES

Just as Ken Campbell had been alarmed by the kind of literature one of his daughters had brought home from school, so also were some other Canadian parents alarmed in the mid-1970s and onwards. The offended parents who took action tended to be conservative Christians.

Early in 1976 in the town of Lakefield in Peterborough County, Ontario, two parents complained about the use of the novel *The Diviners* by Margaret Laurence for grade thirteen students. "The book had been approved by the Ministry of Education and appeared on the supplementary book list, yet the local protest was sufficient to oblige Robert J. Buchanan, head of the English department at Lakefield Secondary School, to remove it from the list until the Textbook Review Committee had evaluated it for use in grade thirteen" (Powers 2003, 418).

Buchanan himself was not in favor of removing the book, and he was supported by all of the English department heads from all of the high schools in Peterborough County. Even the Writers' Union of Canada weighed in in support of *The Diviners*. "Prominent among the book-banners were zealots from some fundamentalist churches. One of them, James Telford, was a Board of Education trustee and a member of the Textbook Review Committee" (Powers 2003, 418).

Of course, no one was actually requesting that the book be "banned." It wasn't as if they wanted the government to step in and forbid anyone from having or reading the book. They just didn't want it used in public schools. But as the Left knows so well, portraying the parents as "book-banners" is an effective propaganda technique to assure widespread public support for using immoral books in the public schools.

In April, 1976, the Textbook Review Committee approved *The Diviners*, and the Board of Education followed suit. However, the concerned citizens were not satisfied, and the "battle was then taken up by 'a number of local fundamentalist churches ... collecting signatures on a petition against' *The Diviners*" (Powers 2003, 420). As Margaret Laurence herself recounted in a newsletter of the Writers' Union,

> One minister, Rev. Sam Buick of the Dublin Street Pentecostal Church, kept his church open from 8 a.m. to 8 p.m. one day, so that people could sign the petition.... Copies of *The Diviners* were on hand, with so-called obscene words marked, and also sex scenes marked. A handy xerox copy of page reference numbers was available (Powers 2003, 420).

James Telford presented this petition to the school board at a subsequent meeting, but a majority of the board still maintained its support of the book (Powers 2003, 420).

This was not the end of the controversy surrounding Margaret Laurence's novels, however.

> In 1978, in King's County, Nova Scotia, a Baptist minister lobbied the local school board to remove *The Diviners* from the classroom, and in Etobicoke, Ontario, a school board trustee attempted to have *A Jest of God* banned from high schools... Also that year a dramatic community meeting took place in Huron County in Ontario, where parents and religious groups demanded that three novels—one of which was *The Diviners*—be removed from the grade 13 curriculum (Cohen 2001, 93).

Apparently all of these efforts were unsuccessful.

To some degree, then, "book banning," or attempts to remove books like *The Diviners*, from public school curriculum, was a hot topic in the late 1970s. One report at the time notes, "In most cases the modern critics have been religious groups, most prominently the Canadian arm of Renaissance International, led by the Reverend Ken Campbell" (*St. John's Report* 1979, 34). The famous Canadian novelist W. O. Mitchell singled Campbell's group out for criticism in a speech to 300 teachers in Waterloo, Ontario. His comments received national attention. In this speech Mitchell "charged that evangelist Campbell was using the book-banning issue for personal profit, soliciting large amounts of money for the cause and distributing book banning lists to the faithful" (*St. John's Report* 1979, 34).

Naturally, Campbell denied the charge. But he did say that Renaissance was actively promoting "book-selection committees."

> Such committees, says Mr. Campbell, would be made up of concerned parents who would advise school boards on the content of books used in the public schools. The committees would be based on two premises: first, that education

> involves the transmission of values; and second, that parents ought to be the ones to determine which values their children are taught. Accordingly, books to be permitted would have to meet three criteria: first, that they be 'great literature,' a term which Mr. Campbell failed to define but on which he thought there would be easy agreement; second, that the values being transmitted were supportive of the family unit; and third, that they follow a policy of 'good-neighborliness' meaning that they could not offend the moral, asthetic [sic] or religious values of the parents (St. John's Report 1979, 34).

The Writers' Union of Canada was very concerned about Campbell's activities. In response, it circulated a 32-page pamphlet entitled *"Censorship: Stopping the Book Banners"* (*St. John's Report* 1979, 35).

W. O. Mitchell had another opportunity to publicly criticize Ken Campbell when he was invited to appear on a television program called *Point Blank*. The topic of the show was the banning of books from schools.

> One of the guests on the program was the Rev. Ken Campbell, founder of Renaissance Canada, which was spearheading many of the book-banning initiatives across Canada. The debate was lively. Mitchell recalled that, after the show, Campbell approached him, all friendly and with a big smile: "Bill, I bear you no animus." Mitchell, refusing to shake his hand, said, "Well, Reverend, I don't bear you any animus either—but my animosity towards you has no bounds." Mitchell took every opportunity he could to attack publicly the book banners, Campbell in particular (Mitchell and Mitchell 2005, 297).

Again, Ken Campbell and the other concerned parents were not "book banners." They simply wanted the literature used in public schools to support rather than undermine traditional Western morality. There are limits to the number of books that can be used in any school, so they might as well be good books. And on this issue, as on the homosexual rights question, Ken Campbell was clearly the point man for conservative Christians in Canada.

CONCLUSION

From the perspective of the Christian Right in Canada, the three most significant features of the 1970s were the rise of the pro-life movement, Ken Campbell's launch into political activism (along with the formation of Renaissance), and the founding of Saint John's Edmonton Report, the magazine that would later become *Alberta Report*. Each of these involved one of the key figures of the Canadian Christian Right, Gwen Landolt, Ken Campbell, and Ted Byfield. All three would make an impact on the nation during the1980s. Although Ken Campbell's prominence would fade somewhat during that decade, Ted Byfield was arguably at the height of his influence as a magazine publisher. While other important players would enter the scene during the 1980s, Campbell and Byfield stood head and shoulders above most of them. There was, however, one exception. Gwen Landolt rose to prominence during the decade, and became a lightning rod for the Left as a founder and early leader of REAL Women of Canada.

REFERENCES

Alberta Hansard. 1988.

Alberta Report. 1980. "Anita Bryant's fall from grace." June 6: 46-47.

Byfield, Mike. 1983. "Preface." In The Deplorable Unrest in the Colonies: A Collection of Ted Byfield's Letters from the Publisher in *Alberta Report*. Edmonton: *Alberta Report*, viii-xiv.

Byfield, Ted. 1965. *Just Think, Mr. Berton (A Little Harder)*. Winnipeg:

Company Of the Cross.

Campbell, Ken. 1975. *Tempest in a Teapot*. Cambridge, ON: Coronation Publications.

Campbell, Ken. 1980. *No Small Stir: A Spiritual Strategy for Salting and Saving a Secular Society*. Burlington, ON: G.R. Welch Company.

Campbell, Ken. 2005. Telephone interview November 23.

Cohen, Mark. 2001. Censorship in Canadian Literature. Montreal & Kingston: McGill-Queen's University Press.

Cuneo, Michael W. 1989. *Catholics Against the Church: Anti-Abortion Protest In Toronto 1969-1985*. Toronto: University of Toronto Press.

De Valk, Alphonse. 1974. *The Unfinished Debate: The Abortion Issue in Contemporary Canadian History. Toronto*: Life Cycle Books.

Gerard, Bernice. 1988. *Bernice Gerard: Today and For Life*. Vancouver: Sunday Line Communications.

Haiven, Judith. 1984. *Faith, Hope, No Charity: An Inside Look At the Born Again Movement In Canada and the United States*. Vancouver, BC: New Star Books.

Hamburg, Harvey. 1977. "Anita takes Miami; gays to fight on." *The Body Politic*. July/August: 1, 12.

Hannon, Gerald. 1979. "Sewell: Unleashing the whirlwind." *The Body Politic*. February: 9-10.

Harrison, Trevor. 1995. *Of Passionate Intensity: Right-Wing Populism and the Reform Party of Canada*. Toronto: University of Toronto Press.

Hedlin, Ralph. 1983. "AR's ten tumultuous years." *Alberta Report*. November 28: 22-35.

Jackson, Ed. 1980. "The Hot Little Issue Gets Big." *The Body Politic*. November: 14-15.

Jackson, Ed. 1981. "Close, But Not Enough." *The Body Politic*. December/January: 9-10, 12.

Laycock, David. 2002. *The New Right and Democracy in Canada: Understanding Reform and the Canadian Alliance*. Don Mills: Oxford University Press.

Leslie, Pat. 1978. "Feminists and faggots unite." *The Body Politic*. February: 7.

Mainse, David (with David Manuel). 1981. *God Keep Our Land*. Toronto: Mainroads Productions Inc.

Mainse, David (with David Manuel). 1983. *100 Huntley Street*. Nashville: Thomas Nelson Publishers.

Mitchell, Barbara, and Ormond Mitchell. 2005. *Mitchell: The Life of W. O. Mitchell: The Years of Fame*, 1948-1998. Toronto: McClelland & Stewart Ltd.

Morton, F. L. 1992. *Morgentaler v. Borowski: Abortion, the Charter, and the Courts*. Toronto: McClelland & Stewart Inc.

Petrasek, Grace. 1991. *Silhouettes Against the Snow: Profiles of Canadian Defenders Of Life*. Toronto: Interim Publishing Co. Ltd.

Powers, Lyall. 2003. *Alien Heart: The Life and Work of Margaret Laurence*. Winnipeg: University of Manitoba Press.

Saint John's Edmonton Report. 1978a. "The Anita issue: Home values versus the New liberty." April 21: 23-26.

Saint John's Edmonton Report. 1978b. "Anita in Concert." May 5: 36.

Saint John's Report. 1979. "Books are not for burning." May 25: 34-35.

Strauss, Marina. 1980. "Majority's silence misled them, Sewell workers say." *Globe & Mail*. November 12: p. 5.

The Body Politic. 1978a. "Our real strength." December/January: 13.

The Body Politic. 1978b. "Bryant hits Canada; Canada hits back." May: 1.

Trollope, Paul. 1978. "Bryant visit sparks largest-ever gay demo; few hear Bryant Pitch." *The Body Politic*. October: 12.

Warner, Tom. 2002. *Never Going Back: A History of Queer Activism in Canada*. Toronto: University of Toronto Press.

Weatherbe, Stephen, and Eric Regaly. 1982. "Dr. Falwell's morality politics." *Alberta Report*. November 22: 40-41.

Wells, Bob. 1980. "CGRO takes aim at Renaissance Int'l." *The Body Politic*. June/July: 14.

CHAPTER 4 | THE FIRST PART OF THE 1980s: THE VOLCANO BEGINS TO ERUPT

The first half of the 1980s was an important period of organizing for the Christian Right in Canada. The most significant new issue at the beginning of the decade was the proposed changes to Canada's constitution by the government of Prime Minister Pierre Trudeau, especially his desire to include a Charter of Rights and Freedoms. On this issue Gwen Landolt was the sharpest mind in the country, at least from a conservative Christian perspective. She boldly predicted that the Charter would lead to left-wing policy-making by Canada's courts. The politicians ignored her. But they didn't ignore the calls by other conservative Christians to have God mentioned in the preamble to the Charter. This symbolic proposal was ultimately accepted.

The early 1980s also saw the revitalization of the Evangelical Fellowship of Canada (EFC), the creation of the Alberta Federation of Women United for Families (AFWUF), and most significantly, the creation of REAL Women of Canada. (The "REAL" was an acronym for "Realistic, Equal, Active, and for Life".) Some Canadians were now beginning to notice the presence of a "new right" in the country.

The 1980s also experienced the greatest period of pro-life activism in Canadian history. The legal cases of Joe Borowski and Henry Morgentaler progressed through the courts, and Morgentaler's illegal abortion activities were the cause of much anger and activism among pro-lifers.

THE PRO-LIFE MOVEMENT ENTERS THE 1980s

One of the biggest differences between the Canadian and American pro-life movements has been the role of the Roman Catholic bishops in each nation. Whereas American bishops became very involved in the abortion issue after the *Roe v. Wade* decision of 1973, Canadian bishops for the most part did not get involved. This was a serious disappointment to many pro-lifers in Canada (Cuneo 1989, 24-25).

Outright conflict erupted between Campaign Life and Cardinal Carter of Toronto during the constitutional debate of 1981. Campaign Life opposed inclusion of the Charter of Rights and Freedoms in the constitution for a number of reasons, one of which was that it did not include protection for pre-natal life. When Ontario premier William Davis publicly declared his support for the Charter, Campaign Life decided to publicly oppose the reelection of the Davis government in the March 1981 provincial election. Although Davis was reelected, Cardinal Carter banned the circulation of Campaign Life material in his parishes. He did not want the group to be using the church for partisan political purposes. Naturally, Campaign Life was very upset about this (Cuneo 1989, 47-49).

Campaign Life maintained a vigorous opposition to the Charter of Rights. Gwen Landolt clearly saw what would happen to Canadian politics if the Charter was adopted. Gwen Landolt is best known as a leader of REAL Women of Canada, the prominent conservative women's organization. In January, 1981, a special parliamentary committee was receiving comments and submissions from Canadians on Trudeau's proposal for a Charter of Rights. Many different groups presented their views. Gwen Landolt was at that time the legal counsel for the pro-life group Campaign Life. Her brief to the committee on behalf of Campaign Life was unbelievably prescient. She accurately predicted what would happen if the Charter was adopted.

Landolt's brief argued that a Charter of Rights should not be adopted because it would be bad for Canada. Landolt hit the nail on the head on the issue of the power the courts would acquire if the Charter was adopted:

> The most important effect of an entrenched Charter of Rights would be that it would give rise to a shift in power from Parliament, which is subject to public opinion, to the Supreme Court of Canada, which is not. This shift in power would then open the door to a wide list of areas in which (for the first time) the judiciary rather than the legislature, will have the final say. We have only to look to the United States, where the U.S. Supreme Court has the final word on any legislation passed by the U.S. Congress, to determine the tremendous consequences that would result from a transfer of this power" (Landolt, 1981, 1-2).

Similarly, Landolt predicted that freedoms Canadians had historically enjoyed would be curtailed by the Charter. She argued that

> [T]he Bill of Rights should not be entrenched in our Constitution. Our present system of Parliamentary supremacy has, during the past 113 years of Confederation, served us well. Individual rights and freedoms have been, with few exceptions, preserved. It is our view that under an entrenched Charter of Rights, many of our fundamental rights and freedoms, which we now take for granted, and which have long

> been established in this country, may be lost, if not permanently, at least until they are restored by the onerous procedure of a constitutional amendment. (Landolt 1981, 7).

This argumentation was presented in January, 1981, months before the Charter was agreed upon. It was dead on, accurately predicting the consequences that the Charter would have upon Canada.

Campaign Life also argued that should Parliament decide to go ahead and adopt the Charter, wording would need to be included protecting unborn children.

> If Parliament should make the final decision, in spite of our protest, that the Charter of Rights be entrenched in the Constitution, then it is necessary that the present proposed Charter of Rights be amended so as to provide protection for the unborn child. It is our view that the present Charter is inadequate to provide this protection (Landolt 1981, 7-8).

The Coalition for Life also wanted protection for the unborn to be specifically written into the Charter. Once it became clear to the leaders of the Coalition that such protection would not be added to the Charter, they decided instead to advocate

> for inclusion within the charter of a clause that would give Parliament ultimate power over Canada's abortion law. What the Coalition had in mind was the epochal 1973 decision (*Roe v. Wade*) in the United States wherein the American Supreme Court declared first and second trimester abortions to be a constitutional right, thereby abolishing state laws restricting abortion and effectively legalizing abortion-on-demand. Coalition leaders realized that patriation of Canada's new constitution, with an entrenched Charter of Rights and Freedoms, would likely lead to numerous constitutional challenges of Canadian laws and thus to an expanded role

for the courts. Specifically, they were concerned that the Supreme Court of Canada might in the future rule that any legislation restricting abortion availability was discriminatory and hence in contravention of the equality guarantees contained in section 15 of the charter. By campaigning for a provision in the charter granting Canada's elected representatives final say on abortion-related laws, then, they hoped to obviate in Canada the scenario which transpired in the United States when existing abortion laws were rendered invalid by judicial decree (Cuneo 1989, 54-55).

The concerns of the pro-life groups were ignored. Cardinal Carter spoke to Trudeau personally, and received assurances that the Charter was neutral on abortion. But Gwen Landolt and the other pro-lifers were right. The Supreme Court, in the "trilogy" of abortion decisions (*Morgentaler, Borowski, Daigle*), would institute a policy of abortion on demand in Canada.

In June 1983 Henry Morgentaler opened the first elective abortion clinic in English Canada, in Toronto. It was closed twice due to charges being laid against Morgentaler, but it opened again in January 1985 and remained open. For the next few years it was frequently picketed. In February 1985 Cardinal Carter encouraged his flock to join the pickets for a few days. Campaign Life was, of course, pleased about this (Cuneo 1989, 57-59). But Carter paid the price for openly supporting the pro-life cause.

> Cardinal Carter took a pummeling in the news media over his sponsorship of the demonstrations. In letters to the editor published by the Toronto dailies, Carter was variously accused of obscurantism, fanaticism, misogyny, hate-mongering, and child exploitation. The sardonic tenor of most commentaries on the cardinal's involvement, in both the electronic and print media, was a lesson likely not lost on the fraternity of Canadian bishops: outright identification

with the pro-life movement was a certain road toward social derision (Cuneo 1989, 65).

Before the Morgentaler Supreme Court victory of 1988, and the subsequent activity of Operation Rescue, there had already been some pro-life civil disobedience in Toronto.

> Canadian activists have staged several sit-ins at the Morgentaler clinic as well as one at the Ontario premier's Queen's Park office; they have twice obstructed vehicular traffic in front of the clinic, and have several times padlocked the clinic's rear gate. Despite frequent charges of harassment and assault brought by clinic employees against pro-lifers, only twice have Canadian activists been imprisoned for convictions related to civil disobedience, and no Canadian activist has yet to spend more than several days in jail. Still, civil disobedience has captured the imagination of the Canadian movement and its practitioners have generally been regarded as anti-abortion heroes (Cuneo 1989, 70).

In August 1985 Cardinal Carter made an agreement with Ontario Attorney-General Ian Scott and pro-choice leader Norma Scarborough of the Canadian Abortion Rights Action League (CARAL) to limit the number of protestors at the Morgentaler facility. Carter had come to the view that the pro-life protests were potential threats to public order and safety. His adoption of this view was likely due to acts of civil disobedience as well as a couple of violent acts that occurred, but which were actually not connected to pro-life organizations.

> Two widely publicized incidents which did occur over a year previously seem to have registered permanently on the public perception of the protest. The first, an attempted bombing of the clinic which resulted in extensive damage to a women's bookstore housed in the same building, was apparently not the responsibility of anyone formally connected to

a pro-life organization. In the second, an elderly man, likewise unaffiliated except in the loosest sense with the movement, made a threatening lunge with a pair of gardening shears at Dr. Morgentaler (Cuneo 1989, 76).

As a result of these incidents, there was a popular media image that the pro-lifers were potentially dangerous. However, as Cuneo points out from his personal experience, the real situation was quite different.

> Ironically, it was anti-abortionists themselves during this period who seemed to face the greater physical danger. The author saw a woman threaten three activists with a shotgun, another woman pull a knife on a middle-aged female picketer, a clinic doctor on two occasions threaten to 'kick the shit out of' activists, and a clinic employee repeatedly promise that he would 'blow the f**king brains out of [the] motherf**king Catholics' (Cuneo 1989, 77).

Nevertheless the leaders of Campaign Life and Toronto Right to Life publicly declared that they were not bound by the agreement made by Cardinal Carter. Apparently the Toronto media were surprised by this because they saw Carter as the "religious leader of the city's anti-choice movement."

> By far the most encouraging event for the movement in 1985 was the 21 September 'Justice for the Unborn' rally which took place in front of the Ontario legislative buildings and culminated in a procession past the Morgentaler clinic. The turnout, estimated by organizers at between twenty and twenty-five thousand, suggested to movement leaders that the time was ripe for the formation of a 'pro-life' political party (Cuneo 1989, 79).

THE CANADIAN CHRISTIAN RIGHT AND
THE CONSTITUTIONAL REFERENCE TO GOD

Prior to 1982 the Canadian Constitution did not mention God. But during the period of constitutional struggle and rewriting, 1980-1982, the question of God's standing in the document arose alongside many other issues.

In 1981 a Joint Committee of the Senate and House of Commons chaired by Liberal Senator Harry Hays and Liberal MP Serge Joyal held hearings on the federal government's proposed constitutional changes. Citizen groups representing many different perspectives appeared before the Committee to advocate their views, and it was in these hearings that religious questions were injected into the constitutional debate. Conservative MPs on the Committee were sympathetic to evangelicals who wanted an explicit reference to God in the Constitution.

Also at this time, "a loose coalition of evangelical, fundamentalist, and pentecostal Christians" was emerging (Egerton 2000, 101). Many of these people were concerned about the direction of Canadian society, especially with regards to such issues as abortion and sexual permissiveness. "They had also witnessed the emergence of the American 'new religious right' in the late 1970s and its powerful role in the election of Ronald Reagan as president in 1980" (Egerton 2000, 102).

The Conservative MPs on the Hays-Joyal Committee supported the desire of evangelical Christians to mention God in the preamble of the Constitution. The Conservative constitutional critic, Jake Epp, had close ties to evangelical groups and was especially supportive. He proposed an amendment to include a reference to God, but it was blocked by the Liberals. NDP MP Svend Robinson was especially outspoken in opposing the reference to God.

At this point the evangelicals became particularly active.

> David Mainse of *100 Huntley Street* appealed to his television followers to join with other evangelicals in writing their MPs and government leaders to press for the reference to God, while Ken Campbell mounted a major newspaper campaign, taking out full-page ads in leading dailies. Leaders of the Evangelical Fellowship of Canada directly petitioned the prime minister, making explicit their reasons for wanting a constitutional reference to God (Egerton 2000, 104).

This, of course, amounted to a significant effort by conservative Christians to influence an important political decision.

But it appears that the most important factor in convincing the Liberal government to accept a reference to God in the new Constitution was the efforts of Ontario MP David Smith, the Liberal Deputy House Leader. Smith was the son of a Pentecostal minister, and he prepared a brief for Prime Minister Trudeau advocating the reference to God. "Smith's brief summarized polling and political reporting on the moral majority phenomenon in the United States, and demographic data on recent Canadian religious trends that held political salience" (Egerton 2000, 104).

This information showed that the conservative segments of Christianity were generally growing while the mainline churches were declining. And there were considerably more students at evangelical and Pentecostal colleges than at mainline seminaries. Another important factor was that the traditional Canadian conflict between Protestants and Catholics was being diminished due to the emergence of a coalition of evangelicals and Catholics on social issues. With these points in mind Smith warned that the Liberals would "pay for this politically for years" if they failed to include a reference to God in the Constitution. In other words, they would lose evangelical voters who appeared to constitute a growing segment of the potential voting population. And what could be more important to a politician's career than voters?

According to George Egerton, "The political considerations raised by David Smith and other Christian Liberals were convincing for the prime minister, and the Liberals inserted their own reference to God in the amendments to the draft constitution" (Egerton 2000, 106). Apparently it was the impressive number of students at evangelical colleges that was most persuasive for Trudeau. Whatever the case, the evangelical campaign to include a mention of God in the Constitution was successful.

Indeed, without the efforts of the activist evangelicals that reference would not exist.

> The inclusion of the reference to God represented a signal success for the evangelical Christian lobbyists, working effectively through sympathetic parliamentarians, especially David Smith and Jake Epp, and demonstrating an ability to mobilize impressive public support. [then-Justice Minister] Jean Chretien would claim that the government received more mail on this issue than any other (Egerton 2000, 106-107).

Egerton is quick to point out, however, that the success of the evangelicals was largely symbolic. The de-Christianization and secularization of Canada has proceeded as quickly as ever. The preamble to the Charter of Rights is not a barrier to those trends. On the other hand, even the powerful Christian Right in the USA has not been able to stem those trends in that country either.

THE UNITED CHURCH OBSERVER ON THE NEW RIGHT

By the early 1980s some people were concerned that a religiously-inspired "New Right" was emerging in Canada as it had previously in the US. The November 1982 issue of *The United Church Observer* featured a long cover story entitled "Religion & Politics: Canada's New Right." On the first page of the article in bold letters it states, "In the U.S., the Moral Majority offers simple solutions to complex issues. Can it happen here?" (Colle 1982, 24). Thus began a ten-page investigation of religion and right-wing politics in Canada.

Although the focus was supposed to be on religiously-influenced politics, the article gave significant coverage to the Fraser Institute, which never has been a religiously-oriented organization. It also mentioned other non-religious organizations such as the short-lived National Foundation for Public Policy Development (an attempt to copy the Washington-based Heritage Foundation), and the Western Canada Concept Party of Alberta. But the main thrust was to determine whether Canada was experiencing the development of a Christian Right paralleling what had been happening in the U.S. There, the article said, "social and religious conservatives, backed by business, helped elect Ronald Reagan and many neo-conservative legislators. The coalition is popularly known as the 'Moral Majority' and its titular leader is the fundamentalist TV preacher, the Rev. Jerry Falwell. Parallel groups in Canada are on the move to effect a similar phenomenon here" (Colle 1982, 25).

To a large degree, readers were assured that such a phenomenon was unlikely to take root in Canada: "The chances of such far-right and even more moderate right-wing religious groups obtaining a massive following in Canada are, however, slim, because the percentage of Canadians belonging to mainline religions is much higher in this country than in the U.S." (Colle

1982, 28). However, this enthusiastic pronouncement was later tempered by the observation that certain regions of Canada might have been more susceptible to conservative religious influences than others:

> But these movements that combine right-wing ideology with religious fundamentalism could be effective in specific parts of Canada, particularly in our 'mini-Bible belt' extending from the West across parts of the Prairies to Southern Ontario and some areas of the Maritimes. Already we have seen movements such as the Western Canada Concept Party and Renaissance Canada emerge (Colle 1982, 28).

Differences between the United States and Canada do hamper the rise of a Christian Right in Canada. As mentioned previously, a higher percentage of Canadians are in "mainline" churches. In the 1980 US election, one successful tactic of conservative groups was to issue "moral report cards" noting the positions supported by sitting politicians. This tactic was credited with helping to defeat more than two dozen liberal congressmen and senators. Renaissance Canada attempted a similar effort in the 1981 Manitoba provincial election, but it apparently flopped. Generally speaking, Canada's parliamentary system of government provides greater obstacles to the success of social movements than the American system. The strong party discipline exercised in the Canadian system hampers the influence that such movements can exert over individual politicians.

Thus, with so many obstacles to face, the article can ultimately assure its readers not to fear for the rise of a Christian Right in Canada.

> The Rev. David MacDonald, PC Secretary of State during the Clark government, says that Canadian groups trying to import American-style right-wing ideology are bound to fail (Colle 1982, 33).

EVANGELICAL FELLOWSHIP OF CANADA

In the early 1960s there were a number of meetings among evangelical leaders in Toronto. As a result of the meetings, a fellowship of pastors was formed in 1964, and the group approved its constitution in 1966. This was the formation of the Evangelical Fellowship of Canada (EFC). The EFC held annual conventions, published a magazine called *Thrust*, and beginning in the mid-1970s would occasionally bring internationally known American and British evangelical leaders to Canada (Stackhouse 1993, 166-168).

The EFC adopted a revised constitution in March 1981 that indicated the organization was moving towards a larger and more active role in society. One thrust of the new constitution was to foster greater unity among evangelicals, and the expectation that

> this unity would be represented to government at local, provincial, and national levels. 'Such relationship with government will assist in practical ways; provide for liaison in united manner with government agencies; and be a means of influence to protect the rights and freedoms of individual Christians, of the Church, and Christian institutions.' More than this interest in defending persons and things Christian, this involvement with government would seek 'to bring moral direction in government decisions' (Stackhouse 1993, 168-169).

Not long after the new constitution and new direction were adopted by the EFC, it hired its first executive director, Brian Stiller, in 1983. Stiller moved boldly and effectively to build the EFC into a prominent voice for evangelicals in Canada. The size of its membership, the size of its income, and the amount of its influence all grew dramatically throughout the 1980s under Stiller's leadership.

Among the changes implemented by Stiller were improvements in the EFC's publications. *Thrust* was replaced by *Faith Today* which had a major focus on current issues.

> Circulation of *Faith Today* by the mid-1980s grew to eighteen thousand and was expected by the EFC to continue to increase. The EFC also published the *Sundial* for Fellowship members, a quarterly newsletter that presented the viewpoints and experience of the EFC's leaders and Stiller in particular on a variety of current topics. And *Understanding Our Times* was published quarterly for members of churches belonging to the EFC and brought news the knowledge of which was expected to help Canadian evangelicals respond better to their world (Stackhouse 1993, 169).

When I interviewed Brian Stiller, he categorically rejected the "Christian Right" label as applying to himself or the EFC. The success of Jerry Falwell and the Moral Majority in the 1980 American elections reflected on Canadian evangelicals, and apparently gave some people the impression that Canadian evangelicals were like their conservative American counterparts. EFC leaders were very unhappy with the tone of the American evangelicals like Jerry Falwell, and wanted to distinguish Canadian evangelicals from the Americans. In this respect, part of the motivation to increase the role of the EFC was to provide a distinctly Canadian evangelical voice that would differentiate Canadian evangelicals from the American Christian Right (Stiller 2006).

This perspective is reflected in media accounts from early in Stiller's tenure. One report notes, "Evangelicals are far from being a monolithic group of lock-step right wingers, says the EFC's Stiller. Though sharing a view of the primacy of Scripture, they differ widely on theological and social matters" (Weatherbe 1983, 20). This article states that these Canadians prefer "to call themselves evangelicals" but nevertheless continues to refer to them as "fundamentalists." With this label in mind, it states that Brian Stiller's

> conversations with government leaders convinced him that they would listen to fundamentalists, just as they now listen to Catholic, Anglican and other mainstream leaders, as long as they were well-informed and "reasonable." Evangelical spokesmen hitherto have sounded shrill, off the wall, and vitriolic, as many characterize government action in the most sinister tones (Weatherbe 1983, 20).

As Stiller recounted in the interview, the American Christian Right leaders were seen as strident, and few people in Canada supported that kind of approach. Canadian evangelicals had to operate differently (Stiller 2006).

Again, in a subsequent report, Stiller distanced Canadian evangelicals and the EFC from what was occurring in the United States. As one writer put it, "Mr. Stiller worries that high-profile American evangelicals such as Jerry Falwell, head of the Moral Majority, provide an image by which the public, led by the news and entertainment media in both Canada and the U.S., stereotype all evangelicals" (Weatherbe 1985, 52). And referring to Canadian evangelicals he said, "far from being right-wingers, 'we are centrists politically'" (Weatherbe 1985, 54).

In January 1984 Justice Minister Mark MacGuigan proposed amendments to liberalize Canada's divorce laws. In one of its first major political efforts, the EFC wanted to thwart such liberalization of the law. This exercise was described as a "groundbreaking crusade" consisting "of a massive letter-writing effort to the justice minister and to MPs" (Orr 1984, 45).

> Some 30,000 brochures are being distributed this month to 15 Calgary and 33 Edmonton evangelical churches. The pamphlets urge parishioners to write asking for a delay in

passing the amendments and, instead, to invite submissions from the public on what route divorce law should take. Hoping to recruit letter writers from throughout the country, Mr. Stiller chose Alberta for his campaign frontier because he found evangelical leaders here "among the most responsive" (Orr 1984, 45).

The Liberal government lost the federal election later in 1984, and it was up to the Mulroney Tories to subsequently implement their own liberalization of the divorce law.

In the Spring of 1985 Dalton Camp, the past president of the Progressive Conservative Party of Canada, wrote a letter on behalf of the Canadian Civil Liberties Association (CCLA). The purpose of the letter was to generate financial support for the CCLA by playing on fear of the Christian Right. Camp wrote,

> Did you breathe a sigh of relief when 1984 was finally over? Maybe you were wrong. Reactionary trends in Canada and the United States are proving a challenge to individual rights and civil liberties through North America. Pick a name—the Moral Majority, the New Right, or whatever they choose to call themselves, these evangelical movements are becoming increasingly well-organized, vocal and influential. Just look at the groups south of the border. They want their religious doctrines enacted into law and imposed on everyone else (Stiller 1986, 32).

Camp then went on to suggest that evangelicals oppose birth control, believe that "the law should punish homosexuals," and that "the law should keep women at home in their place." He also said they want the law to ban books they don't like from libraries and schools, and "they believe that anyone who disagrees with them should be barred from teaching in the public schools." Furthermore, he identified evangelicals with public support for capital punishment, racism against non-whites, and a national security law that would allow government agents to pry into the private lives of Canadians. "Clearly, the danger to our civil liberties right here in Canada is real and present" (Stiller 1986, 32-33).

Although it's understandable that leftists like Camp would be concerned about the rise of the Christian Right, much of the letter was fear-mongering, or worse. In fact, Brian Stiller wrote to Camp on behalf of the EFC strongly protesting this vilification of evangelicals. However, Camp just sent a brief response dismissing the EFC's concerns (Stiller 1986, 35).

In 1986 a major feature article in the EFC's *Faith Today* magazine asked, "Does Canada Need A Moral Majority?" Basically, the answer was "no." The magazine had taken a poll of Canadian evangelicals. It concluded that "Judging by responses to the recent *Faith Today* poll of 126 Canadian evangelical leaders and lay people, this country's evangelical constituency is not eager to import Moral Majority or even to establish a Canadianized version of it" (Tarr 1986, 21).

The next issue of *Faith Today* carried a column by McMaster Divinity College professor Clark Pinnock who wrote approvingly of the Moral Majority. He pointed out that a "hysterical" fear of the Moral Majority was being widely promoted. And this "fear about moral majoritarianism is generated by secularists who fear that these Christians just might stall their own cultural revolution, one they're attempting to perpetrate on the rest of us" (Pinnock 1986, 10). Contrary to the evangelical leaders in the previously mentioned poll, Pinnock wrote that Canada did need a Moral Majority. "I hope moral majoritarianism does come to Canada. We need Christians to organize and say some of the valid and timely things the U.S. movement has been saying" (Pinnock 1986, 10).

Yet a year later, *Faith Today* published a cautiously favorable review of Margaret Atwood's *The Handmaid's Tale*, a novel written to induce fear of the Christian Right. After giving a rather sympathetic portrayal of the novel's theme, the reviewer writes that "rather than react defensively, we can treat Atwood's implied criticism as an opportunity to examine whether our house is in order" (Males 1987, 48). The story of the novel takes place in the United States after it has been taken over in a coup perpetrated by the Christian Right and then renamed "Gilead." Under the new Christian leaders the society has become a totalitarian hell house. The message is that this would be the kind of society favoured by the Christian Right. The *Faith Today* reviewer concluded by saying,

> As to whether well-meaning Christians could possibly be co-opted to a "Gilead," we can reflect on this statement from the German Evangelical Church of the 1930s: "The Holy Spirit is working a great renewal across the nation. The signs of spiritual awakening are everywhere. The evidence is seen blooming in the programs inspired by Hitler and the national party." Perhaps Margaret Atwood has a message for us (Males 1987, 48).

Or perhaps squishy evangelicals are easily absorbed into the fashionable thinking of the day. In any case, it would seem the *Faith Today* review concludes that evangelicals had better be careful lest they become Nazis. So rather than resisting the secularist portrayals of conservative Christians as crypto-fascists, in this instance *Faith Today* encouraged such portrayals.

The EFC certainly made its presence felt in opposing many of the harmful trends in Canadian politics and society such as abortion, homosexual rights, and pornography. In this respect it would be easy to pigeon hole the EFC as being part of Canada's Christian Right. But a more careful analysis would avoid such an easy labeling of the EFC. As Brian Stiller points out, the evangelical community in Canada contains people of diverse political views. And the EFC under Stiller's leadership consciously strove to differentiate Canada's evangelicals from the American Christian Right. *Faith Today* magazine carried articles that were unquestionably unfavourable to the Christian Right at times, such as the positive portrayal of The Handmaid's Tale.

AFWUF

The Alberta Federation of Women United for Families (AFWUF) was formed in 1982 after some pro-life women were thrown out of a meeting of the Alberta Status of Women Action Committee (ASWAC). In November 1981 ASWAC was holding its annual conference. Various workshops were being held at the conference. The feminist view of what happened at the conference is as follows:

> As part of what was later revealed as an organized strategy, three pro-life women joined ASWAC with the intention of attending a workshop on strategizing against pro-life forces led by members of a Calgary group, Abortion By Choice. The workshop moderator chose to cancel the session, however, upon hearing that there were pro-life women in attendance. The moderator argued that the workshop was not intended as a forum for debating the abortion issue, but rather as a discussion of strategy, and that she was not willing to share her strategic insights with these pro-life women (Harder 2003, 54).

One of the pro-life women was Kathleen Toth, the president of Campaign Life. The feminists claim she then vowed to "destroy" ASWAC and then left the conference with the other pro-life women. ASWAC then revoked Toth's membership. Toth and other pro-life/pro-family women then formed the organization

Alberta Women of Worth, which subsequently became the Alberta Federation of Women United for Families (Harder 2003, 54-55).

Wendy Swainson, the founding president of AFWUF, gives a similar account as Harder, but with a few different details. According to this account, it was Swainson who "got the ball rolling" in the formation of AFWUF,

> after being booted out of an Alberta Status of Women Action Committee meeting. "They claim to represent all Alberta women," says Mrs. Swainson, "but when four of us who were pro-life tried to attend a workshop on abortion, they cancelled the meeting, then reassembled down the hall without us." So Mrs. Swainson and her friends decided to start their own women's group to represent the pro-life, pro-family position (Weatherbe and Haiven 1982, 46).

AFWUF held its first annual convention in Edmonton in November, 1982. The featured speaker was American pro-family leader Phyllis Schlafly, fresh from her victory over the Equal Rights Amendment (ERA) in the United States. At the AFWUF conference, attended by about 250 people, Schlafly "warned her listeners of a many-fronted assault on the family and Christian values and exhorted them to fight back" (Weatherbe 1982, 46). "Various feminist groups also showed up for the Schlafly speech, but most stayed outside to heckle, brandishing signs with such messages as 'Ban nocturnal emissions'" (Weatherbe and Haiven 1982, 46).

AFWUF then began advancing the pro-family cause on a number of issues.

> The organization initiated an educational reform campaign specifically targeted at sex education and the morally ambiguous "humanist" curriculum, which it felt should be replaced

by both a stricter attention to "the facts" and an increased emphasis on religious education. AFWUF also undertook an effort to promote the career homemaker primarily through challenging the expansion of child-care facilities, persisted with advocacy around pro-life initiatives, and undertook a multipronged attack against the perceived growth of feminist influence on public policy (Harder 2003, 55).

Since many feminist groups received funding from the provincial and federal governments, AFWUF argued that it, too, should receive government funding. At various times beginning in the late 1980s it did receive some government funding, but the sums were paltry compared to the bucketfuls of cash received by feminist organizations (Harder 2003, 55-57).

AFWUF continued to grow, organize, and communicate its views to government.

> The energy devoted by AFWUF members to letter writing, radio phone-in programs, meetings with elected officials, and political constituency work, as well as the happy coincidence that at least one AFWUF board member was married to a Conservative MLA, made a substantial contribution to the organization's political legitimacy (Harder 2003, 92).

The Conservative MLA was Stockwell Day, later an Alberta cabinet minister, and subsequently leader of the Canadian Alliance.

AFWUF had some success in its efforts. In the early 1990s the board of the Calgary Local Council of Women (CLCW) became dominated by conservative women. "As a result, feminist organizations withdrew their affiliations to the council while conservative women's groups filled their places. From 1992 on, the minutes and resolutions of the CLCW borrow heavily from AFWUF on such subjects as birth control, the family, child care, capitalism, and cultural values" (Harder 2003, 93).

Sometimes success had a price. The Alberta Advisory Council on Women's Issues (AACWI) held a series of meetings around the province in 1988. Late in February it held a meeting in Lethbridge. As it turned out, the majority of presentations made to the Council at that meeting supported conservative positions. Because of that, a number of women who were slated to give presentations at the subsequent Edmonton meeting were contacted by Council staff to see if they were members of AFWUF. Those who were AFWUF members were basically disqualified from presenting since AFWUF itself had already been allotted a 10 minute slot for making a presentation. In this way, a preponderance of conservative presentations could be prevented. As one Council staff member put it, "we don't want the same thing happening in Edmonton that happened in Lethbridge" (Woloshen, 1988, 45).

AFWUF was becoming increasingly prominent by the end of the 1980s. Among the speakers at its November 1989 conference in Edmonton were Chantal Devine, the wife of the premier of Saskatchewan, and John Oldring, the Alberta Family and Social Services minister. AFWUF had received a $2,000 grant from the provincial government and a $3,100 grant from the federal government for this conference. There were 150 delegates. ASWAC had held its conference the previous month, and its attendance "reportedly was less than a third of AFWUF's" (Hutchinson 1989, 36).

John Oldring was a particularly popular speaker at the conference.

> He outlined the Getty government's various pro-family initiatives, but it was in question period that he really became a hit. No, he replied, he did not consider that two homosexuals constitute a family. Yes, he and his wife have long been members of a Red Deer pro-life group. No, he does

not support universal day care ["I don't think we can afford it"], although single parents need day care support. All this brought AFWUF cheers (Hutchinson 1989, 36).

Although organized in only one province, AFWUF was the first significant conservative women's group in Canada. It did not win all of its battles, but it did ensure that pro-family issues received greater attention than otherwise would have been the case. It has played an important role in Alberta. On the national scene, another women's organization, with which AFWUF would become affiliated, made a very big splash.

REAL WOMEN OF CANADA

REAL Women of Canada has been the single most important organization to the Christian Right in Canada. Its intelligent, thoughtful and courageous leadership has been instrumental in keeping the concerns of social conservative Canadians front and centre. Although there have been a number of women who have played important roles in REAL Women, there can be little doubt that the central figure has been Gwen Landolt.

Before REAL Women was formed late in 1983, Landolt had already been a key leader of the pro-life movement in Canada. It was, in fact, the abortion issue that originally motivated her into becoming an activist. As she relates the story,

I probably would have continued to live a quite private life except for a development on the Canadian political scene in the early 1970's, which had a profound effect on me. At that time, the abortion law in Canada had been widened, which resulted in the deaths of thousands of unborn children each year. I made no deliberate attempt to become involved in the issue at first. However, by chance, in 1971 I saw a feminist interviewed on the CBC, claiming a 'right to her own body' and a 'right to abortion.'

In law school I had learned that an unborn child could inherit property and could be the subject of a trust, and suddenly here was someone telling us that the unborn child had no rights and could be disposed of simply because it was inconvenient and unwanted. I was incensed over this injustice. Something had to be done. Shortly afterwards, I founded and became the first president of the Toronto Right to Life Association and was one of the founders of the political arm of the pro-life movement in Canada, Campaign Life Coalition. I also subsequently became National President of the educational arm, Alliance for Life, as well as serving over the years as legal counsel for their organizations (Landolt 2007, 1).

Anne Collins, a Canadian writer and supporter of the "pro-choice" side, gives the following description of and background to Landolt:

> Landolt is the Phyllis Schlafly of Canada: smart, tough, physically imposing, a potent politician. She was a precocious graduate of law school, called to the bar at twenty-three. She was one of three women in a class of 113 ("This is what makes me laugh about these whining feminists these days. I went to law school before it was socially acceptable"). She practiced as a full-time lawyer for seventeen years, including five with the federal justice department specializing in immigration law. She married "late" and, once married, began having children—five in all (Collins 1985, 194).

It was this "precocious" lawyer who initiated the formation of REAL Women in 1983. Betty Steele describes the first events this way:

> [Landolt] was preparing dinner one night in 1983 when she heard on the radio that the federal government intended to remove a tax exemption for dependent, at-home spouses so that more money could be channeled into public day

care, and her concern was galvanized into action. She saw this policy as a design to drive more women out of their homes, encouraging them to abdicate the care of children and husbands. This would eventually undermine marriages and deny children the security of formerly happy and stable lifestyles (Steele 1991, 114).

Besides the proposal to withdraw the tax exemption for dependent spouses, Landolt says that there was also another important factor.

> This was the fact that during the Charter debate, a handful of feminist women were active in the media and especially on the national CBC TV news proclaiming that "the women" of Canada took a certain view on the Charter's provisions and that they were speaking on behalf of 52.4% of the Canadian population i.e. on behalf of all women. It angered me that a handful of government-financed feminists could presume to speak on behalf of all Canadian women. Women do not have a common point of view and differ widely because of our various social, cultural, educational, religious backgrounds. It was an insult to the intelligence and independence of women that these feminists believed that all women thought the same as they. It was obvious to me that the time had come to provide an alternative voice for Canadian women, based on very different values than those espoused so loudly and frequently by the radical feminists on behalf of "Canadian women" (Landolt 2007, 2).

Landolt contacted a number of her friends, and together REAL Women was born in the Fall of 1983.

> To formally announce its existence, REAL Women held a press conference in the Royal York Hotel in Toronto in February, 1984. For many weeks after we received telephone calls from the media across the country requesting inter-

views, and from individuals wanting to become members. It was a great start for the organization. In fact, REAL Women took off like a Roman candle and has never looked back (Landolt 2007, 2).

Betty Steele notes that

> within two years 50,000 women across Canada had joined up to voice their concern. In every province, women, led by other extremely talented women—prominent journalist Doreen Beagan in Prince Edward Island, Lettie Morse in Ottawa, Cecilia Forsyth in Saskatchewan, Lorna LaGrange in Alberta, Peggy Steacy in British Columbia and so many others—were realizing the need to organize, to influence the laws, to save families (Steele 1991, 114).

An early document produced by REAL Women listed the organization's objectives as follows:

> To promote the equality, advancement and well-being of women and recognizing women as interdependent members of society, whether in the family, workplace or community.
>
> To reaffirm that the family is society's most important unit since the nurturing of its members is best accomplished in the family setting.
>
> To promote, secure and defend legislation which upholds the Judaeo-Christian values on marriage and family life.
>
> To support the right to life of all innocent individuals from conception to natural death (REAL Women 1985, 2).

And the family, in the context of point number 2, is defined as "two or more people, living together, related by blood, heterosexual marriage or adoption" (REAL Women 1985, 2).

It's important to note that REAL Women was arguing for the need for real options for women in their career choices. Feminists were arguing that all women should be in the paid workforce. The policies of the federal government supported the feminist view, favoring women working outside the home. REAL Women was not trying to "turn back the clock" and prevent women from pursuing paid employment. It wanted the government, and society generally, to recognize that mothers at home also play a vital role in society and should be recognized and valued as such.

This point is made strongly in a brief presented by REAL Women to Members of Parliament in November, 1985.

> R.E.A.L. Women believes that efforts must be made to reduce pressures on women and their families by allowing women genuine options, including the option of remaining at home full or part-time to care for their families, according to the needs and desires of their families. Full-time parents make a magnificent contribution to society—a fact sadly negated in today's world, rarely recognized or acknowledged. Full-time parenting is all too frequently portrayed and promoted as secondary, to a full-time career in the workplace.
>
> To support homemaking as an option is not to say that we believe every woman should be in the home. We believe that women should have the option to remain in the home, if they so choose. Women are as different and individual in their desires and abilities as men. Neither motherhood nor a Master's degree is for everyone. We would like to see some assistance given to those many women who wish to remain in the home, but are unable to do so because of financial pressures. Indeed, those women who choose motherhood as a full-time career should receive financial and social recognition and assistance from government and from society (REAL Women 1985, 6-7).

The growth and success of REAL Women quickly attracted the critical attention of feminists. Feminists bitterly resented REAL Women and its intelligent and articulate defence of the traditional family. Already in March 1985, at the University of Alberta, Distinguished Visiting Professor Margrit Eichler presented a paper against Canada's pro-family movement, and the paper was subsequently published by the Canadian Research Institute for the Advancement of Women, a feminist outfit largely funded by the federal government.

REAL Women was not the only target of Eichler's paper, but it was a major focus. Eichler pointed out that the Canadian pro-family movement "includes, but is not restricted to, such organizations as the Alberta Federation of Women United for Families (AFWUF), the Saskatchewan Federation of Women, Realwomen of Canada, and Renaissance International" (Eichler 1985, 39).

According to Eichler, the Canadian pro-family movement was attempting "to push a highly restrictive form of sexuality on the entire society, by restricting sexual activity to sex between married partners without using contraceptives" (1985, 23). Apparently the fact that one Canadian pro-family writer (Donald De Marco) publicly opposed the use of contraception was enough for Eichler to categorize the entire movement as holding that view. She also objected to the term "pro-family" because conservatives support only the traditional family, not the diverse family forms favored by Leftists.

> [T]he so-called "pro-family" movement is in fact only advocating one type of family, namely the patriarchal family who can subsist on one income to the detriment of the majority of families in Canada. It is therefore inappropriate to utilize the label of pro-family for this movement. An appropriate label would be the Movement for the Restoration of the Patriarchal Family. I will henceforth refer to them as such (Eichler 1985, 35).

Even worse, the pro-family movement was dangerous to the country, in Eichler's view. This "movement for the restoration of the patriarchal family does constitute a direct threat to democracy, with their insistence of the primacy of one lifestyle over others not just as a personal choice—which must be a fundamental right of every citizen in any democracy—but as something that is legally sanctioned and socially enforced" (Eichler 1985, 36-37). Pro-family activists would not recognize their movement as Eichler describes it since her purpose was not to portray it accurately, but to lambaste it.

In the Spring of 1986 the annual convention of the National Action Committee on the Status of Women (NAC) held a workshop on the "new right" that dealt primarily with REAL Women. The fact that such a workshop was considered necessary demonstrated the rising credibility and influence of REAL Women. One lady who attended the session as a "spy" for REAL Women said "many of those attending seemed to be alarmed that the rival group is gaining far too much support at their expense. Some participants complained that REAL Women is winning the public relations battle because of its pro-family position and moral stand against abortion" (Jenish 1986, 12).

As REAL Women achieved greater public credibility, feminists had to come to grips with the fact that it couldn't simply be dismissed. One feminist activist, referring to REAL Women as "RW," pointed this out in an article in a socialist magazine. As she put it, "There's a tendency in the women's movement to see RW as 'dupes of patriarchy' or 'men in skirts.' That's wrong. It's insulting to those involved and it denies them any responsibility for their actions. These people are not stupid" (Dubinsky 1987, 4). If they were stupid, there would be nothing to worry about from a feminist perspective. But instead, REAL Women was making genuine inroads. "The positions promoted by RW have found their way into government and press. RW has supporters in the Cabinet. It's common to see RW comment included in press reports with a focus on women. CBC's *Morningside*, for example, began an RW panel to 'balance' their regular feminist panel" (Dubinsky 1987, 6).

By far the major controversy involving REAL Women during its first few years of existence, however, was the issue of government funding, especially federal government funding. Many feminist groups were flush with cash provided by the federal government through the Secretary of State. REAL Women's position on government funding was that women's lobby groups should not be funded by the government, but if they were to be funded, REAL Women should be just as eligible as any other group.

> The real issue about funding is whether the government should, especially in times of financial restraint, be funding any women's lobby groups, let alone the radical feminists, who are, in fact, the minority of minorities. In most cases, their organizations have been almost entirely funded by government grants, and as such, can hardly be called non-government organizations. Notwithstanding this, if the government desires to set aside funds for women's groups, then at the very least, it has an obligation to distribute these funds among women's groups having different philosophies—not just that of the radical feminist ideology. In other words, if there is to be funding in all fairness and justice, there should be equal funding for women's groups of various points of view and approaches (REAL Women 1985, 4).

In a presentation made to the Standing Committee on the Secretary of State on December 11, 1986, REAL Women explained and documented how officials of the Mulroney government thwarted its efforts to obtain funding. As the presentation made clear, the Women's Programme of the Secretary of State would only fund groups that supported feminism. REAL Women's experiences with the Secretary of State were as follows:

> R.E.A.L. Women has experienced extraordinary difficulties in working with the Women's Programme, Secretary of State, to the extent that the latter has even refused to forward to us applications for funding. Our association made every attempt in the fall of 1983 and winter of 1984 to receive application forms but none was forwarded to us. We found this difficult to comprehend since we had assumed that the Women's Programme was to represent all Canadian women, and not just a select group with a particular philosophy. We became concerned that there was a deliberate attempt by the Women's Programme to ignore us. In order to ascertain whether this was the case, we advised the Programme that a group of women were organizing a new group called "The National Association of Lesbian Mothers," and requested application forms to apply for a grant. Within a week the requisite application forms, together with the funding guidelines, were forwarded to us…
>
> We completed the application forms under our own organization's name, R.E.A.L. Women of Canada, on August 26, 1984. On December 14, Lyse Blanchard, Director of the Women's Programme, wrote to advise us that we were refused a grant on the grounds that "the promotion of a particular family model is not within the spirit of the objectives of the program. The program concentrates on supporting groups who are working to explore all options for women as they work toward equality in a society that is changing rapidly" (REAL Women 1986, 6).

Despite the fact that REAL Women was supposedly ineligible to receive funding, the Calgary Lesbian Mother's Defence Fund received Women's Programme money to establish a "collective" in 1985 and to hold a lesbian conference in 1986 (REAL Women 1986, 6-7).

REAL Women applied again for a grant in 1985. The Women's Programme sent them an application form, and acknowledged receipt of the completed form. When Walter McLean was appointed as the Secretary of State and Minister Responsible for the Status of Women, REAL Women requested a meeting with him. He claimed to be too busy to meet with REAL Women. But he was not too busy to meet with NAC, to be accessible to NAC, and to support the work of NAC (REAL Women 1986, 7-8).

At this point REAL Women decided to bring its experiences to the attention of other MPs.

> When we received no response from the Women's Programme, Secretary of State in regard to R.E.A.L. Women's application for a grant, our association then wrote to individual Members of Parliament, bringing this matter to their attention. Subsequently, Mr. McLean, together with some of the representatives from his department, arranged to meet R.E.A.L. Women's national executive on April 22, 1985. At this meeting, Mr. McLean resolutely refused to acknowledge or accept our organization as having any validity. Mr. McLean alleged that R.E.A.L. Women did not believe in equality. If such were the case, this would be contrary to our own Articles of Incorporation. In addition, Mr. McLean alleged that funding our association would be contrary to the United Nations Declaration Against All Forms of Discrimination of Women, which was passed by Order in Council by the Trudeau cabinet in 1980 (REAL Women 1986, 8-9).

In July, 1985, REAL Women met once again with representatives of the Secretary of State. Then in February, 1986, they met with the new Secretary of State Benoit Bouchard, and subsequently his Special Assistant in charge of women's issues. As REAL Women pursued the matter, officials with the Secretary of State would request further information from REAL Women, but this was all just part of a run-around. Nothing was actually done for REAL Women (REAL Women 1986, 9-10).

REAL Women wanted to find out what was really going on and therefore pursued another avenue.

> In October 1986, R.E.A.L. Women applied under the Access to Information Act for our file at the Women's Programme, Secretary of State, in order to determine what precisely was behind the difficulties we were encountering with that Department. On November 3, 1986, our file was forwarded to us, in which all documentation, had been removed. The Women's Programme, Secretary of State removed the documentation allegedly pursuant to S. 69 (1) (g) of the Access to Information Act, (which relates to policy matters). On November 21, 1986, we submitted a complaint to the Information Commissioner regarding the exclusion of information from records disclosed to us (REAL Women 1986, 10).

Ted Byfield and *Alberta Report* valiantly took up the cause of REAL Women. Byfield saw the Mulroney government's refusal to fund REAL Women as clear evidence of the government's liberalism. The so-called Progressive "Conservative" Party of Canada, in power at the time, was not a truly conservative party. This was clear from the treatment that REAL Women received.

> It is already obvious, however, that some strong resistance is at work within the federal Tory structure to deny funding to this group. People who campaign on behalf of abortion, prostitution, homosexuality, disarmament may all expect millions in help from the "conservative" government. People who campaign for the preservation of the traditional family may expect nothing (Byfield 1986, 68).

This is indicative of the social liberalism of the Mulroney PC government, and it showed how little had changed despite the ousting of the Liberals.

> It is now becoming evident that, insofar as social values are concerned, in voting for Mr. Mulroney we were in fact bring-

ing upon ourselves four or five more years of Trudeau liberalism. And since not one of Mr. Mulroney's western candidates gave us the slightest inkling of this intention—none of them (with the single and honourable exception of Mr. Joe Clark) said they were social liberals—the reaction of many western conservatives is one of indignation and outrage (Byfield 1987, 52).

The rejection of REAL Women just did not make sense. "If lesbianism gets federal funding—and, in the Trudroney era it certainly does—then why can't traditional motherhood? That this should even become debatable seems bizarre" (Byfield 1987, 52).

The implication of the refusal to fund REAL Women included national exposure of the privileged position of feminists in the federal government. And this exposure helped to set back the feminist cause. Referring to REAL Women Kenneth Whyte wrote,

> In short, the group has touched off one of the noisiest, nastiest and most important political battles in the country today, a battle for the mind, soul and support of the average Canadian woman. Already, says Calgary MP Gordon Towers, the new group has made impressive advances and "undercut the radical feminists, forcing them to be more sensible." But that's only the surface. In broader terms, REAL Women has managed to put the brakes on a feminist-inspired drive towards socialism—with the state as the provider of social welfare and in complete control of the economy—by promoting a popular brand of conservatism in which private arrangements take priority over public, the family is the favoured social unit, and free enterprise is the guiding economic principle (Whyte et al 1987, 8).

Tory MPs such as Gordon Tower and Alex Kindy supported REAL Women. At least one MP claimed that over 75 percent of the Tory backbench supported it. At one point, the Secretary of State David Crombie agreed to give AFWUF an $8000 grant for its annual convention. However, he withheld the money after public complaints by NAC and the NDP (Whyte et al 1987, 12).

REAL Women also experienced some internal growing pains. In mid-1987 a rival organization, Victorious Women of Canada was formed in Saskatchewan. This was the result of a failed attempt to create a Saskatchewan chapter of REAL Women. The driving force and leader of the group was Gay Caswell, a former PC MLA. When Victorious Women held its first convention in Saskatoon in October 1987, a keynote speaker was Beverly LaHaye, the founder of Concerned Women of America and wife of the well-known Christian writer, Tim LaHaye (V. Byfield 1987, 35).

In February 1988 another split led to the founding of Family Forum in Hamilton, Ontario. This group was led by Lynne Scime, a former REAL Women president (Simons 1988, 19). Both Victorious Women and Family Forum seemed to fade from the scene within a relatively short period of time.

BOROWSKI

Joe Borowski began his social activism as a union organizer in Manitoba. He became involved in the NDP and got elected to the Manitoba legislature in the provincial election of 1969. The NDP had won the election, and the new premier, Ed Schreyer, made Borowski a cabinet minister. Borowski was a popular and well-liked politician who was known as a straight talker.

In 1971 Borowski made a trip to Fatima where he recommitted himself to his Roman Catholic faith. A few months later he resigned from his cabinet position over the Manitoba government's failure to take a pro-life stand. Borowski had been increasingly outspoken about his socially conservative views. So much so that a 1972 newspaper editorial said of him, "Today this so-called radical is regarded by many in this province as a reactionary, the Ernest Manning of Manitoba... a bible-thumping, hippy-hating, enemy of pot-smoking, pro-abortion women's libbers and their natural allies, the university professors" (Laurence 2004, 108).

In May 1973 Borowski declared in the Legislature that he was no longer going to pay income tax, as a protest against government funding of abortion. In the mid-1970s he spent a few days in jail as a result. Revenue Canada became more aggressive in trying to collect his taxes in 1978, and due to an altercation with a tax man, Borowski was convicted of assault (Laurence 2004, 126-129).

In 1973 Borowski formed the group Alliance Against Abortion to support his pro-life activities. It began as a group of Borowski's friends who were willing to contribute financially to the cause.

> Eventually the Alliance went public and received donations from thousands of supporters. But these were not tax-deductible donations, nor did they give the donors any right to vote on what the Alliance did. Borowski did not want to have to chair endless meetings canvassing the opinions of the membership. His union days had taught him that democracy and effectiveness rarely coincide. Nor did he want to be tied down by the "educational activities" restrictions that applied to tax-exempt charities. As far as he was concerned, there were plenty of other pro-life groups that were already trying to "educate the public" on the facts of abortion. Borowski wanted to work directly to stop abortions. Alliance Against Abortion was a group designed for "action not talk," with Borowski as its leader-martyr (Morton 1992, 68).

Borowski wanted to challenge Canada's abortion law in court. He recruited a well-known civil rights lawyer from Saskatchewan, Morris Shumiatcher, to argue the case, and raised money for it. By the time Shumiatcher filed a Statement of Claim in Regina, September 5, 1978, Alliance Against Abortion had close to $40,000.

> The Borowski case was simple: the plaintiffs sought a declaration that the 1969 amendments to the Criminal Code which permitted abortion under certain conditions, were in violation of the Canadian Bill of Rights—which guarantees the right to life of every individual... Joe also sought a permanent injunction to prevent the Finance Minister of Canada from providing public money for abortions (Laurence 2004, 143).

The government argued that the Saskatchewan Court of Queen's Bench did not have the jurisdiction to deal with Borowski's case. Later, it added the argument that Borowski did not have standing to challenge the abortion law. However, Borowski won, and on December 1, 1981, the Supreme Court of Canada ruled that Borowski could proceed with his case (Laurence 2004, 143, 144, 147).

It was during 1981 that the Trudeau government's proposals to add a Charter of Rights to the constitution were being discussed. As noted elsewhere, many pro-life groups were concerned about the potential effects of the Charter, especially if it did not include a right-to-life clause. Borowski himself strongly opposed the Charter for that reason, and on May 1, 1981, he embarked on a "protest fast" or "hunger strike" against the Charter. After 80 days, he was persuaded to end his protest fast by Morris Shumiatcher. Shumiatcher pointed out that if Borowski died due to the fast (a realistic possibility by that point) his court case against the abortion law would come to an end without being resolved. That was enough to convince him (Laurence 2004, 151, 152, 163).

In February 1983 Shumiatcher informed Borowski that a trial date had been set for his case on May 9. However, he wanted Borowski to have $350,000 for court costs before he would proceed. Alliance Against Abortion only had $100,000, so Borowski needed to raise $250,000 fast. So he held a news conference to appeal for contributions. He then contacted the editor and publisher of *The Catholic Register* to discuss his problem. *The Catholic Register* then ran a front-page story about Borowski and also urged people to contribute (Morton 1992, 131).

> What happened next exceeded Borowski's wildest imagination. Money began to pour in. For the first time in Borowski's decade-long crusade, the Catholic Church actually provided some support. Sharelife, a Church-sponsored campaign, quietly kicked in $10,000. Local chapters of affiliate groups like the Knights of Columbus and the Catholic Women's League also contributed money for the first time. There were also thousands of individual contributions. But the most remarkable story was the response to Borowski's barnstorm fund-raising campaign through small farm communities on the Prairies (Morton 1992, 131-132).

The prairie meetings raised tens of thousands of dollars. Soon Borowski had more money than he needed.

When Borowski launched his case in 1978 it had been based on an argument about the 1960 Bill of Rights. In the meantime, the Charter of Rights had been adopted, and it replaced the Bill of Rights in Borowski's argumentation. He sought to show that modern medicine:

> had discovered that the so-called "fetus" is indeed a human person. Section 7 of the Charter declared that "everyone has

the right to life." Since section 251 of the [Criminal] Code permitted the aborting—indeed, the killing—of an unborn human child for no compelling reason, it violated section 7 and was therefore invalid. The linchpin of this argument was the claim that the unborn child is indeed a person and thus protected by the Charter (Morton 1992, 135).

Borowski had nine experts who would testify to the humanity of the fetus. The best known of these was Dr. Bernard Nathanson of New York. He had been a famous abortionist and abortion rights crusader before coming to the realization that each fetus is a human being and should not be killed. He then switched and became an internationally famous pro-life activist. "Ironically, he was probably the only man in North America with as much first-hand experience with abortion as Henry Morgentaler, and yet here he was testifying on behalf of the unborn at Joe Borowski's trial" (Morton 1992, 145). The presentation of the arguments went well for Borowski.

At about the same time that the trial got underway, in May 1983 Morgentaler opened an abortuary in Winnipeg. Borowski was the foremost pro-life leader in Winnipeg, and was on the front lines of opposition to the abortion clinic. Morgentaler's activities were clearly against the law. "Borowski and others launched a public relations campaign to force the government to respond, including publishing in the *Winnipeg Free Press* a petition signed by 37,000 Manitobans protesting the Morgentaler clinic. In a province the size of Manitoba, no government can safely ignore a petition with 37,000 names" (Morton 1992, 158). The clinic was raided by police and charges were laid. When the clinic opened again, it was raided again and more charges were laid (Morton 1992, 158-160).

In October 1983 the ruling was handed down on Borowski's case, and he had lost. He appealed to the Saskatchewan Court of Appeal, but that court also ruled against him in April 1987. However, in September of that year, the Supreme Court agreed to hear his case (Morton 1992, 252).

The pro-life movement was heavily invested in the Borowski case, perhaps too heavily. Gwen Landolt believed that pro-lifers should have intervened in the Morgentaler case, but pro-life leaders saw the Borowski case as the key, and the Morgentaler case as less important. Landolt knew otherwise. But as Anna Desilets, executive director of Alliance for Life told her,

> "[A]ll the money, all of the time has gone into the Borowski case, and… the pro-life movement simply could not afford to "shift over and get involved in the Morgentaler case," recalled Landolt. "And I remember putting down the phone… I said, 'Well, that's it.' I knew the game plan." The Supreme Court justices would "shoot down" the abortion law and Joe Borowski's case would be "after the fact. I mean, they wouldn't put Borowski first and have to deal with the abortion law—heaven forbid," elaborated Landolt. "These guys are politicians, really, politicians in lawyer's gowns" (Laurence 2004, 357-358).

As usual, Landolt hit the nail on the head. Morgentaler would win his case and Borowski's case would be dismissed as moot. Borowski's appeal was heard in October, 1988. This time there were interveners involved, the Women's Legal Education and Action Fund (LEAF) opposing Borowski, and REAL Women and the Interfaith Coalition (a hodge-podge of Christian and non-Christian religious groups) supporting Borowski. However, as mentioned, when the decision was announced on March 9, 1989, Borowski had lost due to his case becoming moot. There was no longer any abortion law to be challenged, since it had been struck down earlier in the Morgentaler case (Morton 1992, 261, 262, 271).

HENRY MORGENTALER VS. KEN CAMPBELL

On July 5, 1983, Toronto police raided the Morgentaler Clinic in Toronto. Henry Morgentaler was vacationing in the US at the time, and therefore not present when the raid occurred. The leadership of the pro-life movement in Toronto had decided not to be confrontational regarding Morgentaler's Toronto clinic, believing that protesting would generate support for Morgentaler.

> Quietly but effectively, in January, 1983, the pro-life organizations inundated Attorney-General McMurtry with letters demanding that he enforce the law against any Morgentaler clinics in Ontario. It was not until October 1, 1983, that the pro-life leaders finally called their troops into the streets. Forty thousand pro-lifers, the largest abortion-related demonstration ever in Canada, rallied at Queen's Park and then marched in silent protest down Harbord Street and past the Morgentaler "abortuary" (Morton 1992, 168).

In November 1983, shortly before his trial began, Morgentaler received help from the United States. His effort "got a $50,000 boost from a fund-raiser at a downtown Toronto hotel. A thousand people paid $50 each to hear two leading American feminists, Gloria Steinem and Flo Kennedy, recount the pro-choice struggle to expand and protect access to abortion in the United States and praise Morgentaler for his challenge to the Canadian law" (Morton 1992, 170).

When it came time to select a jury for Morgentaler's trial, a couple of other Americans played a vital role. Morgentaler's lawyer brought two jury selection experts in from Washington, DC to screen people with pro-life views out of the jury. Having successfully prevented anyone who may have had pro-life views from serving as jurors, it was not surprising that the jury acquitted Morgentaler on November 8, 1984.

Pro-lifers were, of course, upset and concerned that Morgentaler was able to hand pick his jury. Ted Byfield wrote a powerful piece analyzing the implications of the decision. He quotes from an article by Anne Collins in *Maclean's* magazine where she claims that the jurors had been "chosen out of a random lot of 132 citizens." This gives a false impression, to say the least. As Byfield pointed out,

> those 12 citizens were in no sense—no sense whatsoever—"randomly" selected. Dr. Morgentaler's lawyer appeared in court with two American experts, imported specifically and solely to assure that the jury did not represent random public opinion. Though in the examination of jurors specific questions as to religious affiliation were prohibited by the judge, any suspicion of religious "taint," or of respect for authority, or of adherence to a strong moral code instantly disqualified any prospective juror. Hence the two experts. Hardly surprising therefore that one of the jurors showed up at a "pro-choice" rally the day after the trial (Byfield 1984, 60).

There was another important issue Byfield identified as well. The jury had acquitted Morgentaler in spite of the fact that he had broken the law. In this case, "the jury refused to convict Dr. Morgentaler because it elected to try not the doctor but the law itself. If our laws are going to be repealed by juries, rather than by parliament, this will make for quite a constitutional change" (Byfield 1984, 60).

If juries can be selected by excluding conservative Christians, and those juries have the power to strike down laws, then Christians will be excluded from an important role in Canadian society.

> If juries are to make laws, and Christians, religious Jews, Muslims and others of "authoritarian" moral suasion are to

be precluded from serving on juries, then what we will have done is effectively deprived religion of any voice whatever in the formulation of public policy. This, of course, is precisely what the likes of Mizz Collins want to see happen. It's up to us to see that it doesn't (Byfield 1984, 60).

Pro-lifers were spurred to action by Morgentaler's acquittal and were especially critical of the jury selection process. Pro-life leaders "promptly organized a 'Jury for Life' project that soon sent over one-million postcards to the Prime Minister opposing 'the choice to kill.' They remobilized the pro-life pickets in front of the Morgentaler Clinic, which once again became the focal point of bitter verbal clashes between pro-choice and pro-life activists" (Morton 1992, 202-203).

The Archbishop of Toronto, Emmett Cardinal Carter, had a pro-life pastoral message read in all of Toronto's Catholic parishes two weeks after the acquittal. It urged Catholics to work to stop abortion.

Morgentaler reopened his clinic on December 10, 1984. Pro-lifers wanted Attorney General Roy McMurtry to quickly shut it down.

> Pro-life picketers returned to the clinic the day it opened. Initially they marched quietly in a circle on the Harbord Street sidewalks. The longer McMurtry procrastinated, however, the more militant they became. By the end of the week, they began to block the steps leading to the clinic in an attempt to prevent women from entering. When some protestors ignored police warnings, they were arrested under the Trespass Act. Infuriated with what they saw as police protection of an illegal abortion clinic, pro-life demonstrators escalated the level of their civil disobedience and more were arrested (Morton 1992, 205).

On December 4, 1984, McMurtry filed an appeal of the Morgentaler acquittal. However, in doing so he declared that the jury selection process had not been illegal and therefore was not a ground for appeal. This upset pro-lifers who therefore decided to take action on this issue.

> In April, four different pro-life groups—Hamilton Right to Life, Alliance for Life, Coalition for the Protection of Human Life, and Catholic Women's League of Canada—filed for intervener status to raise the jury selection issue. Their petition argued that "it is in the public interest that the issue of the jury selection process in this case be considered." If the Crown was not willing to represent the public's interest in this matter, then they would (Morton 1992, 206).

Both McMurtry and Manning opposed this attempted intervention and the judge agreed with them, rejecting the pro-life groups' petition. However, the Ontario Court of Appeal allowed the appeal of Morgentaler's acquittal on October 1, 1985. In allowing the appeal, the acquittal was set aside and a new trial ordered.

Morgentaler appealed this decision to the Supreme Court of Canada, and his case there began on October 7, 1986. Pro-life groups did not intervene in this case because they were already financially committed to the Borowski case, and thought they would have an opportunity to present their views when Borowski's appeal reached the Supreme Court. Morgentaler was being financially supported by the Canadian Abortion Rights Action League (CARAL). Morgentaler's lawyer "was happy that there were no interveners on the pro-life side and wanted to keep it that way. He thought that the government lawyers had not made the strongest possible defence of the abortion legislation and feared that pro-life interveners might bring in new facts and arguments that would strengthen the Crown's case" (Morton 1992, 222).

From the perspective of the Christian Right, one of the important results of Morgentaler's November 1984 acquittal was the effect it had upon Ken Campbell. He heard the news of the acquittal while listening to a car radio.

> As the horrible implications of that news report sunk into my consciousness, I was seized and sickened by the enormity of the threat to life and liberty represented by the outrageous injustice of this acquittal. Surely "the enemy" was coming in "like a flood" eroding the foundations of faith, family and freedom and threatening to sweep away the last vestiges of the ennobling influences of our Judeo-Christian spiritual heritage! The acquittal of Henry Morgentaler on charges of crimes against humanity which he'd fully admitted, was a blow which left me stunned and sickened as if from "a kick in the stomach" (Campbell 1990, 3).

As a result, Campbell vowed to God to be used by Him to oppose abortion in Canada. A few days later he went to visit Harbord Street in Toronto to have a look at "Henry's house of horrors" for himself. He found some office space directly across from the abortuary that was being renovated, and made arrangements to rent that space once the renovations were completed.

Campbell held a meeting of the board of his evangelistic association, to make arrangements for a pro-life ministry. Thus the Choose Life Canada organization was formed as a ministry of the Ken Campbell Evangelistic Association. "On Monday morning, December 10, 1984, the day criminal abortions were scheduled to resume at the illegal abortuary at 85 Harbord Street, we unfurled our 'Choose Life Canada' banner on the wooden fencing protecting the front of the building under renovation at 100 Harbord Street, where we had tentatively arranged to locate our Choose Life Canada office" (Campbell 1990, 17).

Shortly thereafter, an opportunity arose to lease the right half of the building occupied by Henry's house of horrors, 87 Harbord Street. After months of negotiations, red tape and other preparations, Choose Life Canada moved into its new location which it called "The Way Inn." The large front window of The Way Inn was frequently smashed, likely by pro-abortionists. But the police would do nothing about it. "The reluctance of the police to even investigate the repeated smashing of our front window, was in stark contrast to the 24-hour, 7-day per week, million dollar annual protection the police provided the property of our criminal neighbour for over 3 years of his illegal operation until the Jan. 21, 1988 Supreme Court decision which was interpreted as legalizing abortion in Canada!" (Campbell 1990, 28).

Choose Life Canada held a launching rally in March 1985, hosted by the People's Church of Willowdale. The church's pastor, Paul Smith, supported Choose Life Canada. Campbell also acknowledged the public support of David Mainse of *100 Huntley Street*, Jim Hughes, the president of Campaign Life, and Hudson Hilsden, a Pentecostal minister and prominent conservative Christian leader of the 1980s (Campbell 1990, 45-46).

The Way Inn was officially opened on Father's Day, June 15, 1985. Shortly before the official opening, Campbell brought the famous American pro-life activist, Dr. Bernard Nathanson, to the facility for a visit (Campbell 1990, 33-34).

A couple of times near the end of July 1985, Campbell tried to place abortionists from Morgentaler's abortuary under "citizen's arrest." However, in both instances Toronto police thwarted his efforts (Campbell 1990, 97-98).

On September 25, 1986, Campbell staged a citizen's arrest of Ontario Attorney General Ian Scott. Scott had stayed charges against Morgentaler and two of his associates after they were arrested by police on September 24. He wanted to hold off charges until after the Supreme Court's decision in the Morgentaler case. Campbell was upset about this reasoning and wanted to force Scott to do his duty to enforce the Criminal Code. After publicly stating his intent, Campbell went to Scott's office. "I was cordially received by the Attorney General, who observed that I was there to arrest him, extending his right arm for me to place my hand thereon while stating the language of 'the citizen's arrest'" (Campbell 1990, 103).

Campbell then pointed out to Scott his lack of fairness in applying the law.

> I pointed out to him that in our home town, an interdenominational Christian Academy (the Halton Heritage Christian Academy) serving parents from several churches in our community, had been ordered to cease functioning in the Christian Educational facilities provided by the host church, Emmanuel Baptist Church. The Academy had appealed that Court order but had been refused permission to continue operations in that location while its appeal was before the Courts. In contrast, in the same jurisdiction of Ontario, the Attorney General claimed that he could not stop the law-breaking at an illegal abortuary because an appeal of the charges against the abortionists was still before the Courts (Campbell 1990, 103).

Campbell's citizen's arrest of Ian Scott was rejected by the Justice of the Peace. With the assistance of lawyer Angela Costigan, Campbell took his case to the Supreme Court of Ontario, and Appeal Court of Canada, both of which rejected it. Finally, the Supreme Court of Canada refused to hear the case.

> In any case, after exhausting all legal channels in a $100,000 effort to find a Canadian Court which would order the Attorney-General of Ontario to fulfill his oath of office and enforce Section 251 of the Criminal code of Canada, I found

myself, at last, conditioned as a 37 year follower of Christ and 55 year Canadian citizen, to participate in non-violent, civil disobedience in affirming and protecting the humanity of the pre-born! (Campbell 1990, 105).

As the last sentence intimates, after Morgentaler's Supreme Court victory of January 1988, Campbell embraced the civil disobedience tactics of Operation Rescue.

CONCLUSION

The first part of the 1980s was a period of increasing activity and organizing among conservative Christians in Canada. Although the Charter of Rights was adopted contrary to the wise counsel of Gwen Landolt, conservative Christians had managed to influence the federal government to place a reference to God in the preamble of the Charter of Rights.

The EFC stepped up its activities under the stellar leadership of its new executive director, Brian Stiller. AFWUF was formed to provide an alternative to the shrill voices of feminism in Alberta, and not long afterwards, REAL Women was founded to articulate the views of conservative-oriented women in Canada. REAL Women would be the strongest voice for the Christian Right in Canada, at least for the 1980s and 1990s.

Pro-life activism was at its peak during the 1980s. Joe Borowski led an ultimately unsuccessful legal crusade against abortion. Henry Morgentaler, on the other hand, was constantly performing illegal abortions and leading the cause to legalize abortion. With some help from the new Charter of Rights and sympathetic judges, Morgentaler prevailed. But along the way he stirred conservative Christians to various forms of activism to protect the unborn. The late 1980s would seal his triumph and also lead to unprecedented forms of civil disobedience among Canada's pro-lifers.

REFERENCES

Byfield, Ted. 1984. "The appalling implications of Morgentaler's unjust acquittal." *Alberta Report*. November 26: 60.

Byfield, Ted. 1986. "So our Tory members defend the family, do they? Ho, ho, Ho!" *Alberta Report*. November 10: 68.

Byfield, Ted. 1987. "Will some Tory please explain why you're against motherhood." *Alberta Report*. January 19: 52.

Byfield, Virginia. 1987. "Uh-oh, here comes another one." *Alberta Report*. November 2: 35.

Campbell, Ken. 1990. *5 Years Rescuing at "the Gates of Hell"*. Burlington, ON: Acts Books.

Colle, Larry. 1982. "Religion & Politics: Canada's New Right." *The United Church Observer*. November: 24-33.

Collins, Anne. 1985. *The Big Evasion: Abortion, the Issue That Won't Go Away*. Toronto: Lester & Orpen Dennys Limited.

Cuneo, Michael W. 1989. *Catholics Against the Church: Anti-Abortion Protest In Toronto 1969-1985*. Toronto: University of Toronto Press.

Dubinsky, *Karen. 1987. "REALly Dangerous: The Challenge of R.E.A.L. Women." Canadian Dimension*. October: 4-7.

Egerton, George. 2000. "Trudeau, God, and the Canadian Constitution: Religion, Human Rights, and Government Authority in the Making of the 1982 Constitution." In *Rethinking Church, State, and Modernity: Canada Between Europe and America*. Eds. David Lyon and Marguerite Van Die. Toronto: University of Toronto Press.

Eichler, Margrit. 1985. The Pro-Family Movement: Are They For or Against Families? Ottawa: Canadian Research Institute for the Advancement of Women.

Harder, Lois. 2003. *State of Struggle: Feminism and Politics in Alberta*. Edmonton: University of Alberta Press.

Hutchinson, Brian. 1989. "The new wave pounds feminism." *Alberta Report*. November 13:36.

Jenish, D'Arcy. 1986. "Feminists aim at REAL foes." *Alberta Report*. June 16: 11-12.

Landolt, Gwen. 1981. "Brief to the Special Joint Committee on the Constitution of Canada." Campaign Life.

Landolt, Gwen. 2007. "Response to Michael Wagner's Questions." Personal email, February 13: 1-5.

Laurence, Lianne. 2004. *Borowski: A Canadian Paradox*. Toronto: The Interim Publishing Company.

Males, Steve. 1987. "The Handmaid's Tale: A call to action?" *Faith Today*. May/June: 43, 48.

Morton, F. L. 1992. *Morgentaler v. Borowski: Abortion, the Charter, and the Courts*. Toronto: McClelland and Stewart Inc.

Orr, Fay. 1984. "Evangelicals in the lobby." *Alberta Report*. May 14: 45.

Pinnock, Clark. 1986. "Is Jerry Falwell coming to town?" *Faith Today*. May/June: 10.

REAL Women of Canada. 1985. "Brief to Members of Parliament." November 19.

REAL Women of Canada. 1986. "Presentation to the Standing Committee on The Secretary of State." December 11.

Simons, Paula. 1988. "REAL Women fight and split." *Alberta Report*. March 7: 19.

Stackhouse, John G. 1993. *Canadian Evangelicalism in the Twentieth Century: An Introduction to Its Character*. Toronto: University of Toronto Press.

Stiller, Brian. 1986. "Evangelicals: A Threatening Cloud?" *Faith Today*. December/January: 32-33, 35.

Stiller, Brian. 2006. "Telephone Interview." November 28.

Steele, Betty. 1991. *Together Again: Reuniting Men and Women, Love and Sex, Mothers and Children*. Toronto: Simon & Pierre Publishing Company Limited.

Tarr, Leslie K. 1986. "Does Canada Need A Moral Majority?" *Faith Today*. March/April: 18-24.

Weatherbe, Stephen. 1982. "Phyllis' fight for God and family." *Alberta Report*. December 6: 46-47.

Weatherbe, Stephen. 1983. "The new evangelicals." *Alberta Report*. November 28: 20.

Weatherbe, Stephen. 1985. "Beware of evangelicals!" *Alberta Report*. October 21: 52, 54.

Weatherbe, Stephen, and Judy Haiven. 1982. "Out of the closet." *Alberta Report*. December 6: 46.

Whyte, Kenneth, with Phillip Day, Mike Byfield, Steve Weatherbe and Lori Cohen. 1987. "REAlists versus feminists." *Alberta Report*. March 16: 8-13.

Woloshen, Richard. 1988. "The meeting that got away." *Alberta Report*. May 2: 44-45.

CHAPTER 5 | THE LATTER HALF OF THE 1980S: TRYING HARDER, BUT LOSING BIGGER

In September of 1984, Canada elected a Progressive Conservative government led by Brian Mulroney. To some people this represented a shift to the Right, similar to the election of Prime Minister Margaret Thatcher in Britain in 1979 or Ronald Reagan's rise to the presidency in the United States the following year. There was a genuine hope that public policy at the federal level would move to the right after years of Pierre Trudeau's social liberalism. The Progressive Conservatives had previously formed a minority government from June 1979 through March 1980, but it was too short-lived to make any notable impact. Furthermore, the party leader and prime minister at the time, Joe Clark, was notoriously left-wing on social issues. His wife, Maureen McTeer, was one of Canada's most prominent feminist and "pro-choice" activists during the 1980s.

As it turned out, the leadership of the new Mulroney government (which included Joe Clark as a cabinet minister) was also predominantly left-wing on social issues. The new government's willingness to lavishly fund feminist groups while ignoring REAL Women has already been discussed. Its efforts to conform

Canadian laws to the new Charter of Rights and Freedoms led it to embrace homosexual rights. Many backbench MPs were genuine conservatives and were unhappy with the government's positions on these issues, and they did manage to block the pro-homosexual proposals on a number of occasions. The government realized it had to do something to placate those socially conservative caucus members, so it settled on a plan to introduce strong anti-pornography legislation. It introduced two separate bills to do that.

Like the federal government, the new Ontario government of David Peterson embraced some aspects of the homosexual rights agenda in conforming its legislation to the Charter of Rights. Despite considerable controversy and opposition from the Christian Right, the Ontario government succeeded in adding sexual orientation to its human rights law in 1986.

By 1986 some conservative Christians were so upset by the social liberalism of the Mulroney Tories that they decided to form a specifically Christian federal political party. The Christian Heritage Party (CHP) grew rapidly in its first two or three years until the success of the new Reform Party of Canada absorbed many conservative Christians, who saw it as a better vehicle to get MPs elected to Parliament. They were quickly proven correct when Deborah Grey became the first Reformer to win a seat in Parliament in a by-election held in March of 1989.

Abortion continued to be a hot issue for the last half of the 1980s. The *Morgentaler* decision of January 1988 was the defining moment for the abortion issue in Canada. There has been no federal abortion law in Canada since then, but the Mulroney government did try to enact such legislation. One of Canada's greatest thinkers of the twentieth century, George Grant, was a strong supporter of the pro-life cause and a critic of the *Morgentaler* decision

The decade closed with intense conflict over the abortion issue, including the adoption of the civil disobedience tactics of Operation Rescue in Canada. And the international Gay Games aroused significant controversy in BC. Overall, the last half of the 1980s was a period of setbacks for Canada's Christian Right.

ATTEMPTS TO RESTRICT PORNOGRAPHY

The rapid and widespread proliferation of pornographic materials throughout parts of Canada had begun to arouse concern by the 1970s. In 1959 the PC government had passed Bill C-58 which was considered to have a rather conservative approach to opposing obscene material. Nevertheless, due to judicial decisions and "expert opinion," there was a general liberalization in dealing with pornography (Campbell and Pal 1989, 116-119).

By the late 1970s, a number of private members bills were introduced to deal with the spread of pornography. Pierre Trudeau's Liberal government had also proposed three bills that would have dealt with the issue; Bill C-21 in 1978, Bill C-53 in 1981, and Bill C-19 in February 1984. None of these bills went anywhere. However, in December 1980 the Trudeau government created the Committee on Sexual Offences Against Children and Youth chaired by University of Toronto sociologist Robin Badgley. This committee "was directed to investigate the extent of sexual exploitation and abuse of children (including child pornography) and to examine the adequacy of laws in this area" (Campbell and Pal 1989, 123).

In June 1983 the Liberals also established the Special Committee on Pornography and Prostitution chaired by Paul Fraser, the former head of the Canadian Bar Association. This committee held public hearings across the country to ascertain public views on the issue and make recommendations to the government (Campbell and Pal 1989, 126).

In February 1984 REAL Women presented a submission to the Fraser Committee. About three-quarters of the submission dealt with the issue of pornography, and the rest with prostitution. REAL Women argued strongly that pornography contributes to an environment that leads to violence against women, especially rape. They also highlighted the problem of child pornography and recommended specific legislation to stamp out child pornography (REAL Women 1984, 3).

The REAL Women submission also offered responses to common arguments that were used in defense of pornography, including the common argument that governments "cannot legislate morality." The submission responded, "All of Canada's Criminal Code attempts to enforce morality of some kind. It prohibits stealing, killing, fraud and bigamy, etc. In short, it upholds a standard of behaviour or morality in our society". Moreover, "the law serves as a guideline to the conscience. To many, what is legal becomes permissible. The Criminal Code then, serves to educate the public that a certain standard of behaviour is required" (REAL Women 1984, 5).

REAL Women, however, did not have a utopian conception of the law, as if anti-pornography legislation would completely solve the problem.

> It is unlikely that any law will eliminate completely the presence of pornography in society, any more than laws against murder, rape, robbery or simple theft will eliminate those evils. Nevertheless, laws have an educative effect. If there are no pornographic magazines for sale in retail stores, no pornographic movies or movies glorifying violence offered in movie theatres or on television, we will be working to produce a healthier society (REAL Women 1984, 5).

The submission also noted that much of the pornography in Canada was coming from the US and recommended that the

Customs Tariff Act be amended to restrict entry of that material. And it included specific recommendations to change the Criminal Code based on a private members bill from David Kilgour, a PC MP from Edmonton. These recommendations did not include exemptions for literary materials. "We are reluctant to include in legislation a clause which states that the offensiveness or harm of a work may be mitigated by the literary or artistic merits of the work as a whole. Expert testimony in this regard because of the very nature of 'literary merit' is merely subjective" (REAL Women 1984, 8). However, the Fraser Committee did not take the strong conservative stand recommended by REAL Women.

The Badgley Committee, the one appointed by Trudeau's government to look at sexual offences against children and youth, issued its report in August, 1984. It called for specific prohibition of child pornography, as well as strict restrictions on access to pornography by young people. "The committee's approach was tough and was very much in tune with the Conservative government's ideological orientation" (Campbell and Pal 1989, 129).

The Fraser Committee's report was released in February, 1985. It recommended criminal penalties only for hard-core pornography, and decriminalization of soft-core pornography and erotica. Pornography would be classified into three tiers, with different penalties for each tier. The Fraser Committee recommendations "reflected liberal values that insisted that the state should not interfere in individual choices that appeared to cause no harm to others. (The committee had concluded that no link had been established between pornography and anti-social behaviour.)" (Campbell and Pal 1989, 132).

In August 1985 the Interchurch Committee on Pornography was formed as a subcommittee of the Evangelical Fellowship of Canada (EFC). It had the support of the Baptist Convention of Canada, Church of God, Pentecostal Assemblies of Canada, Salvation Army, Elim Fellowship and the Mormon and Roman Catholic churches, and was formed specifically to influence the PC government's pornography legislation (Morris et al 1986, 34).

The PC caucus committee on justice was studying the Fraser Committee report, and many MPs did not like its proposals.

> Then the Interchurch group arrived, bearing graphic samples of (a) what is now permitted by the Criminal Code and (b) what would be everywhere permitted by the Fraser plan. They provided samples of magazines and videotapes now largely restricted to big cities. Recalls Interchurch co-chairman Lois Elliott: 'It was all quite shocking for the MPs' ... Mrs. Elliott says that Interchurch carefully developed a coherent statement of principles and recommendations. Newfoundland MP James McGrath enabled it to deliver these along with visual presentation both to the caucus committee and to an all-party assembly of MPs. Meanwhile Interchurch urged members of supporting churches to write [Justice Minister John] Crosbie and their MPs. The number who did is not entirely certain, but Mrs. Elliott says she has heard it was as many as 37,000, with some 800 to the justice minister alone (Morris et al 1986, 34).

The Interchurch Committee was very pleased with the resulting legislation. Rev. Hudson Hilsden, the committee chairman said, "It's better than we expected" (Morris et al 1986, 34).

An unnamed government policy adviser told Professor Dany Lacombe that the government had been swamped by letters calling for or supporting tough anti-pornography measures. He said that

> The [anti-pornography] community was very, very vocal,

and usually by way of writing campaign letters to ministers and local members. And throughout the history of the subsequent bill the mail to the minister of justice was running overwhelmingly in support of the legislative efforts of the government. And it was not unusual to have the entire membership of a particular church writing to the minister of justice thousands of letters. It was the subject of correspondence for a number of years. Certainly up until the abortion decision in the Morgentaler case, it outstripped everything else (Lacombe 1994, 107).

According to John Crosbie, it was "fundamentalist" MPs within the PC caucus who pushed for the resulting tough pornography bill. He said that "the caucus was divided between the 'liberal sophisticates' like himself, who have few worries about pornography, and the 'fundamentalists' like Jake Epp, who are 'moral-majority type' people, committed to the eradication of all 'evils'" (Lacombe 1994, 109-110). The fundamentalists were upset over the PC government's liberalization of divorce legislation and its proposals to ban discrimination on the basis of sexual orientation. "According to Crosbie, 'the fundamentalists were all full of piss and vinegar' about those reforms. Consequently, when it came time to address the issue of pornography, the 'fundamentalists' were not willing to accept a compromise. They demanded a truly conservative pornography law" (Lacombe 1994, 110).

On June 10, 1986, Crosbie introduced Bill C-114, which would amend the Criminal Code and the Customs Tariff. If adopted, it would have been among the toughest anti-pornography legislation in the Western world. "Human rights activist Jack London described the bill as the product of 'right-wing, fundamentalist, puritanical thought' that 'would give a sense of orgasmic ecstasy to Jerry Falwell'" (Campbell and Pal 1989, 139). Aside from some anti-pornography feminists, the social Left was vehemently opposed to this bill.

Ted Byfield strongly supported Bill C-114 and encouraged his *Alberta Report* readers to write to their MPs about it. He described the opposition to the bill by Canada's arts community as follows:

The soul, if you can believe the nation's editorial writers, is about to be ripped out of the arts in Canada. Something apparently quintessential to Canadian self-expression, indispensable to the film producer, the cornerstone of art photography, the cardinal rudiment of all visual portrayal of that which is enobling in humanity, is to be prohibited from public display on paper or film within the ten provinces and the territories. I refer, of course, to the proposal of the minister of justice, Mr. Crosbie, to draw down the curtain of what a former Manitoba law dean calls "dangerous, right-wing, fundamentalist, puritanical thought" upon the rights of artistic expression in this country. Mr. Crosbie, as we all by now know, actually proposes to prohibit the publication of "any visual matter showing vaginal, anal or oral intercourse, ejaculation, sexually violent behaviour, bestiality, incest, necrophilia, masturbation or other sexual activity." Without these primary artistic constituents, we are solemnly assured in almost every newspaper, the arts in Canada will surely wither and die (T. Byfield 1986c, 52).

At the end of June, John Crosbie was replaced as justice minister by Ramon Hnatyshyn. Hnatyshyn wanted the anti-porn bill to be rewritten, and it died on the order paper when the House of Commons adjourned at the end of August. Many conservative Christians and a number of Conservative MPs wanted the government to reintroduce the bill. The campaign by conservative Christians for strong anti-porn legislation had been effective up to that time. Those Christians, "with the Evangelical Fellowship of Canada in the vanguard, organized a lobby described by some western MPs as the most effective they had ever seen" (V. Byfield 1986b, 34).

The Interchurch Committee wasn't about to give up at that point. It's leader, Hudson Hilsden, promoted a letter-writing campaign to not only bring the anti-porn bill back, but to have it strengthened. He was opposed "to a loophole through which material of 'artistic merit' could pass. 'Clever people' he says, would be able to 'bring just about anything' through with such a clause" (V. Byfield 1986b, 34). His view was shared by Bernice Gerard, at that time a member of the EFC's national council. As she saw it, the "loose wording on artistic merit could be used to justify what C-114's other sections forbade, particularly explicit sexual acts in movies and on television" (V. Byfield 1986b, 34).

During the period between the death of C-114 and the introduction of a new anti-porn law, REAL Women presented a brief to MPs that included a section on pornography. It stated,

> Our association fully supports the intent of the Pornography Bill proposed by former Minister of Justice John Crosbie, on June 10, 1986, which expressly prohibits sexually-explicit material. We support this proposal not only because it prohibits material which is exploitive of both women and children, but also because, according to existing studies, such sexually-explicit material adversely affects behaviour and changes attitudes toward sexuality (REAL Women 1986, 5-6).

On May 4, 1987, Hnatyshyn introduced his anti-porn legislation, Bill C-54. The major difference with Bill C-114 was that C-54 distinguished "erotica" from pornography and did not criminalize erotica. Erotica was, for the most part, just nudity. Aside from that, C-54 was generally considered to be a tough anti-porn bill. NDP MP Svend Robinson described the bill as a "combination of Jimmy Swaggart and Queen Victoria" (Campbell and Pal 1989, 145). He also called it "a right-wing obscenity... [that] will make Canada the most puritanical country in the Western world" (Campbell and Pal 1989, 148). As with the previous bill, the social Left was almost unanimous in its vehement opposition to Hnatyshyn's revisions.

At the outset, because it was believed C-54 was reasonably strong, conservative Christians generally supported it. REAL Women believed it needed some fixing, especially a tightening of the "artistic merit" exemption, but generally supported it. REAL Women's brief on Bill C-54 to the Standing Parliamentary Committee on Justice argued that the bill constituted a reasonable limit on the Charter of Right's "freedom of expression" guarantee.

> This limitation on "freedom of expression" is certainly not without precedent. We have laws protecting society in other areas such as the law prohibiting false advertising, defamation and hate literature, etc. In other words, we already use censorship in many areas because of the values we uphold in our society. Since we already have a law attempting to limit pornography (the obscenity section of the Criminal Code), albeit not too successfully, this indicates that Canadians accept our right to limit freedom of expression in this area. This proposed bill is only a strengthening of the attempt to stop pornography and there is no reason why we should abandon this right (REAL Women n. d., 12).

Ted Byfield was also supportive of Bill C-54, and in the same fashion as he defended C-114, he took aim at the bill's opponents.

> Mr. Ramon Hnatyshyn, Canada's justice minister, has come down on the conservative side of the pornography argument. As a result he has incurred the predictable wrath of that inextinguishable Canadian institution which could be called the "homofemartsyglobe," meaning the homosexuals, the feminists, the artsies and—it goes without saying—Toronto's *Globe and Mail*. I think this word needs to be added to the Canadian vocabulary to save time and space. Rather than quoting them all individually on any issue, they can be

quoted, so to speak, collectively, since they invariably all say the same things anyway (T. Byfield 1987, 52).

The anti-porn bill would restrict too much for these people.

> [T]he homofemartsyglobe apparently fears that Mr. Hnatyshyn's anti-pornography bill has dangerously jeopardized the artistic future of things like anal intercourse, masturbation, ejaculation, mamara-penile encounter and other activities apparently indispensable to the Canadian stage and screen. Mr. Hnatyshyn's bill would prohibit the public depiction of such things, however tasteful (T. Byfield 1987, 52).

Over time, it appeared that opposition to C-54 was growing. Conservative Christians were the most notable supporters. "Leading the support for the bill (though not without several reservations of their own) are the church forces that have backed it from the beginning, people that a journalistic wag early dubbed 'the Moral Majority Munchkins'" (Byfield and Day 1988, 27). This included the Interchurch Committee and the Coalition for Family Values. Despite concerns about the "artistic merit" exemption and a couple of other problems, these groups still supported C-54. And a lawyer for the Coalition, Robert Nadeau, suggested that the PCs would suffer "serious political repercussions" if they let the bill die (Byfield and Day 1988, 27).

Not long afterwards, however, even conservative Christians began to withdraw support for the bill. A few months earlier, in 1987, the Supreme Court of Canada upheld a decision of the Manitoba Court of Appeal that gave a forceful interpretation to the obscenity provisions already in the Criminal Code (*R. v. Video World*). A lawyer hired by the Interchurch Committee analyzed C-54 and concluded that it could actually liberalize the existing provisions against obscenity. As a result, conservative Christians withdrew support for the bill.

> The campaign to proscribe pornography came to an end for religious and family-oriented organizations with the recognition that the present obscenity legislation could still be used to ban sexually explicit material. Suddenly, the alleged subjectivity, vagueness, inadequacy, and unenforceability of obscenity legislation, which created the necessity to reform the law in the first place, vanished (Lacombe 1994, 131-132).

Liberal and loose interpretations of the Criminal Code's obscenity provisions had ultimately led to the campaign for an anti-pornography law. Then a relatively strict and conservative interpretation of the same provisions made the anti-porn proposals potentially counter-productive. Thus the proposed legislation was scrapped. But this was not the end of the story.

> Although the government failed to reform the law on obscenity, the public campaign to criminalize pornography succeeded. In February 1992 the Supreme Court of Canada unanimously declared in the Butler case that while the obscenity provisions of the Criminal Code violated the Canadian Charter of Rights and Freedoms, they were a reasonable and justified limit prescribed by law (Lacombe 1994, 134).

It's important to note that the *Butler* decision was based on feminist argumentation rather than conservative argumentation. Pornography was restricted by the Supreme Court because it was harmful to women. "The feminist attempt to reform the law by constructing pornography as a problem couched in terms of an infringement on women's right to equality succeeded in transforming the law" (Lacombe 1994, 136).

Ultimately pornography was restricted, but largely as a result of the feminist movement, not the Christian Right.

THE EQUALITY REPORTS OF 1985 AND 1986

In March 1985 the Minister of Justice appointed an all-party subcommittee to make recommendations to the government regarding federal laws and policies that would need to be changed in order to conform to Section 15 of the Charter of Rights. That committee released its report in October of that year. It contained a number of recommendations that involved expanding homosexual rights.

In the main, these recommendations required interpreting the Charter as already including protection based on sexual orientation, and amending the Canadian Human Rights Act to also explicitly include such protection. With regard to the former the report states,

> What witnesses told us about the experiences of homosexuals in Canada indicates that they do not enjoy the same basic freedom as others. Their sexual orientation is often a basis for unjustifiably different treatment under laws and policies, including those at the federal level, and in their dealings with private persons. We have therefore concluded that "sexual orientation" should be read into the general open-ended language of section 15 of the *Charter* as a constitutionally prohibited ground of discrimination (Parliamentary Committee 1985, 29).

Similarly, the report concludes "that sexual orientation should be a prohibited ground of discrimination in the *Canadian Human Rights Act*" (Parliamentary Committee 1985, 29). This would bring the Act into alignment with the Charter of Rights. "By amending the *Canadian Human Rights Act* to add sexual orientation as a prohibited ground of discrimination, Parliament would be extending the equal protection and equal benefit of the law, which we take to be guaranteed by section 15 of the *Charter*, to homosexuals" (Parliamentary Committee 1985, 29). It further recommended that the Canadian Armed Forces and the RCMP be prohibited from discriminating against homosexuals (neither would accept homosexuals at that time), and that the legal age for consensual sexual activity be the same for homosexuals as heterosexuals (Parliamentary Committee 1985, 31-32).

The federal government was obliged to respond to the committee's report by February 21, 1986. One committee member, Svend Robinson, urged homosexuals to write to Prime Minister Mulroney telling the government to accept and implement the recommendations. He also noted,

> our sub-committee strongly recommends that courts read into Section 15 of the Charter of Rights a prohibition against discrimination on the basis of sexual orientation. The conclusions of this report can and, I hope, will be cited in Canadian courts in support of this broad interpretation. Thus, if government refuses to act, the courts may order them to do so (Robinson 1986, 19).

The federal government accepted the recommendations of the committee. It's official report responding to the committee states,

> The Government believes that one's sexual orientation is irrelevant to whether one can perform a job or use a service or facility. The Department of Justice is of the view that the courts will find that sexual orientation is encompassed by the guarantees in section 15 of the *Charter*. The Government will take whatever measures are necessary to ensure that sexual orientation is a prohibited ground of discrimination in relation to all areas of federal jurisdiction (Department of Justice 1986, 13).

This response amounted to a considerable victory for homosexual rights activists. As one prominent homosexual activist wrote,

> The declaration of the federal justice minister to Parliament and the country that it is government policy to eliminate discrimination on the grounds of sexual orientation wherever it lies within its constitutional power to do so has to count as a major victory—perhaps the greatest victory gay men and lesbians have won to date. That this declaration has been made by a Progressive Conservative government only enhances the significance of the achievement. Overnight, the debate has been rekindled—with gay civil rights bearing the (reluctant) imprimatur of the state, and our opponents, for once, on the defensive (Popert 1986, 13).

CONSERVATIVE CHRISTIAN RESPONSES

The Mulroney government's decision to back homosexual rights was strongly opposed by many PC MPs as well as conservative Christians. The opposition within the federal Tory caucus was led by Alex Kindy, a medical doctor. The "progressives" within the caucus saw the promotion of "equality" as a high priority. "The conservatives, whose most unbending spokesman is Calgary East MP Alex Kindy, argue that the state's more important duty is to uphold the moral values and Judeo-Christian principles upon which this country was founded and on which, they contend, the very existence of civilized society ultimately depends" (Jenish, 1986, 12).

Justice Minister John Crosbie was not impressed by the response of the conservatives within the PC caucus. In a subsequent book, he refers to Kindy as a "troglodyte" and also singles out another MP as being an outspoken opponent of the proposal to amend the Human Rights Act.

> Another right-wing Tory back-bencher, Dan McKenzie from Manitoba, advised the news media that a majority of caucus members were totally opposed to my proposals to advance the rights of homosexuals and to widen the roles for women in the military. He predicted that my amendment would never pass the Commons (Crosbie 1997, 271).

Crosbie had the support of the highest echelons of the PC Party, most notably the Prime Minister, but it was evident that he lacked support among the party's grass roots and back benchers. Crosbie says that Brian Mulroney "deserves considerable credit for standing up to the reactionaries and fundamentalists in our caucus. Whenever human rights were at issue, the Prime Minister would support a 'liberal' as opposed to a 'conservative' approach" (Crosbie 1997, 271-272).

At the PC national conference in Montreal in 1986, Crosbie's appeal to party members for support of his pro-homosexual proposals was not well received. The conservative Christian view was apparently more popular among the party members attending the conference.

> The Tory crowd reserved their greatest applause for a young minister of the Fundamentalist Christian Assembly Church in Abbotsford, B.C., who argued that homosexuality is something that is learned, and Ottawa should not condone it. He saw a serious danger to Canadian children in pedophilia in the gay community. He said he had children and he wanted to protect them. Those were, and are, the views of many Canadians, and they illustrate why it was so difficult to change the law (Crosbie 1997, 272).

Ted Byfield wrote an especially scathing editorial in response to Crosbie's proposal. He began it with a quote from Crosbie, justifying his moves: "The issue of sexual orientation is very upsetting to some people, but it's a test of tolerance how well we tolerate that which we don't necessarily like." Byfield draws two significant implications from this statement.

> First, it discloses that our minister of justice is curiously keen to gain public acceptability for sodomy. Whether we are able to keep our disgust with this sort of thing to ourselves, he says, is a measure of our civic virtue. Any public condemnation of the practice—one thinks immediately of the Bible's—he asks us to consider contemptible. If two males flaunt their proclivities in public, we had better shut up about it or he will prosecute us. Soon we may expect "affirmative action" for homosexuals. Every school board will be required to hire a certain number. Textbooks will be "cleansed" from intolerance to assure that there are a suitable number of homosexual "families" depicted—boys embracing one another, that kind of thing—and any trustee who speaks out against it will be branded "intolerant" and, if obstinate enough, jailed. For all of this, we may thank a "Conservative" government. The mind reels (T. Byfield 1986a, 60).

The other implication of Crosbie's statement is an embrace of moral relativism.

> What human beings do or do not do, in the opinion of the minister of justice, is not a matter of right and wrong, but merely of what they happen to "like" or "dislike." Some people like olives; some don't. Some people like sodomy; some don't. It's all the same. There can be, in other words, no such things as moral laws or rules to which all human beings are subject. Moral preferences are nothing more than expressions of individual inclination (T. Byfield 1986a, 60).

Two months later Byfield wrote on homosexuality again, this time in response to a letter from a homosexual reader of *Al-*

berta Report. This reader argued that he had a natural affection for members of his own sex. Since the affection was natural, it could not be wrong. In rejecting this view Byfield emphasized the Christian foundation of Canada's society. "Acceptable conduct," he wrote, "cannot be determined by whatever an individual's 'affections' happen to favour, nor by the law, nor by popular opinion. Like it or not, we are driven back to some primal moral authority, something that supersedes popular fad, politics, even majority opinion. For our society there is only one such source, notably the Bible and the Judaeo Christian ethic that has flowed from it" (T. Byfield 1986b, 52).

REAL Women was, of course, one of the organizations that most strongly opposed Crosbie's proposals. The views of this group were communicated to MPs in a brief presented on November 18, 1986. This brief dealt with over half a dozen separate issues, one of which was the proposed extension of homosexual rights. REAL Women argued that the Charter of Rights should not be interpreted as prohibiting discrimination on the basis of sexual orientation since sexual orientation had explicitly been excluded from the Charter by the parliamentary committee considering the Charter in 1981. There were also a couple of court decisions from the late 1970s indicating that the protected category of "sex" in provincial human rights codes did not include sexual orientation (Real Women 1986, 12).

Basically, in the view of REAL Women, giving legal protection based on sexual orientation would mean giving special rights to homosexuals. As the brief puts it,

> Human Rights legislation has always protected a <u>specific morally neutral and unchangeable characteristic</u> which has broad social consensus. Homosexuals are bound together not by a common inherited status, but rather, are linked together because of behaviour or lifestyle. No <u>other</u> minority group is protected by the <u>Human Rights Code</u> on the basis

of behaviour or preference" (REAL Women 1986, 13).

REAL Women argued further that there is much more at stake than a simple claim for equal rights.

> The homosexual community is not asking for equal rights—they already have this. What homosexuals want is official recognition and social acceptance of a lifestyle that is <u>not acceptable</u> to a significant majority of Canadians. To provide this special privilege to the homosexual lifestyle is to use the coercive impact of the law to enforce decisions that are <u>contrary</u> to the beliefs and religious practices of the majority of Canadians. It amounts to government approval of their particular lifestyle. To argue otherwise is to overlook the important role of law in society, which is to serve as an effective teacher and a guideline to the conscience. To many that which is <u>legal</u> is permissible. Therefore, to provide protection for sexual orientation is to adversely affect the social ethic of our society, which has always regarded the heterosexual family as its foundation and most basic unit, and would be a public acknowledgement that homosexuals have an alternative lifestyle which is as valid as that of the traditional family. To this we take strong exception (REAL Women 1986, 13).

Clearly, REAL Women viewed Crosbie's proposals as a significant threat to the privileged position of the traditional family in Canadian society.

The Evangelical Fellowship of Canada also opposed the addition of sexual orientation to the Human Rights Act, but it was also very concerned about being viewed as wanting to deny legitimate rights to homosexuals. As Brian Stiller put it, "The unfortunate part of this debate is that too often broadcasters or journalists imply that evangelical concerns spring from a view that would deny homosexuals equal rights. That simply is not true" (Stiller 1987, 54). He did say that evangelicals view the sexual behaviour of homosexuals as wrong, but added that "We defend their rights to equal access in this society" (Stiller 1987, 54).

Nevertheless, the EFC expressed some of the same concerns as REAL Women. According to Stiller, the homosexuals want "special recognition of their life-style and sexual preference" (1987, 70). Amending the human rights legislation would provide credibility to homosexuality. "To place 'sexual orientation' within the Human Rights Act," he writes, "puts the government in a place where it is called to legislate and legitimize a particular conviction concerning sexual orientation. The government has no right to engage in such legislation of morals" (1987, 54).

The EFC had specific concerns about how amending the legislation would affect social agencies, private schools and businesses. There was a fear that religious agencies would not be allowed to restrict hiring to heterosexuals, that landlords would not be allowed to refuse homosexual tenants, and that schools would be required to teach that homosexuality is a legitimate alternative to traditional marriage. Furthermore, the phrase "sexual orientation" was vague enough to encompass other sexual aberrations (Stiller 1987, 54-55).

Stiller was very prescient in his concern about the impact that sexual orientation protection would have on marriage.

> We are concerned about what the ultimate impact will be on marriage and adoption if this type of legislation is enacted, either federally or provincially. For if "sexual orientation" is added to human rights legislation, pressure will eventually be exerted on the courts to reinterpret the meaning of "marriage." Not only would lesbian and homosexual marriages occur but there also could be a demand on government to

provide family and health benefits to homosexual couples. This would result in the adoption of children in same-sex marriages (Stiller 1987, 55).

When John Crosbie was shifted out of the Justice portfolio later in 1986, to be replaced by Ray Hnatyshyn, the new minister did not pursue the amendments to the Human Rights Act. The strong opposition to Crosbie's proposals likely deterred Hnatyshyn and future PC justice ministers, from pursuing that goal. Kim Campbell did give it a try, but she was also unsuccessful.

BILL 7 IN ONTARIO

In 1985 the Liberal Party was able to form a minority government in Ontario with the help of the NDP. Early in 1986, Bill 7 was introduced by Attorney General Ian Scott to amend various Ontario statutes to conform to section 15 of the (then) new Charter of Rights. (Scott was himself a homosexual.) In response, the Coalition for Gay Rights in Ontario (CGRO) submitted a brief arguing that sexual orientation needed to be added to the Human Rights Code to ensure compliance with the Charter. An amendment to Bill 7 adopting that proposal was passed (Warner 2002, 197).

In 1985, in response to the Federal Equality Committee's recommendations in favour of homosexual rights, an organization called the Coalition for Family Values (CFV) had formed. Its core membership consisted largely of conservative evangelical churches, REAL Women, and the National Citizens Coalition. Led by Rev. Hudson Hilsden, CFV would be in the forefront of opposition to Bill 7.

> By the autumn of 1986, the CFV campaign had gathered considerable momentum as the bill headed back to the

legislature for second reading. The Christian coalition had launched a massive letter-writing and phone campaign, prepared briefs, and courted public opinion, relying upon materials prepared for a previous federal debate which characterized homosexuals as perverted, predatory, paedophiles. However, the formal briefs submitted to politicians tended to avoid such evocations in favour of dry, legal argumentation (Herman 1994, 34).

The stated goals of the CFV were as follows:

1. To address present and prospective laws and public policies relating to the traditional family as the basic unit of society, as well as its economic role and place in society.

2. To promote a balance between individual and collective rights and responsibilities in a rational and responsible framework of law consistent with Canadian legal and democratic traditions, in the least intrusive manner possible.

3. To remove the "sexual orientation" (homosexual rights, etc.) amendment to the Ontario Human Rights Code from Bill 7.

4. To prevent the passage of similar legislation in other jurisdictions (Coalition for Family Values, n.d.a.)

A summary of its reasons for opposing the amendment to Bill 7 was as follows:

The members of the Coalition believe the proposed legislation would unreasonably restrict the freedom and rights of schools, churches, businesses and self-governing professions to the extent that they function as employers. They consider the amendment to be an inappropriate interference with the moral choices and community standards of Canadians (Coalition for Family Values n.d.b., 2).

At one point in its campaign, CFV commissioned a survey of Ontarians by Environics Research Group that showed that people in the province opposed the amendment, 58 percent to 28 percent. As a press release put it, "The notion of widespread public support for pending 'homosexual rights' amendments to the Ontario Human Rights Code is strongly dispelled by a survey of public attitudes towards homosexual behaviour released today by the Coalition for Family Values" (Coalition for Family Values 1986, 1).

Perhaps as a result of CFV's activities, some Liberal MPPs, especially those from rural areas, were under considerable pressure from constituents opposed to the bill. However, the CGRO and the Right to Privacy Committee stepped up their own letter-writing and phone campaigns, and the bill was passed in December (Herman 1994, 34-35).

Although the homosexual rights activists were successful in this struggle, there were bright spots for the Christian Right. In Didi Herman's words,

> It could be argued, for example, that Bill 7 mobilized the pro-family movement more effectively than it did the lesbian and gay movement. Certainly, the Coalition for Family Values was able to initiate a greater letter-writing and phone campaign and succeeded in having the amendment [adding sexual orientation to the Human Rights Code] discussed across a network of conservative churches (1994, 69).

Furthermore, "The CFV's leader, the Rev. Hudson Hilsden, became a prominent spokesperson for the anti-amendment lobby—indeed, of all social-movement actors he as an individual had the most visible role" (Herman 1994, 69).

As Herman notes, the opposition to Bill 7 was a specifically conservative Christian phenomenon; "the Coalition for Family Values was composed almost entirely of Christian organizations, while during legislative debates almost every MPP speaking against the amendment indicated that his or her opposition was also based upon Christian tenets" (1994, 78). But at this point, at least, the CFV had failed to thwart the extension of homosexual rights in Ontario.

CHRISTIAN HERITAGE PARTY

The idea of a specifically Christian political party has been around for a while in Canada. It is likely that some people considered the Social Credit Party to be a Christian party of sorts. By the early 1980s, an Ontario-based federal Social Credit organizer and Baptist minister, Harvey Lainson, was advocating for an explicitly Christian party. Speaking in Edmonton in March 1981, he argued that "a separate party offers the only truly effective route for Christian political action." Christians who are elected as candidates for other parties are held back by those parties. "The Christian candidate may be a good man, and may indeed be elected, but membership in any current political party will inevitably force him to compromise his principles. He needs his own party for support, and Mr. Lainson suggested a name: VOICE, for Voice of Individual Christian Expression" (*Alberta Report* 1981, 25).

Lainson received an opportunity to implement his idea of a Christian political party when he won the leadership of the federal Social Credit Party in June 1986. Even though the Social Credit Party was on life-support by the mid-1980s, the 1986 leadership campaign received some media attention due to the fact that James Keegstra, the Alberta public school teacher who was disciplined for teaching his students about a Jewish conspiracy, was one of the candidates for the party leadership. Lainson beat Keegstra by 67 votes to 38 (Campbell and Orr 1986, 4). However, the party continued to decline and ran only 9 candidates in the 1988 election, its last election as a registered party.

Lainson was replaced as leader of the party by Ken Campbell in 1990. But the party was deregistered in 1993 for failing to field the necessary minimum number of candidates.

In the meantime, however, another explicitly Christian party was being formed by the spring of 1986, the Christian Heritage Party of Canada (CHP). It was officially registered in April 1986, and immediately began to recruit members across the country. The interim leader was Ed Van Woudenberg and the first party president was William Stilwell (husband of well-known activist and school trustee, Heather Stilwell). Both men were from Surrey, BC, the birth place of the party.

The party organizers had previously been active in other parties, but their efforts had been frustrated by those parties. "Mr. Stilwell says that the Surrey founders (all laymen and mostly pro-life, Socreds provincially and Tories federally) first tried to operate within the Conservative party. 'We thought the Trudeau Liberals were the cause of the trouble.' So they worked hard to help nominate and elect good candidates, 'but things keep right on in the same old way. They have to compromise or they are just isolated'" (V. Byfield 1986a, 42-43).

Ed Van Woudenberg traveled to Alberta, Manitoba and Ontario in the Fall of 1986 holding meetings to recruit members. "Mr. Van Woudenberg is finding supporters among right-to-life groups, evangelical churches and such advocates of the traditional family as REAL Women and the Alberta Federation of Women United for Families. Many like him have worked within existing parties but have found conservative moral values unwelcome. In these groups, therefore, the CHP has a ready-made network for publicity and recruitment" (Weatherbe 1986, 41). Many conservative activists had become frustrated with the PC Party, and were looking for an alternative. Elizabeth Green, a pro-life activist in Vancouver, expressed this sentiment well: "The conservative party has proved to be anything but conservative on the moral issues that grassroots conservatives care about" (Weatherbe 1986, 41).

By April 1987 the CHP had 2500 members and had set up dozens of riding committees across Canada. As well, "gatherings in Vancouver, Red Deer, Lethbridge and Winnipeg have drawn from 150 to 500 supporters" (Koch 1987, 10).

The party held its founding convention in Hamilton, November 18-21, 1987. There were 534 delegates at the convention, and they officially adopted the party's constitution and policies. Only conservative Christians would be eligible for membership in the party, although it was hoped that others would also vote for the party's candidates. Members would have to "sign a 'solemn pledge' which vows adherence to the Christian faith, recognizes the family as the foundation of the nation, accepts God as 'author of life,' and binds one's allegiance to God's 'laws of sexual morality for the well-being of society; prohibiting pornography, prostitution, adultery, incest, homosexuality and sexual aberrations which abase man, as well as defile and pollute our nation'" (Gallagher 1987, 15). If elected, the first piece of legislation introduced by a CHP government would be a bill guaranteeing the right to life of the unborn (Gallagher 1987, 16).

In 1989 Ed Vanwoudenberg, the party leader, released a book explaining the CHP's analysis of Canada's problems, the reasons for the party's existence, and the party's proposed solutions for Canada. His party offered a very particular option for Canadians. "The CHP presents to the Canadian people a political choice based on a distinct world-and-life view. This view truly addresses the Canadian scene in spite of the skepticism and deliberate down-playing of our Christian heritage by the secular humanists and advocates of multiculturalism at the expense of national identity" (Vanwoudenberg 1989, 16). All of the other parties subscribed to secular humanism to one degree or another.

Importantly, although the CHP was an explicitly Christian party, it had no intention of forcing Christianity on anyone. Vanwoudenberg and the CHP were dedicated to protecting religious freedom.

> I wish to affirm my deep commitment to the concept of *freedom of religion*. If I discriminate against the religious freedom of another person, what claim can I lay for the defence of my own? I will defend with every means at my disposal the constitutional right of all to have this freedom, the freedom to build mosques, temples, and synagogues. It is the task of government to protect this freedom (Vanwoudenberg 1989, 18).

Although membership in the CHP was not restricted to any particular denomination, its appeal was primarily to conservative Protestants, which is to say, evangelicals. However, some evangelicals were very skeptical about the party. Leslie Tarr, an associate editor of the EFC's magazine *Faith Today*, was not impressed by the party. After mentioning that Christians have a greater responsibility to society than evangelism and church-related activities, he asks if the consequence of that responsibility should "be to create a Christian political party? I think not" (Tarr 1986, 15). In his view, "Whenever the Christian gospel has relied on political forces or legislation to affect and change culture, the results have been disastrous, and in the process the gospel itself has been distorted" (Tarr 1986, 14).

The EFC's executive director, Brian Stiller, similarly expressed concern about the CHP rather than support for it. The party, he said, "will be hampered by its restrictions on membership. It may also ghettoize Christians, keeping them from influence in the mainstream parties. I applaud their primary concerns and desire but I wonder at the value and logic of such a formation." Immediately after this he added, "Nineteenth-century philosopher Friedrich Nietzsche, whose writings became foundational to Hitler's Nazism, said, 'Be careful when you fight dragons lest you become a dragon'" (Stiller 1988, 77). This seems like a rather ominous perspective on the party.

In the 1988 federal election the CHP fielded 63 candidates and received over 100,000 votes. That would be the largest number of candidates it would ever field as well as the largest number of votes it would ever receive in subsequent federal elections. In the 2000 election it didn't even have official party status. But official status was regained for the 2004 and 2006 elections.

The CHP's initial rapid growth was thwarted by the emergence of the Reform Party of Canada. For many conservative Christians, the Reform Party appeared conservative enough and it was much more likely to actually get MPs elected. This issue came to a head for the CHP in September 1991 when seven national board members and the entire Ontario provincial board resigned because the party refused to consider amalgamating with the Reform Party (Cunningham 1991, 19).

FOCUS ON THE FAMILY

In 1977 James Dobson, a pediatrician in California, founded Focus on the Family as an evangelical ministry devoted to strengthening families. A Canadian affiliate of this organization, Focus on the Family (Canada) Association, was founded in Langley, BC, in 1983. Its main purpose is to strengthen family life through radio broadcasts, magazines, books and seminars supporting the traditional family. However, it has also become involved in pro-family activism.

One of its first notable forays in this area was the convening of the first Ottawa Conference on the Family held in June, 1988. This was described as "an historic occasion for the Canadian pro-family movement."

> The three-day conference was the first of its kind for Canada, drawing together representatives from more than 25 family advocacy groups, as well as teachers, administrators and government officials—60 delegates in all. ... The goal of the conference, sponsored by the Canadian Focus on the Family Association, was to form a stronger alliance among the country's many pro-family groups and leaders (Duncan 1988, 2).

The opening night meeting was addressed by the Minister of Health and Welfare, Jake Epp, who was a well-known evangelical in the Mulroney government. Other speakers for the conference included Anna Desilets, executive director of Alliance for Life, Rev. Hudson Hilsden of the Pentecostal Assemblies of Canada, and from the United States, Gary Bauer, a domestic policy advisor to President Ronald Reagan (Duncan 1988, 2-4).

Although not an activist organization as such, Focus on the Family would subsequently become involved as an intervener in court cases, publish a political affairs newsletter and sponsor further meetings to help organize the pro-family movement in Canada.

GEORGE PARKIN GRANT AND THE CHRISTIAN RIGHT

During the 1970s and 1980s, one of Canada's greatest thinkers supported the pro-life movement. Indeed, it would be easy to view him as the most profound thinker among Canada's pro-lifers. George Grant was alarmed by the *Roe v. Wade* Supreme Court decision in the United States, and that event inspired him to write sharply against abortion. Furthermore, through his pro-life efforts, Grant was to be aligned with conservative Christians who, like him, recognized the severity of the situation.

As a result of the abortion controversy, Grant was sympathetic to the kinds of groups that are currently labeled "Christian Right." William Christian writes that Grant,

> signalled his sympathy for the Christian fundamentalist groups who were in the lead in the anti-abortion movement, particularly in the United States. Their consistent, principled stand persuaded him that, although American civilization was in inexorable decline, it might not be decaying as quickly as he had earlier feared (1993, 344).

In a paper delivered to a meeting of the Canadian Political Science Association in 1981, Grant even appeared to speak defensively of the Moral Majority. While mentioning the creationism versus Darwinism controversy in the USA at that time, Grant says, "Let me say in parenthesis that I think the dominant academic community on this continent has been unwise to patronize these people known as the moral majority. My involvement with such people in common Christian tasks has taught me to the contrary" (Grant 1998, 314).

Five years later, in a letter to an American admirer, Grant saw the burgeoning Christian Right in the United States as a possible reason for optimism for the future: "One hopes that the continuing power of the Catholic Church and the new power of the Protestant fundamentalists will give the U.S.A. a shape which sees the danger in the loosing of the passions" (Grant 1996, 359).

In this same letter he makes it clear that he considers abortion to be the salient issue of the time. Furthermore, the strength of the American pro-life movement became a matter of admiration for him.

> As I take abortion to be the great immediate issue for the Western world, it has been a source of the greatest interest to me that the U.S.A. is the only country which has a deep and vigorous anti-abortion movement. In Canada we have some and I work for it, but it is not comparatively vigorous as in the U.S.A. My sense of the greatness of the U.S.A. has been greatly raised by the presence of this anti-abortion movement (Grant 1996, 359).

Clearly, Grant had sympathies for at least the pro-life emphasis of the Christian Right. And he also saw the fight against abortion as the most crucial issue of the time, in the 1980s. In this respect he was at least flirting with the Christian Right. Still, it would not be correct to identify him with the Canadian Christian Right holus bolus. Grant cannot be pigeon-holed as such. He was "the darling of the New Left" in the 1960s, but by the late 1970s "he was being lionized by different groups, theologically conservative Catholics and Protestants and people who might be described as the New Right" (Christian 1993, 314). He had right-wing admirers as well as left-wing admirers by that time, although the two "wings" admired him for entirely different reasons. And William Christian is undoubtedly correct in saying, "The truth is that George remained the lone wolf who defied classification" (1993, 314).

GEORGE PARKIN GRANT ON ABORTION

A fuller discussion of Grant's view of abortion is justified given its significance to the Canadian pro-life movement. His book

English-Speaking Justice contains a powerful section dealing with abortion. It is discussed in the context of criticizing the *Roe v. Wade* decision of the United States Supreme Court legalizing abortion in that country.

In short, the Court ruled that foetuses of less than six months were not persons, and therefore do not have rights. Grant says that this decision "raises a cup of poison to the lips of liberalism" (1974, 71).

Grant bases his argument primarily on the "ontological" issue ("ontology" refers to the "nature of being" of something). The ontology, or nature of being, of the mother and the foetus is the same—both are human beings. By saying that foetuses are not "persons," the Court has determined that some human beings do not have rights. "In negating the right to existence for foetuses of less than six months, the judge has to say what such foetuses are not. They are not persons. But whatever else may be said of mothers and foetuses, it cannot be denied that they are of the same species. Pregnant women do not give birth to cats" (Grant 1974, 71).

Denying some human beings the right to life raises the question as to why any human being has rights. As Grant puts it,

> once ontological affirmation is made the basis for denying the most elementary right of traditional justice to members of our species, ontological questioning cannot be silenced at this point. Because such a distinction between members of the same species has been made, the decision unavoidably opens up the whole question of what our species is. What is it about any members of our species which makes the liberal rights of justice their due? (Grant 1974, 71)

In other words, Grant was asking why people could have rights at all, if abortion, which took away the most fundamental of right to life for the unborn, was being argued as a "human right" for women?

Denying the status of "personhood" to foetuses would open the door to denying personhood to other humans as well.

> If foetuses are not persons, why should not the state decide that a week old, a two year old, a seventy or eighty year old is not a person 'in the whole sense'? On what basis do we draw the line? Why are the retarded, the criminal or the mentally ill persons? What is it which divides adults from foetuses when the latter have only to cross the bridge of time to catch up with the former? (Grant 1974, 72)

This line of reasoning leads to what Grant calls the fundamental questions. "What is it, if anything, about human beings that makes the rights of equal justice their due? What is it about human beings that makes it good that they should have such rights? What is it about any of us that makes our just due fuller than that of stones or flies or chickens or bears?" (Grant 1974, 72)

Thus Grant argued that the abortion issue was really about what it means to be a human being or a person. If we define "person" to exclude foetuses, the same definition could be used to exclude other human beings as well. Furthermore, a definition of "person" that excluded foetuses would invariably involve arbitrary distinctions between human beings, and one set of arbitrary distinctions could easily be replaced by another set of arbitrary distinctions, endangering even more "non-person" human beings. In sum, Grant argued that by permitting abortion, society opened itself up to all kinds of evil possibilities.

Grant tried to make the case for the cogent, consistent application of a principle. By allowing for the execution of one particular group of innocent human beings, there would be no principled basis for opposing the execution of certain other groups of innocent human beings. The determination of which innocent people were to be executed would be entirely subjective. The "solution" for unwanted pregnancies today could become the "solution" to unwanted grandparents tomorrow, and the "solution" to other inconvenient people the following day. If we don't stop abortion and the rationale that justifies it, Grant warned that the killing of innocent people would inevitably increase.

Abortion is often justified on the basis of the argument that each woman has a right to choose what to do with her own body. Thus whether or not to carry a baby to term is a choice that only she has a right to make. But Grant pointed out that "The right of a woman to have an abortion can only be made law by denying to another member of our species the right to exist" (Grant 1986, 117). To justify abortion on the basis of "rights" is especially frightening, in his view. "The talk about rights by those who work for abortion on demand has a sinister tone to it, because in it is implied a view of human beings which destroys any reason why any of us should have rights." (Grant 1986, 119).

Grant was appalled by the *Morgentaler* decision of Canada's Supreme Court in 1988, and he wrote against it. One point he made in doing so was to highlight a specific Christian reason for opposing abortion.

> After the Supreme Court decision, the victorious advocates of abortion on demand paraded with signs, on some of which was the slogan 'Abort God.' They were right to do so. What they meant was 'abort the idea of God because it has held human beings back from liberation.' What is given us in the word 'God' is that goodness and purpose are the source and completion of all that is. Only in terms of that affirmation can we dimly understand why our lives and others' partake in a meaning which we should not hinder but enhance. It is in the name of the fact that the human fetus is a member of

our species, called to partake in meaning, that in the past we have turned away from abortion, except in extreme cases. (Grant 1988, 164).

THE MORGENTALER DECISION

The Morgentaler case was argued at the Supreme Court in October 1986. It's interesting to note that Morgentaler's arguments before the Supreme Court relied heavily on specifically American legal argumentation. The factum of his lawyer, Morris Manning, "cited seventy-one American precedents and twenty U.S. law review articles. The Ontario Court of Appeal had failed to grasp the significance of the new Charter era, which, according to Manning, made *Roe* relevant and the 1975 *Morgentaler* decision irrelevant" (Morton 1992, 224). In his view, the 1973 *Roe v. Wade* decision of the US Supreme Court was more pertinent than the 1975 decision by Canada's own Supreme Court, in which Morgentaler's previous conviction for performing illegal abortions was upheld. US constitutional law should supersede Canadian legal precedents now that the Charter was in place.

Although that line of argument was not influential in the decision, on January 28, 1988, the Supreme Court ruled that Canada's abortion law violated section 7 of the Charter. The majority of judges argued that the abortion law violated the procedural fairness required by the Charter. Needless to say, this was a major victory for Morgentaler and a significant defeat for the pro-life movement.

When Gwen Landolt read the Supreme Court's decision, she noticed something startling. Four of the judges who struck down the law referred to the Powell Report in their decision. Dr. Marion Powell had been commissioned by the provincial government in Ontario to survey the availability of abortion services in that province. Dr. Powell was a "pro-choice" activist, and her report was released on January 27, 1987, three months *after* Morgentaler's case had been heard by the Supreme Court. Landolt reviewed the Morgentaler docket in the Supreme Court archives and "confirmed that the Powell Report was not mentioned once in the thousands and thousands of pages of official court records. Of course, this was not surprising. The report did not even exist at the time of the hearing" (Morton 1992, 247). The Supreme Court, in striking down Canada's abortion law, had relied heavily on social facts drawn from a document that had not been submitted as evidence, and which had been produced by an abortion rights activist.

Landolt shared this information with Laura McArthur, the president of the Toronto Right to Life Association. McArthur then lodged an official complaint with the Canadian Judicial Council.

> McArthur's two-page letter to the Council alleged that what the Court had done was "contrary to long-established procedural rules of accepting evidence off-the-record." By using social facts "not admitted as evidence at the time of the hearings," McArthur argued, the Court had deprived the Crown and other interested parties of the right to challenge the "impartiality of the document." She went on to suggest that its impartiality was very much in question, as Dr. Powell "has a long history (dating from 1972) of pro-abortion activism" and that her findings were biased. (Morton 1992, 248).

The Council replied that the issue raised by McArthur was outside of its mandate to consider, and also that the Supreme Court occasionally relies on materials which have not been introduced as evidence. This is known as "judicial notice." However, as Morton points out, "To justify the Court's use of the Powell Report as an exercise of judicial notice was to stretch the concept beyond its normal scope" (1992, 249).

AFTERMATH OF THE *MORGENTALER* DECISION

The *Morgentaler* decision was clearly a major set-back for the pro-life movement. It, along with the subsequent *Borowski* decision, was the first part of a "one-two punch" that would set the pro-life movement back on its heels. Before *Morgentaler*, despite the availability of abortion, there had been some success.

> While representing a minority of Canadians, pro-life groups could boast of a number of important victories before 1988. At the local level, they were instrumental in restricting access to abortion by electing their supporters to a hospital board and then putting its TAC [Therapeutic Abortion Committee] out of business. This tactic effectively halted abortions in Prince Edward Island and severely limited access in New Brunswick, Newfoundland, and many rural communities throughout Canada. In addition, their constant political pressure intimidated federal politicians, making them reluctant to pursue abortion reform even though the need for reform had been painfully obvious for some years. The activities of pro-life groups also put the pro-choice coalition on the defensive by forcing it to defend the limited gains it had achieved in 1969 as well as its broader feminist-inspired political agenda. Nevertheless, the pro-life coalition had failed in its primary objective—a total ban on legal abortions in Canada (Brodie et al 1992, 62).

As a result of the *Morgentaler* decision it was necessary for the federal government to draft new legislation to regulate abortion in Canada. Naturally, pro-lifers were quick to try to get support for a law protecting all innocent human life.

> The pro-life lobby mobilized a massive public letter-writing campaign which urged MPs to vote for a restrictive abortion law, legalizing the procedure only when the life of the wom-

an was at risk. As important were the intense lobbying activities conducted by pro-life MPs within their respective caucuses. The largest group of pro-life MPs were housed within the Conservative Party, especially on the back-benches. All of them were men and all were very committed to the pro-life cause. Only a year before, one of their most vocal leaders, Gus Mitges, had succeeded in bringing to a vote in the House of Commons a private members bill which ascribed constitutional rights to the foetus. The vote was 62 in favour of creating such rights in law and 89 opposed. Support for the bill came overwhelmingly from the Conservative backbench, none of the eleven Conservative cabinet members attending voted for it. After the Supreme Court decision this group of pro-life Conservative MPs mobilized once again, pressuring fellow MPs to join their ranks. Assisted by pro-life organizations, they called an information meeting for Members of Parliament, with some sixty attending, to hear Dr Bernard Nathanson, an American physician best known for his narration of the graphic pro-life film, *The Silent Scream* (Brodie et al 1992, 66-67).

Due to the deep division over this issue in the Conservative caucus, Prime Minister Mulroney announced that the new abortion law would be put to a free vote in Parliament. On a couple of occasions the government had proposed motions on the abortion issue in the House of Commons, but neither of those motions, nor numerous amendments to them, ever passed in the House. Canada remained without any abortion legislation due to deep divisions among MPs on the issue.

In the Fall of 1988 Mulroney called a federal election. Free trade was the major issue in the campaign.

> In the meantime, pro-life groups were engaging in their campaign to elect a 'pro-life Parliament' but they found the

electorate to be far less concerned about the abortion issue than was the pro-life membership. Public opinion polls, conducted during and after the 1988 campaign, indicated that voters were preoccupied with free trade and not abortion. Only 1.5% of a national sample identified abortion as the most important issue of the campaign but this apparent public disinterest did not deter the pro-life coalition. As promised, it published the position of all candidates on the abortion issue, targeted ridings where pro-choice MPs were contesting re-election, lent its organizational resources to pro-life candidates, and spend [sic] some $400,000 on the election campaign. Pollsters are still uncertain about the impact of these efforts but many pro-choice MPs did not return to the House. Included among these were Ray Hnatyshyn, Lynn McDonald, Flora MacDonald, Lucie Pepin and Marion Dewar. In addition, approximately 74 strong anti-abortion candidates were elected. Twenty were newcomers and all but two of these were Liberals. At least one, Thomas Wappel, gained his nomination because pro-life groups packed the nomination meeting (Brodie et al 1992, 88-89).

In the absence of a federal abortion law, there were considerable differences in access to abortion from province to province. Each province embarked on its own path. When New Brunswick refused to pay Morgentaler for the abortions he performed on three New Brunswick women at his Montreal clinic, he took the provincial government to court, which ruled in his favour. Morgentaler also opened a clinic in Halifax despite a prohibition by the Nova Scotia government. Police arrested and charged him early in November 1989. This case went all the way to the Supreme Court of Canada, which struck down Nova Scotia's prohibition on abortion clinics.

Many pro-lifers were becoming increasingly concerned at the lack of restrictions on abortion. Some became so frustrated that they joined Operation Rescue and engaged in civil disobedience directed primarily against Everywoman's Health Clinic in Vancouver and the two abortion clinics in Toronto. Ken Campbell was one of the Christian leaders supporting this new tactic. It was inspired by the activities of Operation Rescue in the United States. Randall Terry, the American founder of Operation Rescue, was brought to Toronto where he was welcomed and introduced by Ken Campbell at the Queensway Cathedral in January 1989 (Campbell 1990, 125).

> This new pro-life strategy consisted of blocking the entrance to the free-standing clinics so that women seeking abortions could not enter. The tactic inevitably brought in the police to break up the blockade, court injunctions ordering the protestors desist these practices, and defiance of the court orders by the pro-life activists. In Vancouver this predictable succession of events brought protestors the threat of a five-month jail sentence for defying the court's injunctions and a thousand dollar court fine for first offenders. In Toronto, protestors were eventually prohibited from demonstrating within 500 feet of the Morgentaler Clinic (Brodie et al 1992, 90).

The courts in BC were particularly harsh in dealing with protestors who participated in Operation Rescue. The courts upgraded the charges against them from civil to criminal contempt, and denied them a jury trial. However, the rescuers were permitted to make a public statement before being sentenced. They took advantage of this situation and for two days they gave their testimonies which were recorded by the media. This became a public relations success.

> Each of the accused in his own words, some haltingly, some articulately, some rationally, some emotionally, said why he had done what he did. The obvious sincerity and frequent coherence of their convictions plainly impressed, if not the

court, at least the media, and an unparalleled avalanche of pro-life propaganda consequently poured forth through the newspapers and television news as it had never poured before. Whatever the sentence, therefore, "Operation Rescue" had successfully scored a resounding publicity victory. And it was the severity of the courts that helped them do it (Kubish 1989, 32).

The Operation Rescue missions were ideally suited for media attention. As Ken Campbell points out, the pro-abortionists took advantage of this situation.

> The taped telephone message for victims who phone the abortuary seeking counsel and direction, is that they are to come to the abortuary through the back alley using the rear entrance. Yet when there is a "rescue" in progress, the abortionists insist on the theatrics of bringing their victims through the front entrance—the only time the front entrance is used... Moreover, in many instances the "mothers" coming in cabs for abortions during "rescues", are in fact "plants" posing as patients, actresses in the abortionist's "theatre", playing to the pro-abortion bias of the TV cameras! There are other dimensions of the perverse character of the abortion crime syndicate which are particularly evident at "Rescues." The pro-abortionists round up mindless young Trotskyites and anarchists frittering away their lives and public tax monies on nearby university campuses, to harass the "rescuers" during the "rescues". I have never encountered such raw, demonic barbarism! Listening to their "barking like dogs" as hymns were sung by the rescuers, or loudly "hissing like snakes," as the Lord's Prayer was being recited (Campbell 1990, 132-133).

Hundreds of Canadian pro-lifers participated in rescues. They saw this as the only option for stopping abortion at that time. "By the summer of 1989, however, Operation Rescue was winding down; other options were presenting themselves" (Brodie et al 1992, 91).

On July 3, 1989, the Ontario Supreme Court issued an injunction prohibiting Barbara Dodd from getting an abortion. She wanted to get an abortion, but her former boyfriend, Gregory Murphy, went to court seeking the injunction. This was seen as a legal breakthrough by pro-life groups. However, Dodd appealed and on July 11 the Ontario Supreme Court ruled in her favour on the grounds that she had not been given sufficient notice of the original hearing. She thus went to the Morgentaler clinic for her abortion (Brodie et al 1992, 91-92).

However, not long afterwards Dodd had a change of heart. At first Dodd announced that she was going to work for the pro-choice cause.

> Meanwhile, pro-life supporters, including Murphy, held a mock funeral for Dodd's foetus in front of the Morgentaler clinic. Only a week later, and much to the dismay of pro-choice activists, Dodd denounced her decision of the previous week. Granting a press interview from the Toronto office of the Campaign Life Coalition, she suggested that she had been manipulated by pro-choice representatives and that, even though this had been her third abortion, she no longer believed either that women should have them or that they should make the decision without the father. Spokeswomen for the OCAC [Ontario Coalition for Abortion Clinics] steadfastly denied that they had pressured Dodd but the damage to the coalition had already been done (Brodie et al 1992, 92).

On July 7 another injunction preventing an abortion was issued in Quebec. Jean-Guy Tremblay obtained the injunction to prevent his former girlfriend, Chantal Daigle, from getting the abortion she desired. The Quebec Superior Court upheld the injunction 10 days later. Then on July 26 the Quebec Court of Appeal also upheld the injunction.

> In a stunning 3-2 decision, which shocked both the legal community and pro-choice forces everywhere, the Quebec Court of Appeal issued an unprecedented ruling which prevented Daigle from having an abortion. It declared that, in accordance with the Quebec Charter, the foetus was a 'distinct human entity' which 'has a right to life and protection by those who conceive it'. Even though Daigle had told the Court that Tremblay had been abusive and persuaded her to discontinue birth control, it ruled that she had become pregnant voluntarily. Moreover, the court suggested that an abortion was not therapeutic because 'pregnancy is not in itself an attack on a woman's physical well-being'. Instead, it pronounced a biologically determinant rationale that 'rule of nature is that pregnancy must lead to birth'. The rationale provided by the Court clearly echoed the central themes of pro-life discoures (Brodie et al 1992, 93).

Shortly before the initial ruling against Daigle, the US Supreme Court had ruled that states could enact some restrictions on abortion. The US decision, coupled with the Daigle decision, received heavy condemnation from Canadian Leftists. Prof. Allan Hutchinson of the Osgoode Hall Law School in Toronto wrote an article for *The Globe and Mail* arguing that these two decisions indicated that Canada was drifting towards becoming like the state of Gilead, the mythical society in Margaret Atwood's novel, *The Handmaid's Tale*, where the Christian Right held sway.

> The Atwood state, said Prof. Hutchinson, had "evolved out of an apathetic liberal democracy that turned a blind eye to the slow erosion of women's autonomy by neoconserva-

tive fundamentalism. The current erosion of women's hard-won reproductive rights threatens to do the same." He concluded: "The sane and just response is to pull the plug on this rising tide of moralism and to consider seriously giving women control over their own bodies and lives" (V. Byfield 1989b, 21).

The Quebec Court of Appeal decision was immediately appealed to the Supreme Court of Canada. The justices were called back from their summer vacations to hold an emergency session on August 8. A number of groups from both sides of the abortion debate were granted intervener status, including Campaign Life Coalition, Canadian Physicians for Life, and REAL Women of Canada. During the proceedings Daigle's lawyer announced that she had gone to the US and had an abortion there, making the case moot. Despite being moot, the Supreme Court proceeded to strike down the injunction. This contrasts sharply with the *Borowski* decision. When Borowski's case became moot, the Supreme Court refused to proceed with it. When Daigle's case became moot, the Court decided the issue a judgement anyway. The Court certainly left itself open to criticism that it would proceed to judgement on a "moot case" as long as doing so would help the "pro-choice" side.

The mainstream media strongly approved of Daigle's actions and the Supreme Court decision. Ted Byfield clearly pointed out the hypocrisy of the situation:

> It's true that, in aborting the child, she defied a court injunction. In Vancouver, that is a dreadful thing to do, as the judges so gravely aver every time they slam the abortuary rescuers into jail for doing it. [Daigle] receives no such admonition. She has been through enough, the judges decide. So we see how law is administered in Canada. If you defy an injunction in opposing abortion, you are a wretched crimi-

nal and must go to jail. If you defy an injunction in having an abortion, you are a national hero, and warmly commended (T. Byfield 1989, 44).

On November 3, 1989, the federal government presented its proposed abortion law to the House of Commons as Bill C-43. It entailed a general prohibition of abortion, but allowed exemptions to the prohibitions. The pro-abortion side saw it as severely restricting the right to abortion, whereas the pro-life side saw it as providing wide grounds for abortion. Both sides campaigned against the bill. "The politics of Bill C-43, therefore, encouraged an alliance between militant pro-choice and pro-life forces which a spokeswomen [sic] for CARAL admitted was an unusual coalition involving 'two very strange bedfellows'." (Brodie et al 1992, 109).

Bill C-43 would be fought over through 1990 and into 1991 when it was shot down in the Senate. The 1980s concluded with abortion remaining as one of the hottest national issues.

BOB BIRCH

Bob Birch was for many years the pastor of charismatic churches in Vancouver. He was an ally of Bernice Gerard, and they had worked together on moral issues in the late 1970s. Birch had accompanied Gerard on the protest walk on nude beaches in 1977.

Birch became especially prominent due to his activism in attempting to prevent the international Gay Games from being held in Vancouver in August, 1990. The city's approval for the event was announced more than two years in advance, and in September, 1988, Birch spoke to a group of pastors about it. He subsequently helped write and distribute a leaflet to churches in the Lower Mainland encouraging Christians to try to stop the games (Carson 2003, 298-299).

Birch was given a large financial gift to purchase full-page ads in the *Vancouver Sun* and the *Province* in November, 1989. The ads presented the Biblical view of homosexuality, and stated "that because these games will bring God's judgment upon us all in this city, we therefore forbid them in the name and authority of Jesus Christ. We believe that they shall not take place" (Carson 2003, 301).

Birch was in Ottawa when the ads appeared. The ad included a phone number and mailing address, but no name for any person or organization sponsoring the ad. The media immediately began searching for who was responsible, and the answering machine attached to the phone number in the ad filled up with threatening and obscene phone calls.

> Pastor Bob was soon identified as the author. He returned to one of the fiercest onslaughts of his provocative life. He was vilified in the press, regularly hit the headlines and was caricatured in a cruel cartoon in the *Province* as a comic old man at prayer. He was accused of "hate-mongering." He was the "anti-gay minister." Public debates, newspaper articles and pages of letters to the editor chewed over the subject and over him (Carson 2003, 303).

In the context of the struggle over the Gay Games, Birch helped form a prayer group called Watchmen for the Nation. "The Watchmen began to hold a major spiritual-warfare event every month, with crowds of up to 2,000, introducing many believers for the first time to worship and intercession as battle in the Spirit" (Carson 2003, 305). Birch continued to actively oppose the Gay Games, and a flyer entitled "Welcoming the Sodomite Invasion" was widely distributed less than a month before the opening of the Games.

Nevertheless, the Gay Games went ahead as scheduled August

4-11, 1990. An August 1990 issue of *BC Report* contained the following observations:

> Against all the celebration, the only voice raised was that of a small group of evangelical Christians who discerned in the event not the emancipation that it claimed but rather social disintegration. Great societies, after all, had celebrated on the brink of ruin before. Would the historical record show that not one Christian objection had been raised? Thus Reverend Robert Birch, backed by his tiny committee, took a full-page ad in local newspapers in November denouncing the games as a symbol of 'rebellion against God' which will 'bring disgrace to Vancouver' (Carson 2003, 307).

Bob Birch's activism on this issue was not successful in its primary goal of preventing the Gay Games from being held. But he did succeed in drawing attention to the growing power of the homosexual movement and the threat it posed to Canadian society.

CONCLUSION

On the public policy front, the last half of the 1980s was not a particularly good period for the Christian Right in Canada. The *Morgentaler* abortion decision was an unmistakable defeat. Canada has had no federal restrictions on abortion since that time. The aftermath did see an upsurge in pro-life activism, notably the brief involvement of Operation Rescue, but years of continual defeat would subsequently wear down the movement.

The latter half of the 1980s also saw the advance of the homosexual rights agenda in Ontario and at the federal level. Although little was actually done to implement homosexual rights at the federal level, the supposedly "conservative" Progressive

Conservative government had officially embraced homosexual rights. That government attempted to shore up support among conservative Christians by proposing tough anti-pornography legislation, but it was never enacted.

Frustrated by their lack of influence in the PC government, some Christians formed their own federal political party, the CHP. It's initial growth was nipped in the bud by the emergence of the Reform Party of Canada. And the effort to prevent the Gay Games in Vancouver failed.

On the positive side, however, REAL Women did manage to receive a federal government grant of just over $21,000 early in 1989. This was to help fund its annual meeting in Ottawa in April of that year. The grant was very small compared to what feminist groups received, but it was a symbolic success and outraged the feminists (V. Byfield 1989a, 25).

REFERENCES

Alberta Report. 1981. "A Christian political party." March 27:25.

Brodie, Janine, Shelley A. M. Gavigan, and Jane Jenson. 1992. *The Politics of Abortion*. Toronto: Oxford University Press.

Byfield, Ted. 1986a. "The Tories and sodomy: what about right and wrong?" *Alberta Report*. March 24: 60.

Byfield, Ted. 1986b. "Homosexual acts are wrong, 'natural affections' or not." *Alberta Report*. May 26: 52.

Byfield, Ted. 1986c. "The indispensable sordid: how can the arts survive without It?" *Alberta Report*. June 30:52.

Byfield, Ted. 1987. "Now an encyclical from Canada's 'homofemartsy-globe'." *Alberta Report*. June 29: 52.

Byfield, Ted. 1989. "O Canada, where we celebrate freedom by ripping up a baby." *Alberta Report*. August 21: 44.

Byfield, Virginia. 1986a. "Morality-based politics." *Alberta Report*. May 12: 42-43.

Byfield, Virginia. 1986b. "Resurrection of the porn bill." *Alberta Report*. September 22: 34-35.

Byfield, Virginia. 1989a. "REAL Women find the federal tap." *Alberta Report*. March 20: 25.

Byfield, Virginia. 1989b. "Are women putty?" *Alberta Report*. July 24: 21-22.

Byfield, Virginia, and Phillip Day. 1988. "Crucial times for the porn bill." *Alberta Report*. February 1: 26-27.

Campbell, Donald, and Fay Orr. 1986. "Keegstra's loss." *Alberta Report*. July 7: 4-5.

Campbell, Ken. 1990. *5 Years Rescuing at "the Gates of Hell"*. Burlington, ON: Acts Books.

Campbell, Robert M., and Leslie A. Pal. 1989. *The Real Worlds of Canadian Politics: Cases in Process and Policy*. Peterborough, ON: Broadview Press Ltd.

Carson, Beth. 2003. *Pastor Bob: A Statesman of Prayer for Canada*. Belleville, ON: Guardian Books.

Christian, William. 1993. *George Grant: A Biography*. Toronto: University of Toronto Press.

Coalition for Family Values. N.d.a. "Statement of Goals and Objectives." Toronto.

Coalition for Family Values. N.d.b. "Concerned Citizens Called to Action." Toronto.

Coalition for Family Values. 1986. "Survey Results Challenge 'Myth' of Public Support for 'Homosexual Rights.'" November 24. Toronto.

Crosbie, John C. (with Geoffrey Stevens). 1997. *No Holds Barred: My Life in Politics*. Toronto: McClelland & Stewart Inc.

Cunningham, Dave. 1991. "The woes of this world." *Alberta Report*. October 7: 19.

Department of Justice Canada. 1986. *Toward Equality: The Response to the Report of the Parliamentary Committee on Equality Rights*. Ottawa: Department of Justice.

Duncan, Kyle. 1988. "Focus on Ottawa." *Focus on the Family Magazine*. October: 2-4.

Gallagher, Tim. 1987. "Mixing politics and religion." *Alberta Report*. December 7: 15-16.

Grant, George. 1974. *English-Speaking Justice*. Toronto: House of Anansi Press.

Grant, George. 1986. *Technology and Justice*. Toronto: House of Anansi Press.

Grant, George. 1988. "The Triumph of the Will." In *The Issue is Life*, ed. Denyse O'Leary. Burlington, ON: Welch Publishing Company.

Grant George. 1996. *George Grant: Selected Letters*. Ed. William Christian and Sheila Grant. Toronto: University of Toronto Press.

Grant, George. 1998. *The George Grant Reader*. Ed. William Christian. Toronto: University of Toronto Press.

Herman, Didi. 1994. *Rights of Passage: Struggles for Lesbian and Gay Legal Equality*. Toronto: University of Toronto Press.

Jenish, D'Arcy. 1986. "The revolt of the Tory right." *Alberta Report*. March 17: 12-16.

Koch, George. 1987. "More prairie protest." *Alberta Report*. July 6: 10.

Kubish, Glenn. 1989. "Fashioning victory out of defeat." *Alberta Report*. March 13: 32-33.

Lacombe, Dany. 1994. *Blue Politics: Pornography and the Law in the Age of Feminism*. Toronto: University of Toronto Press.

Morris, Leslie, Lori Cohen, Tim Gallagher, and Virginia Byfield. 1986. "How the churches got the porn bill." *Alberta Report*. July 7: 34-35.

Morton, F. L. 1992. *Morgentaler v. Borowski: Abortion, the Charter, and the Courts*. Toronto: McClelland & Stewart Inc.

Parliamentary Committee on Equality Rights. 1985. *Equality for All: Report of the Parliamentary Committee on Equality Rights*. Ottawa: Department of Justice.

Popert, Ken. 1986. "Victory for gay equality." *The Body Politic*. April: 13-14.

REAL Women of Canada. 1984. "Submission of the R.E.A.L. Women of Canada to the Special Committee on Pornography and Prostitution." February.

REAL Women of Canada. 1986. "Brief to Members of Parliament." November 18. Toronto.

REAL Women of Canada. N.d. "Brief Submitted to: Standing Parliamentary Committee on Justice Re: Pornography (Bill C-54)." Ottawa.

Robinson, Svend. 1986. "Write for your rights." *The Body Politic*. January: 19.

Stiller, Brian C. 1987. "Rights or Special Protection?" *Faith Today*. January/February: 54-55, 70.

Stiller, Brian. 1988. "The best way to fight dragons." *Faith Today*. May/June: 77.

Tarr, Leslie. 1986. "A Christian political party?" *Faith Today*. November/December: 14-15.

Vanwoudenberg, Ed. 1989. *A Matter of Choice*. Winnipeg: Premier Printing.

Warner, Tom. 2002. *Never Going Back: A History of Queer Activism in Canada*. Toronto: University of Toronto Press.

Weatherbe, Stephen. 1986. "'Real' political choice." *Alberta Report*. October 13: 41-42.

CHAPTER 6 | THE STRUGGLE AGAINST HOMOSEXUAL RIGHTS TAKES CENTER STAGE

The "pro-choice" side won the important battles of the 1980s, and the homosexual rights activists would win the most significant battles of the 1990s. Whether in the courts or in the legislatures, the homosexual agenda would lose a couple of minor skirmishes but win the big scraps. The politicians and judges cooperated to advance gay rights, and the Christian Right was becoming increasingly marginalized on this issue. The Supreme Court's *Vriend* decision in 1998 would put an end to the Alberta government's opposition to gay rights. Until then it had been the last major government to avoid the gay rights bandwagon.

The 1990s were not kind to the Christian Right in Canada. But the formation of the Canada Family Action Coalition (CFAC) in 1997 did demonstrate that there was further potential for the mobilization of conservative Christians in Canada. This was a positive development and the basis for a certain degree of optimism.

ABORTION LEGISLATION

The decade opened with intense ongoing conflict over the federal government's proposed abortion legislation, Bill C-43. It would have made abortion a criminal offence, except where the mother desired to have one for reasons of physical, mental, or psychological health. Although "pro-choicers" objected to any criminalization of abortion, many conservative Christians saw the law as a virtual legalization of abortion on demand.

Bill C-43 was introduced early in November 1989. Ted Byfield quickly staked out a position strongly opposing it as allowing "wide access to abortion, but not unrestricted access." In his view, Canada was better off without such a law.

> Is it better to have no restriction, or a phony restriction that doesn't restrict? Surely the former. It is easier to contend with an indisputable fact than with a fiction. If there is no law at all, it is true that babies will go on being aborted in their tens of thousands. But as the public becomes increasingly appalled at this spectacle, it will begin to really think the issue through, a process that almost always leads to the pro-life position (T. Byfield 1989, 60).

Both Ken Campbell and REAL Women presented briefs to the Legislative Committee considering Bill C-43 in February 1990, and both opposed the bill. Ken Campbell, with characteristically strong language said, "I must state that it is our conviction that no professing Christian can with integrity support Bill C-43 in its proposed form." In his view, it contained "deceptive double-talk" (Campbell 1990, 292).

REAL Women referred to the bill as a "sham", reasoning that:

> [S]ince Bill C-43 provides absolutely no protection for the preborn child it is nothing more than a calculated attempt

to allow unrestricted abortion in Canada while attempting to hide this fact under cloak of respectability by the pretense that it provides some legal "protection" for the unborn children (REAL Women 1990, 13).

Interestingly, Bill C-43 provides a good example of contrast between Canada's Christian Right and the Evangelical Fellowship of Canada (EFC). In my interview with him, Brian Stiller used this legislation to make that contrast himself. The EFC had supported Bill C-43, seeing it as "gradualism at its best." In Stiller's view, Canadian evangelicals were more comfortable with this gradualist approach than the absolutist approach of the Christian Right (Stiller 2006).

Stiller and the EFC supported Bill C-43 because he believed "it was sending a message that abortion is a criminal act. Over the long-term it would have steered our nation toward a life-protecting direction" (Stiller 1994, 120). In his view, the bill was defeated by a combination of "secular fundamentalism" (the pro-choicers) and "religious fundamentalism" (the Christian Right pro-lifers). "We lost. More importantly, a good bill was lost" (Stiller 1994, 121). This difference in perspective helps to demonstrate that the EFC should not simply be categorized as part of the Christian Right in Canada.

Despite opposition from both sides, the bill passed the House of Commons at the end of May, 1990. Although the bill still had to pass the Senate, many doctors stopped performing abortions, fearing that they would be prosecuted.

> Although pro-life groups had remained silent on the question of prosecutions before the passage of the bill, they now readily admitted that they would try to persuade women, like-minded doctors, and ordinary citizens to lay charges against doctors performing abortions. The national president of the Campaign Life Coalition admitted that 'we've

> told our people to become watchdogs'. They also planned to convince women who had abortions to sue their doctors for medical malpractice. By July, pro-life militants announced that they had already begun to prepare a case against one Toronto doctor whom they refused to identify. By the fall, the Canadian Rights Coalition, modeled on the American Rights Coalition, made available to Canadian women a toll-free number in Tennessee which provided information on how to sue a doctor for malpractice. In response, pro-choice groups began to mount legal defence funds for doctors who might fall victim to these tactics (Brodie et al 1992, 112-113).

Having the bill before the Senate provided another opportunity to prevent it from becoming law. Pro-lifers were quite active at this stage.

> Most active among these was Stanley Haidasz who appeared before the Committee with the Reverend Alphonse de Valk, the editor of a pro-life publication, and later attempted to amend the bill to restrict legal abortions only to cases where the mother's life was threatened. The pro-life forces also recruited Dr Bernard Nathanson to testify before the Senate (Brodie et al 1992, 115).

The Senate vote was held on January 31, 1991, and the bill lost on a tie vote; 43 to 43. That was the last time Canadian politicians would vote on the abortion question, and Canada is still, to this day, one of the only liberal democratic countries in the world without any kind of legislation governing the issue.

THE WAR AGAINST THE FAMILY

Using the term "CCR" as short for the "Canadian Christian Right," Chris MacKenzie states that "If there are two books that can be held up as examples of the fundamental doctrine of the pro-family and CCR movement in Canada, they are William Gairdner's *The Trouble with Canada: A Citizen Speaks Out* (1990) and *The War against the Family: A Parent Speaks Out* (1992)" (MacKenzie 2005, 257). Since the first of those books touches on a broad range of policies, and does comparatively little to address the main social conservative concerns, it's hard to see how it can be said to demonstrate CCR doctrine. Not that members of the CCR would disagree with its contents, but it could just as easily be seen as a book outlining the fundamentals of economic conservatism, rather than any kind of treatise on social conservatism. *The War Against the Family*, on the other hand, is a clear and articulate defense of social conservatism; perhaps the most comprehensive discussion of the pro-family position ever published in Canada.

William Gairdner is a former English professor and Olympic athlete. *The Trouble With Canada* launched his position as perhaps the premier conservative thinker in Canada. At over 600 pages, *The War Against the Family* is a tour de force defending the traditional family and the pro-family agenda.

It's very clear from the outset of the book how Gairdner views the central issue: "[I]n our Western civilization there is an inherent and deadly conflict between statism and the whole idea of the private family" (Gairdner 1992, ix-x). Those who want the government to be the supreme power in society, unrivaled by other institutions, view the family as an obstacle to state power. In Gairdner's view,

> the family as an institution is at the heart of an entire social order. It is no exaggeration to say that the family is the creative engine of all the crucial values of a free and private society. So it follows that for any other social order to dominate—say, any collectivist social order—the family must first be broken down. That is why Canadians—for that matter, all those living under welfare regimes—must realize that if they

have any desire to preserve the cherished life of a free society for their children and grandchildren, they first will have to recognize, then take up moral arms against, all those who wish to destroy the family (Gairdner 1992, 5).

Among those most earnest in their desire to eliminate the traditional family are the radical feminists. Feminists campaign for an all-powerful government. "That's why I say that inside every radical feminist is a little officer of the police State" (Gairdner 1992, 116).

Gairdner is especially adept at painting the big picture about the significance of the traditional family and its role in social order. The traditional family is a bulwark of Western civilization, and the elimination of the traditional family would spell the end of our civilization.

> [A]ll revolutionaries quickly see that to change the *social* order you first have to change the *sexual* order. The traditional family, after all, is a sexual, procreative entity that dictates much of our social reality (sexual roles, economic roles, socialization of gender, etc.). So by redefining the sexual nature of the family, we can redefine society itself. The long and short of this strategy is that those who wish to engineer society in any direction must first break all the traditional moral and religious sexual allegiances. Sexuality must be progressively divested of all its spiritual, procreative, and family meanings, divested even of its connections with romantic love (to which in our culture it has always been inferior), and in its place must be put an increasing emphasis on raw sexuality as a pure and joyous expression of the autonomous self (Gairdner 1992, 246).

Gairdner writes that the strongest support for abortion is from radical feminists who resent child-bearing. Men don't bear children, and radical feminists don't want to be "forced" to bear children either.

Their argument is essentially that men and women are basically the same, but women have always been oppressed victims of male patriarchy because they are stuck with unequal social and domestic duties that arise from the fact that they bear and nurture children. Radicals have aggressively attempted to change this "inequality" by spurning the duties associated with child-bearing—and rearing (Gairdner 1992, 427).

As those familiar with the abortion debate will know, the key slogan for the "pro-choice" position is that women deserve the "right to choose" whether or not to give birth to their children. But Gairdner sees this as unconvincing. "What pro-abortionists want is not the freedom to choose; they already have this. They want the freedom to deny the natural consequences of their own actions or, if you prefer, to undo their original choices. They want Godlike powers" (1992, 430).

The War Against the Family provided a strong case for social conservative forces in Canada in the early 1990s. It spelled out in great detail the strength of the social conservative position. Despite this, however, the country continued down the devastating path of social liberalism.

THE REFORM PARTY OF CANADA AND THE CHRISTIAN RIGHT

Although there were clearly people within the Reform Party who can legitimately be considered to be from the Christian Right, the party itself should not be mistaken as having been a Christian Right party. This point can be demonstrated most clearly from the party's position on the abortion issue and the views of party members on that issue.

The Reform Party held its first full-fledged policy convention in 1989. One of the most significant resolutions passed at that convention was the "Abortion Resolution."

The Abortion resolution followed the precedent established by Reform's only sitting parliamentarian, Alberta MP Deborah Gray, and would apply similarly to other moral issues that MPs would be asked to vote on once they arrived in Ottawa. The process would begin with the Reform candidate stating "clearly and publicly, her/his own personal views and moral beliefs on the issue," typically during the election campaign or while seeking the Reform nomination. Once the issue came before Parliament, Reform MPs would invite public debate and seek a consensus within the constituency. If a constituency consensus could be determined, the MP was obliged to faithfully vote that consensus. If no consensus existed, or was unclear, the MP could vote in accordance with his or her own publicly recorded position on the issue (Ellis 2005, 66).

In effect, this enabled the party to avoid taking a stand on this and other controversial issues. "The Abortion Resolution formed the foundation for Reform policy development, or more importantly, the lack of policy development on specific moral issues such as abortion, capital punishment and euthanasia" (Ellis 2005, 66). With the passage of this resolution, party leader Preston Manning "could control radical elements within the party by arguing that any attempts to develop firm policy stances on these issues would be contrary to the spirit of the Abortion Resolution and would hamper MPs in their ability to faithfully represent their constituents, one of Reform's key populist planks" (Ellis 2005, 66-67). So this resolution was a deliberate dodge of the abortion issue, hardly what one would expect from a party of the Christian Right.

In 1992 the Reform Party held another major Assembly, its last before the 1993 federal election. Each of the 1290 delegates was sent a questionnaire, and over 69 percent of the delegates filled it out. They were asked to agree or disagree with a number of statements, one of which was "Abortion is a private matter which should be decided between the pregnant woman and her doctor." Sixty-one point five percent of respondents agreed with that statement, while only 30.9 percent disagreed. As Ellis puts it, "Contrary to many perceptions about Reform, in 1992 its delegates were pro-choice by a two-to-one margin" (2005, 116).

This survey is not the only indication of party activists' abortion views at the 1992 Assembly.

> After only one strongly worded anti-abortion speech from the floor that received a loud negative response from many delegates, Stephen Harper interjected from the podium. The speech from the floor argued that current Reform policy of constituency representation on moral issues could put its MPs in the position of being forced to support the 'murder of babies' against their own moral convictions. Harper responded by arguing that if Reform candidates were not willing to support the principles of constituency representation then they should not be Reform candidates. After these comments received loud applause, he went on to argue that each MP had the democratic right to argue in favour of his or her position during the debate, but after a constituency consensus had been reached, an MP's duty was to vote in accordance with that consensus. Delegates responded by overwhelmingly endorsing (95 percent support) a populist abortion plank that placed constituency representation above the personal convictions of MPs (Ellis 2005, 133).

Clearly, the Reform Party refused to take a pro-life stand. And this is quite understandable in light of the fact that 2 out of every 3 party activists held a "pro-choice" position. As such, and in spite of repeated media portrayals to the contrary, the Reform Party cannot legitimately be considered to be a party of the Christian Right.

ATTACKS AGAINST *ALBERTA REPORT*

As *Alberta Report* continued to advocate social conservative causes throughout the 1980s and into the 1990s, it became especially hated by many people on the Left. At times, *Alberta Report* had to face consequences for its stand. Occasionally it was vilified in other organs of the media. For instance, after the Montreal Massacre of December 1989, some people wanted to link *Alberta Report* to the murderer of the 14 victims, all of whom were women.

> Thomas Walkom, a columnist in the *Toronto Star*, declared that Ted and Link Byfield on the one hand, and Montreal killer Marc Lepine on the other, "are disparate parts of the same phenomenon." Lepine, says Mr. Walkom, "represents the crazy edge of anti-feminism" while the Byfields "articulate a version which is more acceptable," but both are pursuing the same end (T. Byfield 1990, 44).

Of course, the Byfields and their magazine were not even remotely connected to the killing, but apparently some leftists thought they could score cheap political points by falsely making such a connection.

Sometimes opposition to the magazine was more violent. In November 1991 the Canadian Research Institute for the Advancement of Women (CRIAW) held its annual conference in Edmonton. *Alberta Report* sent a female reporter, Celeste McGovern, to cover the event. McGovern then attended a lesbian workshop at the conference. One of the lesbians there, Houston Stewart,

> was visibly shaken when Celeste McGovern from *Alberta Report* told her that the proceedings of the morning's lesbian workshop would be recounted in the magazine. That

evening Ms. Stewart followed the reporter out of the main conference room and into a deserted hallway of Edmonton's Westin Hotel. The stalwart Ms. Stewart then forcibly ushered the slight Miss McGovern into an empty meeting room, shoved her against a table and wrestled away her note pad and began tearing up the pages (*Alberta Report* 1991, 41).

When McGovern told other women at the conference what had happened to her, she received no sympathy or help at all.

In 1993 some homosexual rights activists contacted businesses that advertised in *Alberta Report* threatening to boycott them if they continued to support the magazine. Many businesses did pull their advertising. Then "Someone started mailing packages containing used condoms and feces to the magazine" (*Alberta Report* 1999, 10). *Alberta Report* was seriously hurt by the loss of advertising revenue.

The Byfields decided to fight back by appealing more directly to its base of Christian supporters, trying to really activate this base. A promotional package for the magazine was put together containing a sample copy, a brochure touting the magazine's conservative Christian credentials, and a cover letter from Link Byfield. These materials were enclosed within a large envelope. The cover of the envelope read: "Christianity under attack in Alberta? Are you serious? Dead Serious."

The cover letter from Link explained the situation as follows:

> I am the publisher of *Alberta Report*, a weekly newsmagazine that for the last 20 years has sought to cover the news of the province from a traditional Christian perspective—not just religious news, but also developments in education, law, politics, economics, the arts, everything. Hence when the homosexual lobby sought to have "sexual orientation" included under the human rights code, we ran a cover story

on this subject, explaining the implications: The homosexual "lifestyle" for example could be taught and advocated in public school sex-ed classes. We also included a description of homosexual practices, taken from gay publications. No other Alberta media have carried this information. Since then, our advertisers have been assailed with letters from the gay lobby, calling our coverage "hate literature," and urging them to stop advertising in the magazine. Understandably, businesses serving the public do not want to involve themselves in controversy, so that this campaign will certainly hurt us. Many Christians ask: What can we do to help? The answer is: Subscribe to *Alberta Report*. If we can replace the lost advertising revenue with added circulation revenue, we will certainly survive this attack (L. Byfield 1993).

Slowly, however, the magazine began to succumb to lower advertising revenues and gradually shrinking circulation. It continued to champion the same causes it had from the start, but the culture was changing and the potential market for a Christian-based conservative newsmagazine was getting smaller. As Link perceptively saw things, Canadian society was shifting from its Judeo-Christian foundation to a new religion of secular humanism.

In a terrific essay commemorating *Alberta Report*'s twenty-fifth anniversary, Link defended the magazine's Christian basis and commitment to Western morality, especially the traditional family. The traditional family was now in the forefront of the culture war.

[T]he family, more than any other institution, is what the new religion must destroy. The schools it captured long ago, and the media. The social authority of the church is gone, having been reduced mainly to Catholic bishops and Protestant moderators uttering socialist irrelevancies. But the family, though badly weakened, remains in place. And as long as it remains, the new religion is not secure (L. Byfield 1999, 21).

And so *Alberta Report* would stick to its guns: "Defending the family will be this magazine's central purpose over the next quarter-century, as it has been for the last" (L. Byfield 1999, 21). And so it was until the untimely death of the magazine in June 2003.

INTERVENING IN IMPORTANT COURT CASES

Just as Gwen Landolt had predicted back in January 1981, the adoption of the Charter of Rights had led to a situation where the courts were increasingly involved in public policy decisions. One of the most significant consequences of this was the advancement of the pro-abortion agenda in the late 1980s. In a similar way, a series of Supreme Court decisions would push the homosexual rights agenda throughout the 1990s.

One aspect of the increased role of Canadian courts under the Charter was the correspondingly increased role of third party interveners in cases involving policy matters. Perhaps the best example of this phenomenon is the role of the Women's Legal Education and Action Fund (LEAF), a feminist organization.

> No group has been more active in using litigation than organized feminists. Feminists played an influential role in the framing and adoption of the Charter. They were the first to form a United States-style litigation organization—the Women's Legal Education and Action Fund (LEAF)—with the objective of using "test cases" to pursue "systematic litigation" strategies. LEAF has gone on to become the most frequent non-government intervener before the Supreme Court of Canada and the most frequent recipient of CCP [Court Challenges Program] funding (Morton and Allen 2001, 56).

The Court Challenges Program was essentially a federal government funding mechanism for left-wing interest groups to pursue social change through litigation under the Charter. LEAF was very successful in using that funding to bankroll litigation to achieve a whole host of changes to public policy. For example, "In three policy fields—pornography, immigration and abortion/fetal rights—feminists have not lost a single case" (Morton and Allen 2001, 76).

By the late 1980s Gwen Landolt realized that it was necessary for conservative groups to become interveners as well, despite the lack of government funding for them.

> I became aware of the lack of pro-life interventions in the courts just after the abortion law was struck down by the Supreme Court of Canada in January 1988 in the *Morgentaler* case. A few weeks after that decision, I went up to Ottawa to review the Supreme Court of Canada dockets on the case. I read every piece of paper and every document in the six or so dockets that I had been provided by the Registrar of the court. I was dismayed to learn that not one word or document was included in the dockets in support of the pro-life position. I promised myself then, that from that time on, never again would a pro-life/pro-family case be argued before the courts without an intervention from our perspective. I believed this was important so that history would show that there were individuals in Canada who did not accept the anti-life/family position promoted by the courts, government and media. Also, I did not want to provide the courts with an opportunity to later exonerate themselves for their disastrous decisions by claiming that no one had presented opposing arguments to them. As a result, REAL Women has been involved in all the major pro-life/pro-family cases argued in Canada. We have done this at our own expense, unlike those opposing us who had access to the government funded Court Challenges Programme and also from generous funding by the Status of Women (Landolt 2007, 3).

Although it is difficult to judge the influence of interveners on many court cases, the conservative side won in the *Mossop* homosexual rights decision of 1993. However, in three subsequent cases, the homosexual side won. In *Egan v. Canada*, the Supreme Court decided in 1995 that "sexual orientation" should be seen as being included in section 15 of the Charter. In *Vriend* (1998), the Court read "sexual orientation" into Alberta's human rights legislation. And in the 1999 decision *M. v. H.*, the Court ruled that the failure to include same-sex couples in its definition of "spouse" rendered Ontario's Family Law Act in contravention of the Charter of Rights. The Supreme Court was driving the advance of homosexual rights in Canada.

In 1995 the Canadian Centre for Law and Justice (CCLJ) was organized by Ottawa lawyer Gerard Guay to support litigation on behalf of conservative Christians. Its initial focus was on helping the cause of Christian broadcasting in Canada, but it also became involved in other issues of concern to conservative Christians. It was modeled after the American Center for Law and Justice (ACLJ) headed by Jay Sekulow in the United States. Prominent American television evangelist Pat Robertson offered support to the CCLJ, as printed on the organization's promotional brochure:

> Canadian Christians now face the same kind of hostility and difficulty we Americans face. It is time for Canadian Christians to stand up and make their views known to their leaders, and their fellow Canadians. The best way to do this is within the Canadian legal system, which is why I am pleased to respond to a request for assistance in establishing the CCLJ.(Canadian Centre for Law and Justice n.d.)

Unfortunately, the CCLJ quietly folded after just a few years in operation.

THE MOSSOP CASE

In 1985 Brian Mossop, a federal civil servant, attended the funeral of his male lover's father. Since this entailed absence from his job, he applied for bereavement leave, but it was rejected because his homosexual relationship was not recognized as constituting a family. Mossop then laid a complaint of family status discrimination under the Canadian Human Rights Act. "For Christian activists, the Mossop case was a natural rallying point. Unlike superficially less provocative campaigns for sexual orientation amendments, this sort of litigation threatened to undermine, indeed to overturn, the traditional family unit" (Herman 1994a, 274).

Focus on the Family took the lead in organizing a response from conservative Christians.

> When Jim Sclater, Focus's public policy director, heard that the tribunal decision had been in Mossop's favour, he called the Justice Department and spoke to the senior counsel on *Mossop*, who told him that the 'government didn't have much of a case.' Focus, which believed that a strong argument against the redefinition of family to include gay couples could surely be made, began to contact fellow Christian activists. The strategy decided upon was to become official intervenors in the litigation (Herman 1994a, 274-275).

Because a number of sympathetic organizations were involved in other legal intervention already, Focus took the lead in the Mossop case. Sclater first contacted REAL Women.

> REAL Women had worked with Focus in the past and both were at that time involved in setting up the Legal Defense Fund (an umbrella organization established to solicit litigation funds from a broad range of Christian groups), so that it was a natural partner. A less obvious choice was the Sal-

vation Army of Canada. That organization became involved in the case through its law firm which had been consulted by Focus and had relayed to it Focus's interest in *Mossop*. The Army had serious reservations about joining together with two such overtly right-wing groups, but Salvationists' anti-homosexuality eventually overrode this concern and it went on to take a leading role in the litigation. Shortly thereafter, two others, the Pentecostal Assemblies of Canada and the Evangelical Fellowship of Canada, both with active histories in opposing lesbian and gay equality, joined up as well. Activists had thus realised their desire to have a mix of organizations known to the courts as intervenors (e.g. REAL Women) but also with long, respectable histories (e.g. the Salvation Army) (Herman 1994, 275).

The side supported by the Christian intervenors won at both the Federal Court of Appeal and the Supreme Court of Canada.

In a four-three decision the court turned down Mr. Mossop's appeal to have his relationship to Ken Poppert recognized as a family with accompanying benefits. The appeal was dismissed more on technical than substantive grounds. Writing for the majority, Chief Justice Antonio Lamer broadly hinted that if rechallenged under the Charter of Rights the outcome might be very different (Demers 1993, 20).

BILL 167 IN ONTARIO

In 1990 the NDP won the Ontario provincial election and Bob Rae became premier. The NDP had long supported homosexual rights, so activists were hopeful about achieving some of their goals under the new government.

In September 1992 a Human Rights Board of Inquiry ruled that the provincial government had discriminated against Crown prosecutor Michael Leshner by denying survivor benefits to his same-sex partner under the pension plan. This ruling bolstered the campaign of homosexual activists to obtain the same employment benefits as heterosexual couples.

In April 1993 a by-election was held in a Toronto constituency with a large homosexual population. In order to increase her party's chances of winning the by-election, Liberal Party Leader Lyn McLeod made strong public statements in favour of homosexual rights. The Liberal candidate, Tim Murphy, won, and shortly thereafter he introduced a private member's bill, Bill 45, to bring Ontario's laws into conformity to the requirements of the Leshner decision. This bill received NDP support and passed both first and second readings.

Active conservative Christian opposition to the extension of benefits to same-sex couples began with the *Leshner* decision. Subsequently,

> [S]ocial conservative forces began organizing with more vigour upon the arrival of Bill 45, claiming it represented 'an attack on freedom of religion' and the right to express the view that Christianity 'does not condone homosexuality.' In November and December 1993, thirty petitions were read in the legislature, most being from church congregations in small towns or rural areas. One petition bearing 2,200 signatures from the Family Coalition Party claimed, 'The Ontario legislature is out of control,' and asserted, 'Marriage and the family are the rock all civilizations are structured on.' Well-organized, face-to-face encounters with churchgoers opposed to gay rights confronted MPPs from rural and suburban ridings (Warner 2002, 229-230).

In 1994 another by-election was held, this time in a rural constituency. The Liberals had a lead going into the campaign, but the Conservative Party made an issue of the Liberal leader's public support for homosexual rights. The Conservative candidate won the by-election, and his victory was widely seen as the result of the homosexual rights issue. Many Liberals shared this interpretation (Rayside 1998, 146-147).

In May, 1994, Attorney General Marion Boyd introduced Bill 167 to extend the same benefits to same-sex couples as heterosexual couples.

> There had been lobbying against gay rights since the introduction of Bill 45 in mid-1993, much of it organized by Protestant fundamentalists. Shortly after Bill 167's first reading, the Roman Catholic archbishop of Toronto urged parishioners across the archdiocese to write to their provincial representatives protesting the proposed legislation as "a matter of considerable urgency." Shortly after, the Ontario Conference of Catholic Bishops joined the archbishop in opposition to Bill 167 (Rayside 1998, 148).

MPPs from rural and suburban constituencies received numerous letters on both Bills 45 and 167, with the vast majority opposing the bills. According to David Rayside, this "vocal opposition in part reflected the capacities of right-wing Christians to mobilize their grassroots" (1998, 156). And with apparent widespread opposition to Bill 167, it was defeated on a free vote at second reading on June 9, 1994. Christian activism had scored a victory.

HATE CRIMES AND HUMAN RIGHTS ACT AMENDMENT BILL C-33 (1996)

Among the Liberal Party's promises in the 1993 federal election was the enactment of legislation that would include tougher sentences for people convicted of committing crimes motivated by hatred against certain categories of people. Among the protected categories listed in the resulting legislation was sexual orientation (Warner 2002, 212). According to Rayside, this was the first piece of federal legislation ever to include the words "sexual orientation" in a positive sense (Rayside 1998, 112).

The hate crime legislation was introduced as Bill C-41 in September, 1994. The sexual orientation component of the bill was the most controversial aspect and it was strongly opposed by some Liberal backbenchers, especially Tom Wappel and Roseanne Skoke. "Wappel, Skoke, and fellow Liberal backbencher Dan McTeague led a public campaign against the sexual orientation provision of Bill C-41, and were joined by about a dozen other MPs… . [I]n the end, the bill, with sexual orientation included, was passed by Parliament in June 1995" (Warner 2002, 213).

In December 1993 Justice Minister Allan Rock also announced that the Liberal government would amend the Canadian Human Rights Act (CHRA) to include protection on the basis of sexual orientation. This commitment was mentioned in the subsequent speech from the throne. The goal of adding sexual orientation to the CHRA had been shared by the previous Mulroney government, but had been thwarted by backbenchers within the government caucus.

REAL Women had been in the forefront of that battle.

> Another active group, the Evangelical Fellowship of Canada, mounted a fund-raising and petition campaign in 1995 that declared ominously that 'inclusion of sexual orientation could affect the freedom of speech and religious freedom of many Canadians who believe homosexual practice to be immoral.' Later, once a CHRA amendment was introduced, REAL Women and the Evangelical Fellowship were joined by the Canadian Conference of Catholic Bishops, which warned that amending the CHRA would lead to the social legitimization of relationships the church could not condone.

Another group, the Coalition of Concerned Canadians, ran a full-page national newspaper advertisement opposing the sexual orientation amendment. Declaring themselves as being dedicated 'to clarifying and reinforcing the continuing importance of the traditional family in Canadian Society,' they proclaimed the CHRA amendment 'is the product of myth and is a serious threat to marriage and family (Warren 2002, 213-214).

On April 24, 1996, the Senate passed Bill S-2 adding "sexual orientation" to the CHRA. Shortly before it was passed, REAL Women was able to make a presentation to the committee considering the bill, despite the fact that the hearings were not advertised and were only three hours long. The presentation pointed out that even Max Yalden, Chief Commissioner of the Canadian Human Rights Commission, believed adding sexual orientation to the CHRA would lead to homosexual couples achieving "marital status." The phrase "sexual orientation" was undefined, and critics said that would leave the door open for subsequent interpretations that might cover ever more deviant forms of sexual behaviour. Furthermore, REAL Women made the case that, since homosexuals are more highly educated and affluent than the average Canadian, they actually had equal or better access to the levers of political and legal power than most "average Canadians".

> Finally, it should be noted that to exclude "sexual orientation" from the CHRA Act does not deprive homosexuals of one single constitutional right. Moreover, to exclude sexual orientation from the CHRA does not mean to "discriminate" against them for their sexual practices, since they already share all the fundamental rights of other Canadians and in fact, have far more advantages (economically, educationally, politically and culturally) than do most Canadian citizens. Homosexuals are not being singled out for unfair treatment:

in fact, they have singled themselves out for privileged treatment by aggressively pursuing special protected status to which they demonstrably have no valid claim (REAL Women 1996, 9).

In April of 1996, very shortly after Senate passage of S-2, another law was introduced in the Commons. Bill C-33 proposed to amend the Canadian Human Rights Act to include, among other things, "sexual orientation" as a protected right. About two dozen Liberal MPs opposed the inclusion, but the main opposition to Bill C-33 came from the Reform Party. The ability of the Reformers to successfully mobilize opposition to the bill was undercut by concentrated media attention on a couple of Reform MPs who made particularly controversial remarks about homosexuals. With the Reform Party on its heels, the Liberals were able to rapidly push Bill C-33 through Parliament.

As the bill moved quickly through parliamentary processes, "opponents outside the legislature were marshaling their forces. Letters, phone calls, and petitions continued to flow in, mostly mobilized by the religious right" (Rayside 1998, 117).

There were a few Liberal MPs opposed to C-33, none more forthright than Roseanne Skoke, a conservative Catholic. In her view,

> To confer homosexuality as a human right on the basis of sexual orientation will provide homosexuals with a special legal status that will allow them to redefine the family, to redefine spouse, to enter into the realm of the sanctity of marriage, to infiltrate the curriculum of our schools and education and to impose an alternative lifestyle on our youth... Homosexuality is unnatural and immoral (Hansard 1996, 2453).

Reform MP Dr. Grant Hill's statements about the health consequences of homosexuality created a firestorm.

> My specific problem with this bill is that it will produce and allow a promotion of an unhealthy lifestyle, a behaviour that is unhealthy. I am speaking now as a physician with a physician's specific knowledge and experience. The specific problems promoting this lifestyle relate to HIV, gay bowel syndrome, increasing parasite infections, lowered life expectancy and finally, the one I have chosen to highlight today, an increase in hepatitis in Canada (Hansard 1996, 2405).

He then went on to cite data from a study conducted by the U.S. Center for Disease Control.

These comments created a media controversy and Hill's comments were said to "promote bigotry and hatred." The Canadian Medical Association even released a statement contradicting Hill and stating that "there is no scientific evidence" to say "that homosexuality is an unhealthy lifestyle." And a complaint against Hill was laid with the Alberta College of Physicians and Surgeons (Verburg 1996, 36).

In the midst of the controversy over the CHRA, Ted Byfield took a careful look at the transformation of attitudes towards sexuality since the 1960s.

> Morality serves always as a restraint on human desire, which usually means on human aggression. When you remove the morality, therefore, you remove the restraint. And it is this, not any new scientific or moral enlightenment, that accounts for our revision of attitude. The rules inhibited us, so we got rid of the rules. No longer must women bear the children conceived within them. No longer need men or women heed vows of sexual exclusivity. No longer need these ancient curbs against sodomy, bestiality, pederasty and other assorted sexual delights confine and restrict us. So we steadily rid ourselves of the laws, and then make it illegal for anyone to oppose or criticize what we have done. (T. Byfield 1996, 44).

Reform Party leader Preston Manning tried to temper his party's opposition to homosexual rights by changing the nature of the debate from "human rights" to "equal opportunities," but this did not seem to impress anyone, least of all his supporters. Link Byfield even wrote an editorial entitled, "Mr. Manning's evasive ideas about 'rights' are worse than [Liberal Justice Minister] Mr. Rock's" (L. Byfield 1996, 2).

The opposition to Bill C-33 had some effect since "to appease family values MPs and social conservative groups, the bill was amended to add a preamble stating the government 'recognizes and affirms the importance of family as the foundation of Canadian society and that nothing in this act alters its fundamental role in society'" (Warren 2002, 214). The government also allowed a free vote on the bill. "Finally, on 9 May 1996, Bill C-33 was adopted in the House of Commons, on a vote of 153 to 76, ending the long and torturous campaign commenced by gay and lesbian activists over two decades earlier" (Warren 2002, 214).

Political scientist David Rayside drew the following conclusions about the Christian Right in Canada from his study of the conflicts over Bill C-41 and Bill C-33:

> There is no question that gay/lesbian activists, even with such allies, were outgunned by anti-gay opponents, particularly from the religious right, in mobilizing the weaponry of letters and phone calls to politicians. Though not nearly as powerful a set of political players as their American counterparts or with nearly as large a constituency, the various components of the religious right in Canada are still able to motivate large numbers of citizens to register their opinions with elected politicians in a political system in which only a small proportion of the population does so. Like the lesbian/gay movement, the religious right's strength is primar-

ily at the local level, but unlike political groups representing feminist, racial minority, and sexual diversity concerns, its grass roots support is widespread geographically rather than concentrated in large urban centers, and more easily coordinated. Those grassroots can be mobilized from local pulpits as well as by fundamentalist Christian broadcast media emanating from both Canadian and American centers. Its network can generate passionately written letters from individual voters in a large number of constituencies, in addition to even larger numbers of form letters and petitions. The religious right swamped pro-gay forces in sending letters and petitions to Parliament Hill. On hate crimes, for example, one MP reported that by the final vote, the total number of signatures on petitions opposing the inclusion of sexual orientation stood at over 83,000, whereas those on petitions favouring the move totalled only 7,250. At one point Roseanne Skoke reported receiving 10,000 letters and phone calls in support of her anti-gay position. In the case of the Human Rights Act amendment, pro-gay petitions totalled 20,000 signatures, but were still vastly outnumbered by the other side. The influence of such voices is evident in the number of parliamentarians in English Canada who are nervous about constituency reactions to pro-gay legislation. It [sic] rural areas in particular, where support for such measures is weak, the mobilizing capacity of the right can easily convince legislators that it represents the overwhelming majority of constituents even when it does not (Rayside 1998, 122).

Grant Hill's controversial statements in the debate over C-33 about the unhealthy nature of homosexual behaviour were vindicated by the Alberta College of Physicians and Surgeons, but his colleagues were not about to support him publicly. In February 1997,

He was called into the office of the Alberta College's deputy registrar and was told the inquiry had found his assertion to be backed by overwhelming evidence, and had confirmed that the gay lifestyle is indeed dangerous from a health viewpoint. Dr. Hill had been cleared. Fine, said he, so now would the college make an announcement to this effect? No, he was told, it would not. He would have to do it himself. The court had found the defendant innocent, so to speak, but wasn't about to say so publicly (T. Byfield 1997, 44).

ORIGIN OF CFAC 1997

During the controversy surrounding Bill C-33, a number of small groups of Christians across the country organized to oppose the bill. Roy Beyer, Brian Rushfeldt and a few people from Medicine Hat began to discuss the possibility of uniting these groups to operate together. This was the beginning of CFAC. As Rushfeldt himself puts it, "The issue that really triggered the formation of the Canada Family Action Coalition (CFAC) was Bill C-33, the sexual orientation legislation that the Liberals jammed through on Canadians... That was the final wake up call for a number of people across Canada" (*ARISE* 1998, 19).

The idea was to network the local groups in order to coordinate their efforts. The result was the formation of CFAC which was incorporated as a non-profit organization in March, 1997.

CFAC was the brainchild of Brian Rushfeldt and Roy Beyer. Both had been pastors with the Victory Churches, a Calgary-based charismatic denomination, and Rushfeldt had been dean of Victory Bible College. Before the early 1990s, Rushfeldt basically had been uninvolved in politics. But Bill C-33 changed that. He saw it

> as leading to an erosion of religious freedoms; as well as un-

dermining family and morality through the inevitable consequences to the education system. That was the catalyst that spurred me into political activism. [Roy Beyer] and I decided we needed to do what we could to oppose this and so we looked at ways we could organize across Canada to mobilize the voice of social conservatives. I wanted to do whatever I could to make society a better place for children and future generations. I felt an obligation to at least prevent further erosion of morality and democratic freedoms and responsibility (Rushfeldt 2007, 1).

In contrast to Brian Rushfeldt, Roy Beyer had been involved as an activist off and on over the years. In the early 1980s, for example, he led a petition effort in Lethbridge against an upsurge of perverse strip shows. The petition gathered 6000 signatures, the largest petition ever gathered in the city to that point. Beyer was encouraged in his activism by the leadership of his church, particularly Pastor George Hill, the founder of the Victory Church movement.

> One of Pastor George's key statements on the vision of the Victory Church was along the lines of the following—there are three arenas of influence in society that have been abandoned by the church—the schools, the media and the politics. He believed that Victory Churches was called to impact all three arenas of influence (Beyer 1999, 173).

This perspective was very significant to the subsequent founding of CFAC. Beyer states that

> It was the fullness of the vision in Victory that allowed me to expand myself and prepare myself for the work of Canada Family Action Coalition (CFAC). I shared the vision of CFAC with Pastor George and other members of the Victory Churches Board nearly five years before I stepped into it on a full time basis (Beyer 1999, 178).

Together, then, Roy, Brian, Brian's wife Judy, and five businessmen formed CFAC (Rushfeldt 2007, 2).

CFAC would be very prominent in leading the opposition to the Supreme Court's *Vriend* decision in 1998. It would also be very active in campaigning for Christian television and against child pornography.

> When John Sharpe of B.C. tried to get the child porn law struck down we acted quickly. That was our largest campaign and we won it, overall. Our petition with over 500,000 signatures was called one of the "largest petition efforts in Canadian history" by the Library of Parliament (Rushfeldt 2007, 2).

Charles McVety, the president of Canada Christian College in Toronto, was a founding board member of CFAC. He would become president of the organization in 2000 when Roy Beyer left that position. Before that, however, CFAC helped McVety overcome an Ontario ministry of education effort to shut down his college.

> [When] Canada Christian College (CCC) applied, after 25 years of receiving annual licences from the province to hold classes, for the right to become a degree-granting institution, it got a letter from the universities branch of the Department of Education and Training, ordering the school to "immediately cease and desist all activities." Only a CFAC-led avalanche of e-mail and faxes aimed at the minister overcame the bureaucracy's antipathy (Parker 1999, 33).

Canada Christian College generated considerable support from evangelical churches in Ontario, the government backed down, and CCC received legislative approval (McVety 2007).
The first major project undertaken by CFAC was the production of an Alberta Voter's Guide for the Alberta provincial election of

April, 1997. This effort generated a considerable amount of interest in the province. Nothing like it had been done on such a large scale before. "CFAC began receiving feedback from various groups and individuals who told them that they had been waiting for something like it to get started" (*ARISE* 1998, 19).

Shortly thereafter a federal election was called. In spite of the daunting task, CFAC undertook to produce a federal voter's guide for the provinces West of Quebec. With the help of numerous volunteers this goal was accomplished. As Rushfeldt put it, "Prior to the federal election, we really had no money, no manpower and no network. So it was a miracle that we were able to raise the money, put all the data together and get 500,000 of the voter's guides distributed" (*ARISE* 1998, 19).

CFAC received a lot of positive feedback from this project. Some people even said that they voted for the first time as a result of the voter's guide. This was a significant achievement for Rushfeldt. "Of course, this is one of our key concerns: that the Christian community is not really involved in democracy, even in the sense of voting once every four years. We need to do whatever we can to motivate them and get them involved" (*ARISE* 1998, 20).

In its early stages, CFAC also focused on setting up chapters in communities across Canada, and networking with other pro-family organizations.

Unquestionably, the formation of CFAC was one of the most important events for the Canadian Christian Right in the 1990s.

THE *VRIEND* CASE

Delwin *Vriend* began working as a lab instructor at King's College in Edmonton in early 1988. *Vriend* had been raised in the

Christian Reformed Church, which is affiliated with the college. Thus *Vriend* was very familiar with the college's code of conduct. In early 1990 the administration learned that he was living a homosexual lifestyle, contrary to the code. When the college president discussed the matter with him, *Vriend* demanded that the college alter its code.

> "Delwin could have remained teaching at the college, if only he hadn't insisted on living that lifestyle," says King's vice-president John Rhebergen. "But what he was doing was contrary to our Statement of Faith. If a heterosexual couple had been doing the same thing, we'd have done the same thing. Christian morality is a requirement of teaching here." By late 1990, Mr. *Vriend*'s lifestyle had become an open issue around the school. He began wearing a T-shirt announcing "Nobody knows I'm gay," and at his invitation, the media started to haunt the place. "The students had a pretty good idea what was going on," says a former student, who wishes to remain anonymous. "You couldn't miss the CBC cameras in the lobby. Some conservative Christian students demanded that he be fired and a pro-gay lobby demanded he be kept on." With its moral commitment and its credibility with students on the line, the college asked Mr. *Vriend* to resign in January 1991. When he refused, he was fired (Woodard 1998b, 14).

Vriend then took his case to the Alberta Human Rights Commission, but the Commission rejected it because sexual orientation was not covered by Alberta's human rights legislation, the Individual Rights Protection Act (IRPA). Thus *Vriend* launched a legal challenge against the Alberta government, "arguing that omitting sexual orientation from the IRPA violated the equality guarantees in the Charter of Rights and Freedoms" (Woodard 1998b, 14).

In an April 1994 court ruling, the judge agreed with *Vriend* that sexual orientation must be included in the IRPA, and that he had been discriminated against on the basis of sexual orientation. However, the Alberta government appealed the decision, and in February 1996 the Alberta Court of Appeal overturned the previous decision, ruling that this was an issue that should be determined by the legislature.

The Alberta Court of Appeal decision was particularly noteworthy, as University of Calgary political science Professor Ted Morton indicated in his analysis of it. First of all, he pointed out how *Vriend* was trying to use the Charter, which is supposed to restrict the state, to actually empower the state.

> The Charter applies to "state action." That is, it protects citizens from governments, not citizens from other citizens. HRAs [human rights acts] apply to "private action," by prohibiting discrimination in private sector employment, credit, housing, and so forth. That is, HRAs expand the scope of government and restrict freedom of association—another Charter right. *Vriend*'s claim amounts to asking the courts to use the Charter—a state-limiting instrument—to order the expansion of government (Morton 1996, 121).

Justice John McClung (grandson of famous suffragette Nellie McClung), who wrote the Court of Appeal decision, argued that the Charter applied to government action, not inaction, and that *Vriend* was challenging the Alberta government's failure to act, not something it had actually done. Furthermore, since Alberta's human rights legislation did not distinguish between heterosexuals and homosexuals, it did not discriminate against the latter.

McClung also went out of his way in this decision to criticize judicial activism based on the Charter, especially the tendency of judges to legislate through judicial interpretation. And he specifically criticized gay rights cases.

> These cases are not just about whether "sexual orientation" should be added to a list of prohibited grounds of discrimination. Justice McClung goes out of his way to point out that they are also about "the validation of homosexual relations, including sodomy, as a protected and fundamental right, thereby 'rebutting a millennia of moral teaching'" (Morton 1996, 123).

Vriend appealed to the Supreme Court of Canada, which heard the case in November 1997. There were a number of interveners on the side of the Alberta government, "the Alberta Federation of Women United for Families (AFWUF), the Christian Legal Fellowship (CLF), the Evangelical Fellowship of Canada (EFC), Focus on the Family Canada, and the Ontario attorney-general" (Torrance 1997, 30). The Supreme Court ruled in Vriend's favour in April 1998. It said that the omission of sexual orientation from the IRPA violated section 15 of the Charter, and therefore it would read sexual orientation into the IRPA (Warner 2002, 210).

Social conservatives in Alberta were furious about the Supreme Court's decision.

> Outside the legislature, the most visible opposition came from the Canada Family Action Coalition—led by a Christian minister claiming support in up to one thousand churches—that ran full-page advertisements in two daily newspapers. The Alberta Civil Society Association broadcast advertisements on several radio and television stations, claiming the decision would infringe religious freedom and undermine the family (Warner 2002, 211).

Roy Beyer of CFAC was prominent in the opposition to the *Vriend* decision. So was Hermina Dykxhoorn, president of AF-

WUF. But the media reaction was largely supportive of *Vriend* and hostile to its opponents.

> The [Edmonton] *Journal* was especially unrelenting in its editorial condemnation of alleged anti-*Vriend* homophobia. Its editorial cartoonist, Malcolm Mayes, cast *Vriend* opponents as Ku Klux Klansmen, and columnist David Staples likened them to Nazis... Edmonton TV station CFRN refused to run an ad from Mr. Morton's Civil Society group, and self-described civil rights lawyer Brian Edy of Calgary mused about the need for laws to restrict "misleading" advertisements from groups like CFAC (Woodard 1998a, 17).

The media storm against people opposed to the decision became so intense that Ted Byfield was led to observe,

> By far the most shrill language occasioned by the *Vriend* decision came from those who were deeply deploring shrill language, and the most righteous of indignation emerged from those vehemently deploring righteous indignation. Obviously nobody can hate quite as fervently as the denouncers of hatred (T. Byfield 1998, 44).

Indeed, some of the supposedly "anti-hate" supporters of *Vriend* were willing to demonstrate hatred to their opponents.

> CFAC co-founders Brian Rushfeldt of Calgary and Roy Beyer of Edmonton were instrumental in generating 3,700 faxes and phone calls a day to Premier Klein during the first week after the Supreme Court of Canada ruled in *Vriend* that the province must protect homosexuals in its human rights code. Their work did not go unnoticed. After the campaign, which urged the premier to employ the notwithstanding clause to avoid the court's order, Mr. Rushfeldt says he received a number of "negative, nasty letters," as well as a death threat from the homosexual group Queer Nation. "But I know where

I'm going in eternity and I have no fear of death," says Mr. Rushfeldt. "I think being ready to die for the truth is the very essence of a healthy society" (Parker 1999, 35).

Besides the grassroots mobilization against the decision, there were also members of the government who wanted to negate its affect on Alberta.

Many PC caucus members, led by Provincial Treasurer Stockwell Day, a social conservative champion, publicly urged invoking the notwithstanding clause of the Constitution, under which the legislature could vote to override the decision for five years. Premier Ralph Klein and MLAs, mainly from rural areas, were deluged with angry phone calls. Many callers urged use of the notwithstanding clause, while others merely read 'church bulletins or scripted comments verbatim over the phone.' Klein's office reported about one thousand calls, with two-thirds opposing the *Vriend* decision. Stockwell Day reported about 1200 calls, most of which were negative. In the end, the Klein government did not invoke the notwithstanding clause, despite opposition form [sic] about one-third of the caucus (Warner 2002, 211).

Many conservatives in Alberta were angry over Klein's decision. For many of them, their anger stemmed from their opposition to the homosexual rights movement. But others just hated being told what to do by Ottawa.

Other Canadians imagine that Albertans get angry about gay rights because we hate gays. This is not true. We couldn't be bothered hating gays. We get angry because we don't like—and don't accept—being told by outsiders how we will live, what we will think, and what our provincial laws will say. And this goes double when the people doing the telling are a panel of fat-headed, overpaid Ottawa lawyers in red suits who alter our laws at a whim and answer to no one. Our laws do not belong to these Ottawa lawyers, whose stupidity about charter rights grows more wanton and reckless by the year. Our laws belong to us. And we can't understand why Ralph Klein sides with the court against us (L. Byfield 1998, 2).

For Link Byfield, the decision by Ralph Klein to accept the *Vriend* decision was a watershed event. He knew there had been a significant change in the province when Klein refused to invoke the notwithstanding clause to opt out of *Vriend*. In his view, up until then, Alberta would have opted out (L. Byfield 2007).

Later the same year Senator Ron Ghitter, a Progressive Conservative from Alberta, delivered the Dr. Bernie Vigod Memorial Lecture at the Atlantic Human Rights Centre. This lecture constituted an all-out attack on Canada's Christian Right and was entitled, "Theo-conservatism: A Threat to Human Rights." Unlike other conservatives, the theo-conservatives' "agenda relates to morals, infidelity, honesty, abortion, family cohesion and homosexual legitimacy, and their remedies strike at the very foundations of human rights in Canada." Ghitter identified Canada's Theo-conservatives as "Preston Manning, Ted Byfield, the Christian Heritage Party, R.E.A.L. Women and many others who find their sanctuary in the Reform Party of Canada."

Ghitter was convinced that human rights were being threatened in Canada. And "the imminent threat to human rights in my respectful opinion is that which comes from what are known as the theo-conservatives, sometimes called the moral majority." And to drive the point home, he stated that these people "more than any other grouping in Canada, pose the greatest threat to the maintenance and advancement of human rights in our nation."

Ghitter used the *Vriend* case and the inclusion of sexual orientation in human rights legislation as one example of theo-conservative opposition to human rights.

The lightning rod in Alberta is sexual orientation. This is the issue which brings out the theo-cons in remarkable force and visibility. When the Human Rights Commission timidly proposed that gays and lesbians should be treated the same as everyone else, and should be included in the Individual Rights Protection Act, the moral majority screamed foul and acted to stop such heresy. In Alberta they won, but thanks to the Supreme Court of Canada their victory was short lived (Ghitter 1998).

CONCLUSION

During the 1990s the Christian Right in Canada continued to lose the important battles. With a legal regime protecting unrestricted abortion, the pro-life cause was unable to make any inroads for the unborn. In effect, the pro-life movement was marginalized to a large degree.

On the issue of homosexual rights, the Christian Right was in constant retreat. The addition of sexual orientation to the Canadian Human Rights Act in 1996 was a major symbolic loss. And the *Vriend* decision of 1998 was a knock-out blow, indicating that the Supreme Court would enforce the homosexual rights agenda whenever given the opportunity. Alberta, the last bastion against the gay agenda, caved in. Politicians and judges were cooperating to implement homosexual rights at both the provincial and federal levels.

The most hopeful event of the 1990s was the formation of CFAC. A national organization capable of rapidly mobilizing conservative Christians on issues of concern was a promising development. And it has not disappointed its supporters.

This pattern, of continued losses on policy issues, accompanied by the creation of new conservative Christian organizations, would continue in the early part of the new millennium.

REFERENCES

Alberta Report. 1991. "Manhandling the press." November 25: 41.

Alberta Report. 1999 (Supplement). "*Alberta Report* turns 25." January 11:3-14.

ARISE Magazine. 1998. "Family Action Coalition: Getting Christians Involved in The Political Process." Winter: 19-20.

Beyer, Roy. 1999. "A Nation Changing Vision." In George Hill and Hazel Hill, *Adventure, Romance & Revival*. Calgary: House of Victory Publishing.

Brodie, Janine, Shelley A. M. Gavigan, and Jane Jenson. 1992. *The Politics of Abortion*. Toronto: Oxford University Press.

Byfield, Link. 1993. "This letter is addressed to Alberta Christians who are concerned about some of the directions society is taking and want to do something about it." Edmonton: *Alberta Report*.

Byfield, Link. 1996. "Mr. Manning's evasive ideas about 'rights' are worse than Mr. Rock's." *Alberta Report*. May 27:2.

Byfield, Link. 1998. "Albertans have to tell Ralph to give them a direct vote on gay rights." *Alberta Report*. April 27: 2.

Byfield, Link. 1999. "Our next 25 years." *Alberta Report*. January 11: 18-22.

Byfield, Link. 2007. Personal interview. Edmonton: January 31.

Byfield, Ted. 1989. "No law at all is surely better than a law that doesn't work." *Alberta Report*. November 20: 60.

Byfield, Ted. 1990. "I've been convicted of murder but I'd like to make a point." *Alberta Report*. January 22: 44.

Byfield, Ted. 1996. "What exactly was it that gained for sodomy such a fine reputation?" *Alberta Report*. May 20: 44.

Byfield, Ted. 1997. "While medicine's officialdom dodges or lies two courageous doctors declare the truth." *Alberta Report*. March 3:44.

Byfield, Ted. 1998. "The media's inquisitional court has handed down another denunciation of inquisitions." *Alberta Report*. April 27:44.

Campbell, Ken. 1990. *5 Years Rescuing at "the Gates of Hell"*. Burlington, ON: Acts Books.

Canadian Centre for Law and Justice. N.d. *For Family Freedom and Life*. Ottawa: Canadian Centre for Law and Justice.

Demers, Jim. 1993. "Brian and Ken are not a family ... yet." *Alberta Report*. March 15:20-21.

Ellis, Faron. 2005. *The Limits of Participation: Members and Leaders in Canada's Reform Party*. Calgary: University of Calgary Press.

Gairdner, William. 1992. *The War Against the Family: A Parent Speaks Out*. Toronto: Stoddart Publishing Co.

Ghitter, Ron. 1998. "Theo-conservatism: A Threat to Human Rights." Fredericton, NB: Atlantic Human Rights Centre.

Hansard. 1996.

Herman, Didi. 1994. "The Christian Right and the Politics of Morality in Canada." *Parliamentary Affairs*. Vol. 47, No. 2, pp. 268-279.

Landolt, Gwen. 2007. "Responses to Michael Wagner's questions." February 13:1-5.

MacKenzie, Chris. 2005. *Pro-Family Politics and Fringe Parties in Canada*. Vancouver: University of British Columbia Press.

McVety, Charles. 2007. Telephone interview. June 22.

Morton, F. L. 1996. "Canada's Judge Bork: Has the Counter-Revolution Begun?" *Constitutional Forum*. Vol. 7, No. 4: 121-125.

Morton, F. L., and Avril Allen. 2001. "Feminists and the Courts: Measuring Success in Interest Group Litigation in Canada." *Canadian Journal of Political Science*. March: 55-84.

Parker, Shafer. 1999. "The lesson of the Resurrection." *Alberta Report*. April 5: 32-33, 35.

Rayside, David. 1998. *On the Fringe: Gays and Lesbians in Politics*. Ithaca, NY: Cornell University Press.

REAL Women of Canada. 1990. "Presentation to the Legislative Committee on Bill C-43 An Act Respecting Abortion." Ottawa: Real Women of Canada.

REAL Women of Canada. 1996. "Bill S-2, An Act to amend the Canadian Human Rights Act (sexual orientation)."

Rushfeldt, Brian. 2007. Email interview. July 19.

Stiller, Brian C. 1994. *Don't Let Canada Die By Neglect and other essays*. Markham, ON: *Faith Today* Publications.

Stiller, Brian. 2006. Telephone interview. November 28.

Torrance, Kelly. 1997. "A Supreme display of judicial prejudice." *Alberta Report*. November 17:30.

Verburg, Peter. 1996. "The dirty politics of homosexual health." *Alberta Report*. June 3:36-37.

Warner, Tom. 2002. *Never Going Back: A History of Queer Activism in Canada*. Toronto: University of Toronto Press.

Woodard, Joe. 1998a. "Ralph gets moral, and Alberta gets gay rights." *Alberta Report*. April 20:12-17.

Woodard, Joe. 1998b. "The strategy of a human-rights ambush." *Alberta Report*. April 20:14.

CHAPTER 7 | THE END OF TRADITIONAL MARRIAGE AND THE GROWING ATTACK AGAINST CHRISTIANS

The new millennium opened on a largely hopeful note for conservative Christians. A new national political party was being formed, and there was considerable interest in the party's leader in many parts of English Canada. Stockwell Day had a proven track record of public support for the traditional family and other issues dear to the heart of the Christian Right; he had also been very clear in his position against abortion. He was young, charismatic, telegenic and even seemed to have support among some elements of the media.

Unfortunately, that media interest and support was short lived. The Canadian Alliance under Day's leadership did not meet expectations in the federal election of November 2000. Disillusionment set in among many prominent party members, and Day's leadership was quickly undermined. In a leadership ballot early in 2002, Day lost to former Reform MP Stephen Harper who subsequently managed to merge the Alliance and federal PC Party. Harper's commitment to social conservative causes had been ambiguous, and he harshly punished MP Larry Spencer for his outspoken opposition to the homosexual movement.

If Stockwell Day's short tenure proved to be a disappointment, there was nevertheless much worse to come. Somehow homosexuality became virtually synonymous with "human rights" so that public opposition to homosexuality was frequently portrayed as some kind of "human rights" violation. The irrepressible Ken Campbell spent four years fighting off a "human rights" challenge. He ultimately won his fight. Others were not so lucky. And with the addition of sexual orientation to the "hate propaganda" provision of the Criminal Code in 2004, homosexual activists potentially had an even stronger weapon with which to punish dissent from their agenda.

But the biggest setback for Christian activists would come the following year with the legal establishment of same-sex marriage. The fight leading to that event would mobilize conservative Christians like never before, but it was not enough. Nevertheless, the mobilization held out hope that the Christian Right was organizing to such a degree that it would remain a more significant force in Canadian politics. The emergence of new leaders, such as Tristan Emmanuel, indicated that a new stage in the Canadian Christian Right had been reached.

STOCKWELL DAY

In the early to mid 1980s Stockwell Day was an assistant pastor at the Bentley Christian Centre in a small town in central Alberta, about halfway between Calgary and Edmonton. The church had a private school and Day was the school administrator. Private education was a controversial issue in Alberta during the early 1980s, and Day was actively involved in defending Christian schools during that period.

In 1986 Day was elected as a member of the Alberta Legislature for the Progressive Conservative Party. He was a backbencher for the first few years, but became increasingly known for his defence of the traditional family. When Premier Don Getty formed the Premier's Council in Support of Alberta Families, Day was made the Council's chairman. In the summer of 1992 *Alberta Report* featured a cover story on Day (Gunter 1992).

When Ralph Klein became premier in December 1992, he appointed Day as labour minister. Day later served briefly as social services minister, and then in March 1997 he became the provincial treasurer. He oversaw a number of budget surpluses and tax cuts. But he also publicly supported traditional moral causes such as opposing abortion and homosexual rights. Day had excellent credentials as both an economic and social conservative.

In 1997 the Reform Party emerged from the federal election as the official opposition. Despite continued electoral gains, the failure to win the election and the failure to win seats in Ontario were seen as tremendous disappointments. The party would need to change significantly to appeal to Eastern voters and become a genuine national party.

At the Reform Party's Assembly in May 1998, leader Preston Manning proposed the creation of a new and bigger political party. In effect, the idea was to unite the Reform Party and the national Progressive Conservative Party under the banner of a new political party. The new party would then presumably be a genuine national party able to form the government in Ottawa.

This project was known as the "United Alternative" or UA, and at a convention in January 2000, the Canadian Alliance Party was born out of the Reform Party and some former Progressive Conservatives. The new party would need a leader, and so a leadership election was scheduled for the summer of that year. The main leadership contenders were former Reform leader Preston Manning, prominent Ontario Tory Tom Long, and Stockwell Day.

A large number of conservative Christians mobilized to support Stockwell Day's leadership campaign. Although Preston Manning was also an evangelical Christian, he did not receive the widespread conservative Christian support that Day did. Claire Hoy quotes Link Byfield as explaining why this was so. When Manning punished a couple of his own Reform MPs for making anti-homosexual remarks, he

> lost his luster. You'd never see Stock openly kick his own supporters in the head. You may disappoint your own core, but you don't want to insult them. Manning buckled to this militant secularism. Burn a little incense here. You really have to piss on the Christians. What he was really saying is we don't want Judeo-Christian conservatives in our party. He painted them as extremists. Stock won't do that. Everybody understands you've got to stay as close to the middle as you can sometimes, but as long as the cock crows three times and he's not denying us as Manning did, Stock will get that kind of support (Hoy 2000, 157-158).

Charles McVety worked hard to support Day's campaign. He was a major player for Day in Ontario, delivering 10,000 Alliance memberships for Day (McVety 2007). Roy Beyer left his position in CFAC to form an organization called Families for Day, which signed up at least 6500 new party members (Geddes 2000, 20). Day also received the support of Father Alphonse de Valk, editor of *Catholic Insight* magazine and a long-time pro-life leader, as well as the support of Campaign Life Coalition (Harrison 2002, 54). Clearly, the Stockwell Day campaign was heavily populated by conservative Christians.

However, Day also received considerable support from other, non-Christian elements of the conservative movement. For example, Day's campaign manager was Rod Love, Ralph Klein's top strategist and well-known opponent of social conservative goals (Bunner 2000, 11).

On the first leadership ballot in June 2000, Day came first with 44 percent of the votes, but fell short of the majority necessary to win. A second ballot, between Day and Manning, was held on July 8 and Day won easily (Bunner 2000, 10). Needing a seat in the House of Commons, he ran in a BC riding where the sitting MP, Jim Hart, had resigned to make way for Day's candidacy. Day easily won the seat in a September by-election, and subsequently arrived at his first news conference by riding a jet ski across a lake, wearing a wetsuit. This image would embed itself in the minds of many voters, and led to some serious questioning within the party about the caliber of advisors Day had surrounded himself with.

But Day's ascension to the leadership was widely interpreted as catapulting conservative Christians into a new place of political prominence in Canada. An article in *Maclean's* magazine stated that social conservatives "believe that with Day in charge, the time is right to get serious about shoring up the Alliance as a political base for their values, including staunch opposition to abortion" (Geddes 2000, 20). American–based scholar Dennis Hoover, who had written his doctoral dissertation on conservative Christian political activism in Canada wrote, "a religious right has arrived in Canadian politics. And Canadian journalists have found this very hard to swallow—something like getting down a sacred cow." He went on to observe,

> On May 27 *The Globe and Mail*'s John Ibbitson wrote that the Alliance would have trouble beating the rap that had dogged the Reform Party—that the religious right had exercised "a disproportionate influence." The question that the Canadian media have yet to face, and which will not go away, is what amount of social conservative influence *would*

be proportionate in a united Canadian right? After the recent elections the answer is: a lot more than most Canadians thought (Hoover 2000).

Day's victory created a sense of hope and optimism among many Alliance supporters. A new party with a fresh, young, charismatic leader could expect to appeal to many voters and perhaps win an election. The possibility of growing Alliance support may have slowed the advance of homosexual rights, at least in one instance.

> CFAC boasts its lobbying influenced at least some of the backbench Liberal MPs who pressured federal Justice Minister Anne McLellan to drop a plan to change the legal definition of marriage to include same-sex unions. McLellan's move left gay-rights advocates convinced that top Liberals are spooked by the Alliance. "The Liberals caved in to the perception that there would be a backlash," said Kim Vance, president of Equality for Gays and Lesbians Everywhere. "I certainly think they can see the writing on the wall about the support the Alliance is going to get in the next election." (Geddes 2000, 21).

With support for the Alliance building, Prime Minister Chretien called an election for November 27, 2000. Trevor Harrison writes that, "In general, social conservatism was not a telling issue in the campaign" (Harrison 2002, 81). Nevertheless, the campaign did not go well for the Alliance. The CBC's Rick Mercer made fun of the Alliance position advocating referendums for moral issues such as abortion, and the CBC's news program *The National* highlighted Day's conservative religious beliefs to generate public disapproval. The Liberals made some political hay out of this, with party hack Warren Kinsella going on *Canada AM* one morning to display a purple "Barney the Dinosaur" doll. With his tongue just barely in his cheek, Kinsella accused Day of believing The Flintstones cartoon was a documentary. It was another way of mocking Day's belief in the Biblical account of Creation. The Liberals easily won the election (Harrison 2002, 82-85).

Within a short time after the election, considerable opposition to Day's leadership arose within the Alliance Party. One notable problem was an incident left over from Day's tenure as an Alberta cabinet minister. Day had written a letter to a Red Deer newspaper about a local lawyer that led to a costly lawsuit against Day, with the Alberta government picking up the tab. There were many controversial aspects to this situation, especially the high cost of Day's lawsuit at the taxpayers' expense, and a subsequent large donation to the Alliance by one of Day's lawyers (Harrison 2002, 93-110).

In the spring of 2001, a number of high level party officials quit their posts. This apparently reflected disenchantment with Day's leadership. The disenchantment also affected Day's own caucus. Some Day supporters believed the simmering discontent was being fomented by supporters of former leader Preston Manning. At an April caucus meeting, five MPs called on Day to resign as leader. Discontent continued to spread, and in May, 8 MPs left the caucus. Later that month, The Alliance's national council met in Calgary. In a tight vote, Manning supporter Rick Anderson was suspended from the council. (Harrison 2002, 126-141).

The resignations of MPs from the caucus and subsequent expulsion of Rick Anderson marked "a turning point in the Alliance party's ongoing crisis and set off an almost daily round of resignations, expulsions, accusations, and fresh rumours" (Harrison 2002, 143). The party continued to unravel, and with Day losing more and more caucus support he finally resigned in July to make way for a leadership vote to be held in March 2002. Day ran again, but lost to his main competitor, Stephen Harper, on the first ballot.

Many conservative Christians helped Day in this second leadership campaign, including Roy Beyer and his organization Families for Day, as well as Charles McVety. However, Day had also lost the confidence of some of his previous supporters.

Stockwell Day's original leadership campaign certainly led to the mobilization of many conservative Christians into Alliance politics. Had his leadership not been undermined, this would likely have led to an increase in political influence for conservative Christians. While some of that Christian support has likely transferred into the new Conservative Party (formed by an amalgamation of the Alliance and federal Progressive Conservative Party in late 2003), the long-term effect of the Day campaign does not appear to be large. As the experience of Larry Spencer would show, the new Conservative Party had limited tolerance for conservative Christians.

LARRY SPENCER

Larry Spencer was an American Baptist pastor who moved to Regina in 1974 to found and build Baptist churches. After 25 years in Saskatchewan, he became a Canadian citizen in 1999, and the following year he ran as the Canadian Alliance candidate for a Regina constituency in the federal election, and won. In the subsequent leadership squabble, Spencer supported Stockwell Day.

Nevertheless, Harper allowed Spencer to remain as the party's Family Issues Critic, a position he had been given under John Reynold's interim leadership. In this role he was expected to give the Canadian Alliance Caucus' Social Committee weekly updates on issues impacting families. Due to the federal government's apparent interest in changing the definition of marriage to include same-sex couples, Spencer prepared a "marriage backgrounder" for the Social Committee to consider.

The response of the Committee to his report demonstrated a strong aversion to Spencer's social conservative priorities. As he recounts it,

> Paranoia was already setting in as some caucus members felt the pressure being sent down from the OLO [Opposition Leader's Office] to avoid comment on the definition of marriage. The Caucus Chairman was a member of the Social Committee. I was caught completely by surprise when he recoiled from the marriage document I was presenting. He took a very quick glance at its contents, but it wasn't the content that seemed to be the problem, just simply the fact that we would put anything of substance regarding this sensitive issue into print. He slid his copy back to me as if it had burned his hand and stated his reluctance to have such a document circulated. One by one, the others slowly nodded in agreement and returned their copies as well (Spencer 2006, 69).

Clearly, the party leadership was hesitant to deal with this issue.

Apparently not long afterwards, Spencer spoke by phone with reporter Peter O'Neil of the *Vancouver Sun*. O'Neil wrote an article based on this interview that appeared on November 27, 2003. Unfortunately for Spencer, O'Neil inaccurately reported that Spencer had claimed there was a homosexual "conspiracy" and misrepresented Spencer's views on other matters dealing with homosexuality as well.

This article embarrassed the Canadian Alliance leadership and potentially imperiled the merger of the Canadian Alliance and Progressive Conservative parties that was in the works at that time. Harper immediately fired Spencer from his Family Issues Critic position and Spencer agreed to a temporary resignation from Caucus. He also agreed to issue a public statement of apology written by members of Harper's staff:

> I slowly read through the proposed statement. It sounded like a bit of over-kill to me, but it did give me a clearer picture of the perceptions that were flying around. I began to realize that not only had Peter O'Neil laid me on the cross of political death, but that my own party was going to furnish the nails that would keep me there to the last breath (Spencer 2006, 76).

There was a "media frenzy" over Spencer's alleged comments, but the Canadian Alliance leadership insisted that Spencer avoid talking to the media at all. The media coverage was negative for the most part. But Spencer did receive public support from the Christian Right.

> Some organizations like the Christian Heritage Party, Real Women of Canada, Concerned Christians Canada, LifeSiteNews.com, along with several others were very supportive. The gag order the party had placed me under prevented me from responding even to these who were trying to help (Spencer 2006, 84).

Although Spencer had only agreed to a temporary resignation from caucus, there was mounting evidence that the party leadership wanted to keep him out of caucus permanently. "There was apparently no desire—certainly no effort made—to ascertain what the real truth about what I had said. Mr. Harper was quite content to drive in the nails and offer me up as a sacrifice with no further hesitation" (Spencer 2006, 100).

In February 4, 2004, Spencer was allowed to speak to the new Conservative caucus for five minutes, after which a secret vote was taken concerning his re-entry into the caucus. The caucus voted to keep him out. In the subsequent election in July, 2004, Spencer ran as an Independent, but was defeated.

If this incident demonstrates anything, it shows that the Canadian Alliance Party was losing interest in the issues associated with the Christian Right after Stockwell Day resigned as leader of the party. And the new Conservative Party was so concerned about its public image that it was willing to jettison MPs who were too critical of the homosexual movement.

KEN CAMPBELL BEFORE THE HUMAN RIGHTS COMMISSIONS

In April 1998 Ken Campbell placed a full-page ad in the national edition of *The Globe and Mail* criticizing the Supreme Court's decision in the *Vriend* case. Campbell wanted to encourage the Alberta government to nullify that decision by invoking the notwithstanding clause of the Charter of Rights. The ad used some rather strong language to describe the homosexual rights movement.

A few weeks later, in June of that year, a homosexual filed a complaint against Campbell with the Ontario Human Rights Commission (OHRC). And then in November, another homosexual filed a complaint against Campbell (for exactly the same ad) with the BC Human Rights Commission (BCHRC), even though Campbell was living in Ontario at the time.

The complaint in the Ontario case was three pages long. Among other things it alleged that Campbell's ad was designed to "spread harmful misinformation, foster discriminatory attitudes, besmirch and hurt people who are not heterosexual, muster public opinion against treating people equally who are not heterosexual, and promote hatred against people who are not heterosexual." It also claimed that the ad "includes allegations of fact which are false, misleading, and/or discriminatory and seeks to base legislative and social conduct upon these false allegations of fact" (Campbell 2004, 17).

Of course, Campbell in his official reply denied the charges and astutely pointed out that the "complainant has not identified a single misrepresentation of fact or of a misleading statement" (Campbell 2004, 27). Furthermore, Campbell suggested a different way of dealing with this dispute, one that was much more consistent with the principles of a free country:

> I submit that the appropriate recourse to which the complainant has ready access, is the same public space in which I published the truth which the complainant has found offensive, namely, that the complainant prepare an equally civilized expression of the philosophy to which he is committed, and purchase space and publish the same in a full-page ad in the national edition of *The Globe and Mail* (Campbell 2004, 29).

This was a very reasonable suggestion. If the complainant didn't like Campbell's ad, he was free to publish an ad with a contrary message. But instead, he wanted to have Campbell punished for placing an ad opposing the homosexual rights movement. Campbell saw this for what it was and made no bones about it in his official reply:

> [T]he complainant's apparent determination to obstruct the dissemination of ideas which he finds offensive, reflects a fascist inclination all-too-characteristic of the special interest lobby he represents, to squelch public debate and the ventilation of alternative view-points on the issues at hand (Campbell 2004, 29).

After Campbell had presented his arguments, the Ontario Human Rights Commission decided not to proceed with the complaint. It issued a ruling in April 2000 stating that "while the advertisement is highly offensive, it is nevertheless an expression of opinion that does not fall within the purview of the [Human Rights] Code" (Campbell 2004, 115). Thus Campbell had won in Ontario.

However, unlike the Ontario case, the BC case proceeded to a tribunal. As Campbell stated at the time, "it is lawless for the BC Human Rights Commission to refer this complaint to the Tribunal for a hearing, when the same complaint essentially, had already been investigated and dismissed by the Ontario Human Rights Commission" (Campbell 2004, 183).

Tribunal hearings were held in the fall of 2001, with Campbell acting in his own defence because he could not afford a lawyer. The complainant was seeking an order prohibiting Campbell from placing such an ad in the future, as well as ordering Campbell to pay about $85,000 in penalties, some of which would be used to pay for a pro-homosexual ad in *The Globe and Mail*, some of which would be used to fund a pro-homosexual organization, and the rest of which would be used to line the complainant's own pocket. Campbell replied that he would rather

> submit to the inevitable incarceration as a prisoner of conscience for a principled refusal to pay (even if I had the resources to do so) or to allow anyone else to pay, on my behalf, one penny of the penalty exacted from me by the Tribunal as a "remedy" to the complainant for the evil cause he represents and which brings us here (Campbell 2004, 169).

The main thrust of the complaint was that Campbell's ad amounted to discrimination or an intent to discriminate against homosexuals. The official Tribunal ruling, in October 2002, dismissed the complaint, stating that the charges regarding discrimination were not demonstrated by the complainant. Thus Campbell had won in BC as well.

However, there really wasn't much to celebrate in the ruling. Apparently after the Tribunal process was underway, the complainant had tried to amend his charges against Campbell by adding an allegation that the ad was "hateful." But for procedural reasons the amendment was not accepted by the Tribunal.

And in the official Tribunal ruling, there is a cryptic reference to this issue, implying that Campbell may well have lost had the charge of "hate" been raised in the proper way. The Tribunal ruling states that it should not "be read as a determination that the advertisement, or others like it, are permitted under the [Human Rights] Code." The question of hatred "was not properly before me and I have made no determination of that issue" (Campbell 2004, 240). So it may be that Campbell won due to a procedural blunder on the complainant's part.

BILL C-250

On November 22, 2001, NDP MP Svend Robinson introduced a bill in Parliament that would add sexual orientation as a protected category under the genocide and hate propaganda provisions of the Criminal Code. This bill, C-415, was selected as a votable bill as a result of receiving unanimous consent of all parties in the House of Commons. It then passed second reading in the House on May 29, 2002, and was referred to the Standing Committee on Justice and Human Rights.

Pro-family groups were very concerned that this bill would stifle debate on homosexual issues by making opponents of homosexual rights liable to charges of committing "hate" crimes. Nevertheless, the Canadian Alliance (CA) party was unwilling at this point to try to stop the bill. On May 2, 2002, a delegation from REAL Women met with the CA justice critic, Vic Toews, and the CA family critic, Larry Spencer. Gwen Landolt recounts that,

> We were advised that the Alliance caucus had decided not to call for a vote on Bill C-415 on second reading, but hoped to make amendments in committee or at the time of the third reading of the Bill. It was made clear to us that this decision was a political decision so as to prevent the party from being

attacked by the media (and the Liberals) for its "homophobic" rejection of protection on the grounds of sexual orientation (Landolt 2002, 4).

When Robinson's bill came up for debate in the House on May 29, "Mr. Toews, Alliance spokesperson on the Bill, responded by stating that the Bill should not be limited to sexual orientation but should be expanded to include all the enumerated groups set out in S. 15(1) of the Charter" (Landolt 2002, 4). The NDP, PC, Liberal and Bloc Quebecois parties all supported the bill, so the CA did not actively oppose it. "When the Speaker called for a vote from the scanty number of MPs present in the House (no more than 15 MPs were present), the Bill passed second reading with no dissent" (Landolt 2002, 4-5).

More conservative Christians became involved by this point, contacting their MPs to oppose the bill due to the threat it posed to their freedom. Svend Robinson referred to this activism as "a campaign of distortion, of lies, by the religious right that is unbelievable" (Stock 2002, 9). The CA changed its position on the bill and issued a press release on November 21, 2002, declaring, "It is the Canadian Alliance position that the bill should be defeated because it will substantially interfere with the right of religious and educational leaders to communicate essential matters of faith" (*REALity* 2003a, 8).

On May 6, 2003, REAL Women was able to present a brief on the bill, now known as Bill C-250, to point out its potential dangers. The brief pointed out that even Justice Beverly McLaughlin of the Supreme Court saw the Criminal Code restrictions on hate propaganda as a threat to freedom of expression in Canada. Also, the term "hate" was vague and subjective. For example, Svend Robinson considered Liberal MP Roseanne Skoke's public statements opposing the addition of sexual orientation as a protected category in federal legislation to be "hateful" and "homophobic hate mongering." On December 7, 1999, Robinson even grabbed a sign from a Catholic priest, broke the sign and threw it, claiming it was "hateful." The sign merely contained quotes of Catholic teaching on homosexuality. These are examples of what is "hateful" by Svend Robinson's standards (REAL Women 2003, 3-6).

Yet angry attacks upon Christians are not considered to be "hate" according to the authorities.

> On March 9, 2000, a group of feminists, calling themselves the "Collectif Autonome Feministe," were in Phillips Square in Montreal to protest their alleged oppression by the patriarchy. Following their protest, they donned ski masks and launched an assault on nearby Mary Queen of the World Catholic Cathedral. They spray-painted on the church, "Religion—A Trap for Fools," and erected a burning cross outside. Inside, they disrupted worshippers by spray-painting slogans on the altar, overturning flower pots, sticking used sanitary napkins on pictures and walls, and throwing condoms around the sanctuary—while screaming in foul language their opposition to religion and claiming the right to abortion and freedom of speech. The Montreal police did not lay charges against these women because, according to the police spokesperson, there was no evidence of a hate crime, but merely a political statement being made by these women. Hate crimes apparently only become "hateful" when the attacks are made on favoured, protected identifiable groups: attacks on all other groups are not apparently, "hateful" (REAL Women 2003, 6-7).

The brief goes on to point out that the defences set out in the Criminal Code to prevent abuses of the hate propaganda provisions are illusory. Religious freedom protections had failed to protect a Catholic school in the Marc Hall incident of May 2002, where the school had been compelled to allow Hall to bring his "boy friend" to an official school event. Toronto printer Scott Brockie also received no help from the supposed safeguards. Brockie had refused to print pro-homosexual literature, and he had essentially been told that while he was free to practice his religion in private and in his church community, he would be forbidden from applying his religious principles to his business. And there were other cases. "Even if proceedings are not directly instigated against pro-life/family organizations or religious leaders, for example, it is clear that, inevitably, if the proposed amendment becomes law, it will have a chilling effect on public debate" (REAL Women 2003, 15).

The REAL Women delegation was pleased with their efforts that day and were optimistic that the bill would go no further.

> Our presentation was well received by the Alliance members on the Committee, as well as a majority of the Liberal MPs. They understood and shared our concerns about this controversial bill. Mr. Robinson, the sponsor of the bill, did not have a good day. When we left the Committee hearings on May 6, we were confident that the bill would not be returned to the House of Commons for third and final reading. We believed that the Committee would recommend that the bill not be proceeded with (*REALity* 2003d, 1).

What they didn't know at the time was that Justice Minister Cauchon had decided to treat C-250 as a government bill. Vic Toews tried unsuccessfully to kill the bill in the committee. The bill went back to the House of Commons, was amended to exempt statements based on "religious texts," and was then passed on September 17, 2003, by a vote of 145-110 (*REALity* 2003b, 1-4).

Having passed the House of Commons, the bill was then sent to the Senate.

In the Senate, the bill was delayed several months due to the heroic efforts of Senator Anne Cools. It finally slipped into the Standing Senate Committee on Legal and Constitutional Affairs for review in early February. All the time the bill was proceeding through Parliament, the media maintained a steely silence on the bill and its implications with few Canadians knowing about it. To offset this, REAL Women placed a full-page advertisement in the National Post on March 17, 2004, in which we set out the dangers of the bill. The advertisement was published on the second day of hearings by the Senate Committee on the bill (*REALity* 2004a, 6).

The ad encouraged people to contact the Senators about the bill, and some people apparently did so. REAL Women was able to appear before the Standing Senate Committee on Legal and Constitutional Affairs, along with a few other groups, to oppose the bill. But the Senators were not interested in their concerns (*REALity* 2004a, 6).

The final vote on Bill C-250 in the Senate was held on April 28, 2004, and it passed easily by a vote of 59-11. REAL Women speculated that the law would not be used immediately. "Homosexual activists will be very careful, at least for a while, having this law enforced. They do not want to take chances that it will be overturned by the courts" (*REALity* 2004b, 8).

TRISTAN EMMANUEL

After completing high school, Tristan Emmanuel began attending the Ontario Bible College in 1989. While there he became involved in political activism through a pro-life organization. Political activism remained an important part of his life over the next few years, and he became active in the Christian Heritage Party as well as the Family Coalition Party of Ontario, of which he served a stint as deputy leader. He also ran for an Ontario PC Party nomination at one point.

When he became a pastor of an Orthodox Presbyterian Church in 1999, he gave up political activism, although his interest in political affairs did not wane. And when Svend Robinson's Bill C-250 gathered steam, he jumped right back into activism.

He explains the situation in detail in his book *Christophobia*, where he states that

> on June 7, 2003, when I heard that Members of Parliament were going to vote in the House of Commons on a bill that would radically challenge Christ's authority in my country and aggressively attack His gospel, I had to act. There really wasn't a choice. Once again the words of the Great Commission echoed loud and clear: "All authority has been given to me." That was all I needed to know. I had to get involved. I felt that if I, a pastor, did not defend my Lord's interests here in Canada, if I did not defend the right to freely proclaim the gospel, and if I did not defend the need for homosexuals to hear the gospel, then I would be denying the Gospel of Christ. I would never again be able to hold my own office as a minister of this Gospel in high esteem. You see I believed then, and I still believe today, that Bill C-250 was designed to criminalize the gospel message about homosexuality. I have never been more convinced of anything. In response to the threat that this bill might pass, I organized a town hall meeting in my constituency of Lincoln, not far from Niagara Falls, Ontario. I invited our local MP and two other dear friends, Reverend Royal Hamel and Mrs. Lynne Scime. Together we decided to deal head-on with the issue of Bill C-250. We would begin by educating our local Christian community. We'd tell them about the bill, its serious flaws, and its dangerous implications for freedom. We wanted Christians to band together to oppose the passage of Bill C-250 in the House of Commons. We resolved to do everything we could, democratically, to ensure that the bill would not become law.

But there was one big problem. One town hall meeting wasn't enough. There was just too much work to do. There were too many Christians to educate, motivate, and mobilize. As a result, we embarked on a whirlwind town hall tour of Southern Ontario. We visited more than a dozen different federal ridings and conducted 15 town hall meetings. The basic strategy was to lobby the Christian community to get serious about its faith. Our goal was to urge the Christian community across denominational boundaries to tell their elected officials to represent their views in Ottawa. As a result of that political action, I'm even more convinced that motivating the Christian community is the key to changing our nation (Emmanuel 2003, 17-18).

It was also during this time that the traditional definition of marriage was struck down by an Ontario court, and the same-sex marriage issue became especially hot. Tristan formed the Equipping Christians for the Public-square Centre (ECP Centre) in 2004, and began discussions with the elders of his church regarding the career implications of his political activism. He came to the conclusion, in conjunction with the elders, that God was calling him to go full-time with the ECP Centre. He approached some businesses and convinced them of the need for an organization that would operate as a Christian lobby group to defend the freedoms of Christians and educate Christians about the problems they are facing in Canada. This was successful, and Tristan resigned from the pastorate to pursue his ECP Centre activities full-time.

SAME-SEX MARRIAGE

In May 1999 the Supreme Court of Canada handed down its decision in the *M. vs. H.* case. M and H were lesbians whose relationship had broken down. M wanted alimony from H but was denied because women in lesbian relationships did not count as "spouses" under Ontario's Family Law Act (FLA). M went to court claiming that the heterosexual definition of "spouse" in the FLA discriminated against homosexuals. The Court ruled in her favour. The benefits accorded to common law couples under the FLA had to be extended to same-sex couples. People in same-sex relationships were to be given the same status as spouses that people in heterosexual relationships had.

Justice Gonthier, the only Supreme Court judge to dissent from this decision, referred to it as a "watershed." And this is certainly how REAL Women viewed it as well.

> [T]his decision has released a pack of hound dogs prepared to attack and destroy the traditional family. Put another way, the reasoning in *M and H* has slipped a noose around the neck of the traditional family and it will only take one more court challenge to pull the rope tight and kick the chair from under it, leaving the traditional family limp and lifeless (*REALity* 1999a, 3).

This would prove to be prophetic, as the "one more court challenge" overturned the exclusive heterosexual definition of marriage in June 2003.

As a result of the *M. vs. H.* decision, Reform MP Eric Lowther (Opposition Critic for the Family) introduced a resolution in the House of Commons as follows:

> That, in the opinion of this House, it is necessary, in light of public debate around recent court decisions, to state that marriage is and should remain the union of one man and one woman to the exclusion of all others, and that Parliament will take all necessary steps to preserve this definition of marriage in Canada (*REALity* 1999b, 1).

Liberal Justice Minister Anne McLellan announced that Jean Chretien's government supported the motion because it accepted the historic definition of marriage in Canada. (Within four years or so, however, the Liberal government would claim that the historic definition of marriage was unconstitutional and violated "human rights"). With Liberal support, Lowther's motion passed easily, 216-55 (*REALity* 1999b, 2).

Another response to *M. vs. H.* was a private member's bill from Liberal MP Tom Wappel to confine marriage exclusively to one man and one woman. This proposal was strongly supported by Gwen Landolt who wrote a paper arguing for the need to act quickly to prevent the courts from legalizing same-sex marriage. If the courts strike first, it would be virtually impossible to invoke the notwithstanding clause to protect traditional marriage. In such a case homosexual activists, with help from much of the media, would be able to portray use of the notwithstanding clause as bigotry and discrimination (Landolt 1999, 6).

But if the Marriage Act could be amended along the lines advocated by Wappel, and the notwithstanding clause written into the amendment, things could be quite different.

> [I]f a notwithstanding clause were to be included with the amendment to the *Marriage Act* prior to the issue of same-sex marriages becoming a high profile political issue, by way of a Supreme Court of Canada ruling on it, it may be possible, if not highly likely, that the notwithstanding clause could be passed by Parliament. This conclusion is based on the fact that the Reform Party's resolution on marriage of June 8, 1999 passed overwhelmingly in a vote of 216 to 55. This indicates that the House of Commons, at this time, at least, believes that marriage should be restricted to members of the opposite sex (Landolt 1999, 6-7).

This strategy could only succeed if Parliament acted immediately.

> [T]he time to proceed is now. Action should be taken prior to any further deterioration of resistance to such an amendment and to any coalescing of support within the homosexual community. Certainly, an amendment should be pursued before any ruling on the issue by the Supreme Court of Canada (Landolt 1999, 8).

Once again, Gwen Landolt correctly sized up the situation, but her solution was not enacted.

As a result of the *M. vs. H.* decision, the Ontario government was required to amend its laws to conform to the Court's ruling within six months. Together with the Catholic Civil Rights League and CFAC, REAL Women submitted a brief to the Ontario government providing advice on how to obey the court order while doing minimum damage to the traditional form of marriage. This brief argued that,

> since the institution of legal marriage is the foundation of society and in the best interests of children, this institution should be distinguished from all others and should be given special recognition and support to promote and encourage its formation. The appropriate course of action to give effect to this principle is to provide separate statutory protection to other interdependent couples by way of enacting a separate statute (REAL Women et al 1999, 3).

This advice was ignored.

On October 25, 1999 the Ontario government introduced Bill 5 which amended the definition of "spouse" in 67 provincial laws. It created a marriage-like status for same-sex partnerships and gave these partnerships most of the rights and benefits of marriage. This bill was rushed through the legislature, and passed third reading on October 27. The following day it received royal assent. Pro-family advocates felt betrayed (Rogusky and Stirk 1999, 1-3).

The push towards same-sex marriage was moving rapidly. In 2001 the Law Commission of Canada, a federal government agency, released a major report arguing for the legalization of same-sex marriage. It stated that,

> whether or not denial of same-sex marriage infringes the Charter, adherence to the fundamental values of equality, choice and freedom of conscience and religion requires that restrictions on same-sex marriage be removed; the status quo reinforces the stigmatization felt by same-sex couples (Law Commission 2001, 130).

In short, "fundamental Canadian values and the secular nature of the state's interest in marriage require that the state not discriminate against same-sex couples" (Law Commission 2001, 131). It does seem strange, however, that for most of its history, Canada did not realize its "fundamental values" required same-sex marriage. How did generations of Canadians fail to recognize their very own "fundamental values"?

By this time, there were court actions aimed at overturning the opposite-sex requirement for marriage in three provinces, BC, Ontario and Quebec. Although a decision in the BC case upheld the traditional definition of marriage, that decision was appealed. And courts in both Ontario and Quebec ruled against traditional marriage (Department of Justice 2002, 12).

Due to the increasing controversy over the definition of marriage, the House of Commons Standing Committee on Justice and Human Rights decided to hold hearings across the country on this issue and then form recommendations for the government. REAL Women made its presentation to the Committee on

February 12, 2003. As this brief made clear, "The promotion of homosexual marriage has little to do with expanded regard for marriage and everything to do with an attempt to gain social approval of same-sex unions" (REAL Women 2003, 13). And the implications of such a move were extremely serious.

> In short, claims for same-sex marriage not only demand a radical redefinition of marriage, but are predicated on a foundation of relativism that compels almost unlimited extension and virtually unrestricted restructuring of marriage as a legal and social unit. Marriage will then become just another socially created institution that can be shaped by the power-builders. By keeping the label and the legal status of marriage, but changing the meaning and concept, legalization of same-sex marriage necessarily involves rejection of what marriage means and has meant for millennia, replacing it with relativistic, post-modern extensions of private preference (choice) or personal intimacy (commitment) relationships. Thus, legalization of same-sex marriage entails a radical rejection of marriage by redefinition and replacement. If marriage means everything, and includes anything, it means nothing (REAL Women 2003, 15).

The Committee hearings proved to be a waste of time, since before the Committee could even write its report, the Ontario Court of Appeal struck down the traditional definition of marriage on June 10, 2003 in the *Halpern* decision. The *Halpern* case had originally been decided in favour of same-sex marriage in July 2002. However, in that decision the court gave the federal government a two-year period in which to change the law regarding marriage. The same-sex couples involved in the case appealed the decision (because they opposed the two-year delay), and the June 2003 ruling mandated that same-sex marriage be immediately valid within Ontario.

On June 17, 2003 Prime Minister Jean Chretien announced that his government would not appeal the *Halpern* decision. Instead, the government would introduce legislation authorizing same-sex marriage. Also, the government would seek a Reference from the Supreme Court of Canada to ensure that religious beliefs against marrying same-sex couples would be protected. The legislation was introduced on July 17, 2003 (*REALity* 2003b, 6).

It is interesting to note that on June 26, 2003, a number of the judges involved in the *Halpern* case celebrated their precedent-setting cases with homosexual rights advocates. The judges clearly saw themselves as part of the homosexual rights campaign and not impartial to the issues they were deciding (*REALity* 2003c, 8-9).

THE 2004 FEDERAL ELECTION

At this stage in the debate an election was called for June 2004. Shortly before the election was called, the Liberal Party had conducted "push polling" against evangelical Christians in Ontario. As the *National Post* put it,

Push polling is a technique for planting suggestions in the minds of voters under the guise of collecting their opinions. A pollster contracted by the Liberals was asking voters the sort of question cited above—specifically, whether they would be "more or less likely to vote for the Conservatives if you knew they had been taken over by evangelical Christians?" Such leading questions are intended as much to plant the idea that such a "takeover" has already occurred as to solicit people's voting preferences (*National Post* 2004).

Indeed, this poll "was clearly an attempt to demonize evangelicals in order to scare voters away from the Conservative party—

to incite religious bias for partisan gain" (*National Post* 2004).

During the campaign the Liberals, along with their media allies, continued the strategy of portraying the Conservatives as "scary." When the Conservative Health Critic suggested that counselling would be valuable for women contemplating abortion, a media chorus of condemnation erupted.

> *The Globe and Mail* considered this worthy of front page coverage in its June 1 edition. It then followed the abortion issue with story after story on the "intolerance" of the conservatives towards a woman's "choice" on abortion. The left-wing *Toronto Star* followed suit. The CBC was delirious with joy over this breakthrough on abortion, which naturally led to the CBC and the newspapers reporting on the Conservatives' other "scary" views on same-sex marriage, marijuana, and the recently passed homosexual hate crime amendment. This latter issue was deemed front-page news in the June 9th edition of *Globe and Mail* (*REALity* 2004c, 2).

Nevertheless, the Liberals lost their parliamentary majority and had to settle for a minority government under Prime Minister Paul Martin.

GAY MARRIAGE BATTLE RESUMES

The government did little to advance same-sex marriage legislation until the Supreme Court reference was handed down on December 9, 2004. The Court determined that the federal government had sole jurisdiction over who could marry in Canada, that the proposed same-sex marriage legislation was constitutional, and that churches did not have to marry same-sex couples. As a result, Bill C-38 was introduced in February 2005 to legalize same-sex marriage.

Four major pro-family organizations, REAL Women, CFAC, Campaign Life Coalition and the Catholic Civil Rights League formed the Defend Marriage Coalition to oppose the legislation. It would establish a website, distribute brochures and lawn signs promoting traditional marriage, purchase full-page ads in the *National Post*, rent a bus with the Defend Marriage logo, organize rallies supporting traditional marriage, and lobby MPs on the issue (*REALity* 2005a, 6).

Roy Beyer served as the Operations Director of the Coalition and Charles McVety was its Senior Director. According to McVety, the Coalition was quite active.

> As the president of Canada Family Action Coalition I have the privilege of talking with many leaders who fight for marriage and that is how the Defend Marriage Coalition was birthed. To date the Coalition has seen over 200,000 people attend approximately 300 prayer rallies. The largest rally, with over 20,000 in attendance, was held on Parliament Hill on April 9th, 2005. The Coalition has printed and distributed 1.4 million brochures in five languages. Ten full page advertisements have been displayed in *The Globe and Mail* and the National Post. Over 1 million telephone calls and hundreds of thousands of emails and faxes have been sent. A massive effort to save marriage has gone forth (McVety 2006, 4).

Besides the rallies, advertisements and such, Christian Right organizations also had the opportunity to present their views to the Legislative Committee on Bill C-38. REAL Women presented a brief on May 30. It provided considerable documentation demonstrating that homosexual relationships were inferior to committed heterosexual relationships and that same-sex unions were harmful to children. It also argued strongly that accepting same-sex marriage would ultimately lead to an unlimited extension of the concept of marriage (REAL Women 2005, 4-16).

Interestingly, the Minister of Justice, Irwin Cotler, had deceptively argued that same-sex marriage would not lead to an expansion of marriage to include other groupings just a few days earlier.

> In this regard, it was disingenuous of a Minister of Justice to argue in his testimony before this Committee on May 12, 2005 that polygamy, incest, etc. will not result from the passage of Bill C-38, since "bigamy and incest are criminal offences in Canada. That is the law of the land. That will not change." Perhaps Mr. Cotler believes Canadians are easily confused. It would be extraordinary if the government could make the revolutionary change in the definition of marriage, by opening it up to two "persons," but is incapable of making further amendments to the legislation at a later date. ... Does one not recall that, prior to 1969, all homosexual acts were deemed to be criminal acts contrary to the Criminal Code? This provision was subsequently amended. Further, the Criminal Code provisions on abortion, prostitution, pornography, etc., have all been amended over the years. What is a criminal offence today may well not be one tomorrow. It seems clear that the definition of marriage can and will also be changed to expand to other relationships (REAL Women 2005, 16).

Roy Beyer and Charles McVety were both able to speak to the Committee on June 9. McVety emphasized the threat to religious liberty posed by Bill C-38. As he stated to the Committee,

> If this bill does become law, remember that the law is universal. It is for everyone in the country; it is not just for a special interest. This law will be imposed on every single member of our society. We see this as clever legislation that attempts to ghettoize people of faith. We see this legislation as an attack on our freedom. We see this legislation as an attack on our right to participate in democracy. Currently

> we are already under attack, even though this has not even become law. I am the president of Canada Christian College. The Liberal Party discussed this at their caucus meeting and they came out with an attack on the charitable registration of our institution. If this becomes law, recognize the fact that under charity law, a charity cannot engage in activities to change the law. It is not the law yet, so charities can engage in these activities. But if it becomes law, charities will certainly be subverted (CC38-17, 5).

Roy Beyer's comments focused more on finding a "compromise solution" to the redefinition of marriage. He proposed legal recognition of same-sex relationships as "civil unions."

> When we discuss this, terminology is very important to people of faith. That's exactly why we need to seek a creative solution. Allow the definition of the word "marriage" – as they have in France – to remain as being a union between a man and a woman, whether it's for the purpose of producing future generations, or it has to do with religion. It's important to people to keep the word "marriage" as marriage, defined as being between a man and a woman. The term "civil union," in a separate category of relationships, can be used to provide exactly what it is that you want those unions to provide. Civil unions and marriage: this is the solution that would avoid the inevitable conflict with religious tradition (CC38-17, 13).

Here was the leading edge of the Christian Right in Canada offering a significant compromise on this issue.

Besides Beyer, McVety, and REAL Women, Tristan Emmanuel was a major leader in the opposition to same-sex marriage while this issue was before the House of Commons in 2005. The media recognized that he had become a significant player in the national debate. On June 13, 2005, he was the topic of a prominent article in *The Globe and Mail* as well as the topic of a feature on the Canadian Broadcasting Corporation's *The National* television newscast. Besides commenting on his influence in organizing opposition to same-sex marriage, *The Globe and Mail* piece described him as "an engaging, intelligent, charming, sincere man with unparalleled oratorical skills" (Valpy 2005). And *The National* feature concluded by stating, "this may not be the last you ever hear of him. He's already come a fair distance in a short time on the strength of his personality, his conviction, and the simple fact that the same-sex marriage issue may offer him something all politicians crave: the chance to broaden his base" (Boag 2005).

RESULTS OF THE SAME-SEX MARRIAGE FIGHT

In spite of the extensive work done by conservative Christians and others to oppose same-sex marriage, their efforts were not successful. On June 28 the House of Commons passed Bill C-38. The Senate passed the bill on July 19, and the following day it was signed into law by the Chief Justice of the Supreme Court of Canada. This was a major defeat.

The silver lining in it all, however, was a new vitality for the Christian Right in Canada. This was widely noticed by the media. One of the first articles appeared in the homosexual newspaper *Capital Xtra* (and subsequently reprinted in *REALity*) on July 14. It pointed out that the same-sex marriage debate had galvanized the Canadian Christian Right.

> A sleeping giant has been awoken by Canada's debate about same-sex civil marriage rights: the Christian right. Their engagement in the political arena threatens to change a lot in Canadian politics over the next generation. Perhaps—if we don't figure out how to deal with this—this emerging

> religious extremism will wreak the same havoc upon civil debate in this country as in the US, where religious extremists hijacked the Republican party and re-wrote the nation's agenda in biblical terms (Kirkby 2005, 3).

The article pointed out that new organizations were being created, such as a new think tank funded by Focus on the Family Canada, and the Institute for Canadian Values. It also pointed to the work of the ECP Centre.

> Christian conservatives are re-engaging in the political process. And many of them have found their leader in Tristan Emmanuel, an evangelical who founded, and now works full-time for, an organization called Equipping Christians For Public Life (Kirkby 2005, 4).

Basically, homosexual activists were being warned that they would be facing a much stronger opponent in future battles.

> The landscape of Canadian debate is being re-engineered by social conservatives on a scale we haven't experienced here for decades. US groups are setting up shop here and Canadian groups are adopting US-style confrontational activism (Kirkby 2005, 4).

Pollster and long-time political observer Allan Gregg also pointed to the growing power of conservative Christians in Canadian politics. He noted the activity of Tristan Emmanuel in organizing Christian activists to participate in Conservative Party candidate nominations.

> Emmanuel, the founder of the Equipping Christians for the Public Square Centre in southern Ontario, travels across Canada to spread the message that Jesus commands Christians to be politically engaged. These developments in Christian circles (to say nothing of those within other faiths) have

many voters and pundits calling for reinforcements to the "great wall" separating church and state (Gregg 2005, 21).

The *Western Standard* also focused on the new strength of Christian activism in a cover story in the fall of 2005. This article also featured Tristan Emmanuel prominently, quoting him as saying, "The sleeping giant is awake," referring to increased Christian activism as a result of the same-sex marriage debate. Like the *Capital Xtra* article, this one highlighted the side effects of the same-sex marriage fight.

> Ironic as it may be, the same-sex marriage law passed in June may have had the unintentional effect of rousing the Canadian religious right to become more allied and galvanized than ever. "The seeds are there: it's brought people together, it's made them vocal in a way they've never been vocal before, and it's helped bring a lot of relatively disparate groups together under one umbrella," says [Ipsos-Reid vice-president Andrew] Grenville. "The potential is there for this to be huge" (Johnson 2005, 38-39).

In December 2005 the Liberal minority government of Paul Martin lost a vote of confidence and a federal election was called for January. Some Christian Right leaders, such as Tristan Emmanuel and Charles McVety, strongly supported the Conservative Party. Conservative leader Stephen Harper had announced that he would revisit the same-sex marriage debate if elected. The Conservatives won a minority government.

Some people on the Left were very concerned that Canada's Christian Right would have considerable influence in the new government. This fear was most prominently displayed in a cover story in *The Walrus* magazine in October 2006. This article highlighted the role of Charles McVety, who it described as "the lightning rod of the Christian right" (McDonald 2006, 47). This article drew the attention of *Maclean's* columnist Paul Wells who refuted the claims of its author, Marci McDonald: "McDonald believes the Prime Minister is in the pocket of religious extremists. She fails quite spectacularly to prove it" (Wells 2006, 15).

In December 2006 Prime Minister Harper called a free vote in the House of Commons on whether to re-open the same-sex marriage debate. The vote went heavily against re-opening the debate, and Harper declared the issue closed. The way he handled this issue alienated some of the conservative Christians who had previously supported him.

AMERICAN INFLUENCE ON THE SAME-SEX MARRIAGE DEBATE

One of the claims made by some same-sex marriage supporters was that the American Christian Right was trying to influence Canadians to reject same-sex marriage. For example, there was the case of James Dobson, the American founder of Focus on the Family. In 2005, "Focus on the Family Canada bought time on 130 radio stations for an appeal from Dobson urging Canadian voters to contact their MPs and kill Bill C-38" (McDonald 2006, 52). It was alleged that Focus on the Family Canada was receiving hundreds of thousands of dollars a year from the US to influence Canadian politics.

However, the allegations about the American money were false. As the president of Focus on the Family Canada, Terence Rolston, explained,

> The financial support noted in the Focus on the Family U.S. annual report refers primarily to costs incurred in the U.S. from which Focus Canada benefits. These are services and not, as the stories suggest, a massive infusion of cash. Fur-

> ther, this annual support has been provided to us since our inception 22 years ago, long before gay marriage hit the airwaves in Canada. The services this support provides are related primarily to our radio broadcasts. Those broadcasts provide daily help for families dealing with subjects like strong-willed children, family health, faith and from time-to-time family policy (Rolston 2005).

Rolston also pointed out that Justice Minister Irwin Cotler took the allegations of American interference seriously enough that he said he would examine the issue and possibly do something to prevent foreign interests from influencing Canadian policy. But the fact is that American influence has been around for a long time.

> Americans and their political leaders have long exerted influence, both accidental and intentional, on Canadian debates. This is true on an ongoing basis in the Canadian environmental lobby, as well as questions on drug laws, terrorism, and the military. In fact, even EGALE Canada, a prominent advocate for same-sex marriage, openly acknowledges on its website the "generous support" of individuals from "across Canada and around the world" for donating to their cause (Rolston 2005).

Thus to suggest that the Christian Right was unique in receiving support from outside Canada was entirely false. There have been many instances where groups on the social Left in Canada have received American support.

THE GROWING NUMBER OF "HUMAN RIGHTS" CASES

By the late 1990s a number of Human Rights Commission cases as well as some court cases, were of serious concern to conservative Christians. Ken Campbell's experience has already been noted. In each case, homosexual activists were using agencies of the state to punish Christians for their opposition to homosexuality.

Many of these cases are already familiar to conservative Christians in Canada. Scott Brockie was punished by the Ontario Human Rights Commission for refusing to print materials for the Canadian Lesbian and Gay Archives. London Mayor Dianne Haskett was punished by the Ontario Human Rights Commission for refusing to declare a gay pride proclamation. Hugh Owens faced a 10-year battle in the Saskatchewan Human Rights Commission and then the courts because he placed an ad in the *Saskatoon Star-Phoenix* in June 1997 expressing the Bible's opposition to homosexuality. Activist Bill Whatcott is still fighting in the courts of Saskatchewan as a result of anti-homosexual flyers he produced and distributed. And Trinity Western University in BC almost lost its ability to offer the final year of teacher training over its insistence on a student code of conduct that included a comprehensive ban on sexual activity outside of marriage, including homosexual relations.

As this book is going to print, Alberta pastor Stephen Boissoin is in the midst of a very serious "human rights" case for writing a letter to the editor of Red Deer's daily newspaper opposing homosexuality. And at one Calgary meeting held to support him, homosexual rights activists calling themselves the "Gay Militia" forcefully disrupted the meeting. The meeting was held by the Concerned Christian Coalition, and the speaker for the event was Tristan Emmanuel (*The Interim* staff 2004, 1).

BC teacher Chris Kempling has had his teaching license suspended for writing letters to the editor of the *Cariboo Observer* expressing opposition to homosexuality. At least one of the complaints levelled against Kempling was for comments he made as a representative of a political party, the Christian Heritage Party.

The Catholic bishop of Calgary, Fred Henry, was investigated by the Alberta Human Rights Commission for a pastoral letter he wrote in January 2005 opposing Bill C-38. Previously, in June 2004, the Canada Customs and Revenue Agency had threatened "to revoke the charitable status of the Roman Catholic Diocese of Calgary if Bishop Fred Henry did not withdraw a pastoral letter that criticized Prime Minister Martin for professing to uphold the Catholic faith while flouting the teaching of the Church on vital moral issues like abortion and gay marriage" (Leishman 2006, 192).

Besides agencies of the state like human rights commissions, some conservative Christian organizations have also had run-ins with the Canadian Broadcast Standards Council (CBSC), a voluntary association of broadcasters that practices self-regulation. In 1997, an episode of the Focus on the Family radio show was deemed by the CBSC to have violated the Canadian Association of Broadcasters (CAB) Code of Ethics due to its criticism of aspects of the homosexual rights movement. The Laura Schlessinger Show received the same judgment in 2000 for an episode that had criticized homosexual behaviour (Grace 2000, 18-19). And an episode of the television program *John Hagee Today* which was broadcast in September 2004, was ruled in 2005 to have violated the CAB Code of Ethics for negative comments Rev. Hagee made about homosexuals. To be fair, the CBSC has also dismissed some other complaints against conservative broadcasts as unfounded.

CONCLUSION

From the perspective of the Christian Right in Canada, the first few years of the new millennium have been rather depressing. The bright light of Stockwell Day's leadership fizzled quickly due to party infighting. Homosexual activists have been very effective through the use of "human rights" commissions and tightening the criminal law to restrict opposition to their lifestyle. And then, to top it all off, the federal government determined that restricting marriage to heterosexual couples constituted discrimination, or worse.

From this perspective, the future looks bleak for the Christian Right in Canada. But this is not the correct perspective from which to make a judgment about the future. The "lifestyle" encoded in the Ten Commandments (thou shalt not kill, thou shalt not commit adultery, etc.) is the lifestyle most conducive to the thriving and flourishing of the human race. Living honestly, non-violently, with married couples in a life-long mutual commitment (and no sexual activity of any kind outside of marriage) leads to physical, mental and social health. Naturally, this lifestyle conflicts with the dominant modern notion of "sexual freedom" practiced by homosexuals and heterosexuals alike.

But you reap what you sow, and modern Western societies are increasingly reaping the bitter fruits of the Sexual Revolution. These fruits sometimes include physical and mental health problems, as well as decreasing population growth. Over time, the practitioners of sexual freedom will likely experience numerical and demographic decline, while on the other hand, those who reject the Sexual Revolution and live by the traditional code of the Ten Commandments are likely to thrive. This is the real hope and basis for optimism for the Christian Right.

REFERENCES

Boag, Keith. 2005. "Canada's Evangelical movement: political awakening." *The National* (CBC TV). June 13.

Bunner, Paul. 2000. "Stock Mania." *The Report*. July 24: 10-17.

Campbell, Ken. 2004. *Not You But Your Father*. Tumbler Ridge, BC: Coronation Publications.

Department of Justice Canada. 2002. *Marriage and Legal Recognition of Same-sex Unions: A Discussion Paper*. Ottawa: Department of Justice Canada.

Emmanuel, Tristan. 2003. *Christophobia: The Real Reason Behind Hate Crime Legislation*. Jordan, ON: Freedom Press (Canada) Inc.

Emmanuel, Tristan. 2007. "Personal interview." Edmonton, May 31.

Geddes, John. 2000. "New Might on the Right." *Maclean's*. September 11: 18-23.

Grace, Kevin Michael. 2000. "When in doubt, censor." *The Report*. June 5: 18-22.

Gregg, Allan. 2005. "The Christian Comeback." *Saturday Night*. November: 21-22.

Gunter, Lorne. 1992. "The family re-asserts itself." *Alberta Report*. July 6: 36-40.

Harrison, Trevor. 2002. *Requiem for a Lightweight: Stockwell Day and Image Politics*. Montreal: Black Rose Books.

Hoover, Dennis R. 2000. "A Religious Right Arrives in Canada." *Religion in the News*. Summer. Vol. 3, No. 2.

Hoy, Claire. 2000. *Stockwell Day: His Life and Politics*. Toronto: Stoddart Publishing Co. Ltd.

Interim Staff. 2004. "'Gay militia' attacks Christian activists meeting." *The Interim*. May: 1, 3.

Johnson, Tim. 2005. "Onward Christian Voters." *Western Standard*. October 17: 33-39.

Kirkby, Gareth. 2005. "Christian Right Sets Up Shop." *REALity*. July/August: 3-4.

Landolt, C. Gwendolyn. 1999. "Upholding the Integrity Of Traditional Marriage." REAL Women of Canada.

Landolt, C. Gwendolyn. 2002. "Closing Down Public Debate on the Homosexual Issue." Ottawa: REAL Women of Canada.

Law Commission of Canada. 2001. *Beyond Conjugality: Recognizing and supporting close personal adult relationships*. Ottawa: Law Commission of Canada.

Leishman, Rory. 2006. *Against Judicial Activism: The Decline of Freedom and Democracy in Canada*. Montreal & Kingston: McGill-Queen's University Press.

McDonald, Marci. 2006. "Stephen Harper and the Theo-cons." *The Walrus*. October: 44-61.

McVety, Charles. 2006. "The Government Changed the Definition of My Marriage." *Evangelical Christian Magazine*. November/December: 4-5.

McVety, Charles. 2007. Telephone Interview. June 22.

National Post. 2004. "Stop Christian-Bashing." May 15.

REAL Women of Canada. 2003. *Brief on the Study on marriage and the legal recognition of Same-sex unions*. Ottawa: REAL Women of Canada.

REAL Women of Canada. 2003. *Brief on Bill C-250 An Act to amend the Criminal Code (hate propaganda)*. Ottawa: REAL Women of Canada.

REAL Women of Canada. 2005. *Brief on Bill C-38, An Act respecting certain aspects of legal capacity for marriage for civil purposes*. Ottawa: REAL Women of Canada.

REAL Women of Canada, Catholic Civil Rights League, Canada Family Action Coalition. 1999. "A Suggested Approach by the Government of Ontario to the Supreme Court of Canada Decision in M v. H."

REALity. 1999a. "M and H: A Tale of Judicial Prejudice." May/June: 1-4.

REALity. 1999b. "Parliament Upholds Traditional Marriage." July/August: 1-2.

REALity. 2003a. "A Report on Svend Robinson's Hate Bill (Bill C-250)." March/April: 7-10.

REALity. 2003b. "The Sordid Story of How the Same-Sex Marriage Issue Was Manipulated in Canada." July/August: 4-7.

REALity. 2003c. "Judges Party With Homosexual Activists." July/August: 8-9.

REALity. 2003d. "Manipulation and Deceit Gives New Life to Bill C-250 (Amendment to Hate Propaganda Provision)." September/October: 1-4.

REALity. 2004a. "Update on Bill C-250." March/April: 6.

REALity. 2004b. "Bill C-250 The Battle Finally Over." May/June: 7-8.

REALity. 2004c. "The Bizarre 2004 Federal Election." July/August: 1-2.

REALity. 2005. "Pro-Family Groups in Canada Organize Against the Anti-Marriage Bill C-38." March/April: 6.

Rogusky, Derek, and Frank Stirk. 2000. "In Name Only." *Citizen*. February: 1-3.

Rolston, Terence. 2005. "Distorting U.S. Role in Canadian Debate." *Vancouver Sun*. February 10.

Spencer, Larry D. 2006. *Sacrificed? Truth or Politics*. Regina, SK KayteeBella Productions.

Stock, Peter. 2002. "Just trust me, says Svend." *The Report*. December 2: 9.

Valpy, Michael. 2005. "Spreading the gospel of political evangelism." *Globe and Mail*. June 13.

Wells, Paul. 2006. "Well, so much for the power of God." *Maclean's*. October 2: 15.

CHAPTER 8 | HUMAN FLOURISHING THROUGH TRADITIONAL FAMILY LIFE

Human beings flourish and thrive when their lifestyles lead to mental, physical and social health. Many unavoidable events occur throughout our lives that reduce health, such as accidents and illnesses. These are common to all people. But there is also a "cause-effect" relationship in terms of health. There are ways of living that are demonstrably less healthy than other ways of living; smoking or drinking to excess, for example, have demonstrable and unquestioned negative health effects. So it is no exaggeration to say that health can be significantly affected by a person's lifestyle choices.

As Leon Kass puts it, "the claim is that health is at least in large part affected by or dependent upon virtue, that being well in body has much to do with living well, with good habits not only of body but of life" (Kass 1985, 175). A large body of social science research has been accumulating over the last 30 years or so indicating that traditional family life is healthier than other ways of life. Yet it is this way of life that has been under attack since the sexual revolution began in the 1960s.

As the negative consequences of this revolution become increasingly apparent, there is reason to believe that many people will see the necessity and appeal of traditional family life. It will appear more and more obvious that traditional morality, the kind favoured by the Christian Right, is the surest path to human well-being.

Sexual freedom appeals to the base desires of human beings, but it does not lead to the good life. And this reality cannot be ignored forever.

THE SEXUAL REVOLUTION

All Western countries have been affected by the Sexual Revolution. As Australian Barry Maley writes, the 1960s "marked a turning point in Western civilization."

> The cry against repression in favour of sexual liberation has, in the name of freedom of expression, trumped all attempts at restraint and modesty and effected a transformation in values and sexual mores. This has penetrated deeply into the relations between men and women and into family life, not to speak of its often coarsening effects more generally – on ordinary language, for example. Those who resisted or complained, those who sought to defend the decorous and the restrained, were soon silenced by accusations of hypocrisy, conservatism, defence of capitalism and patriarchy, religious fundamentalism, a wish to censor, and sexual 'hang-ups' (Maley 2001, 41).

It's interesting to note that many of the most important leaders of the Sexual Revolution, such as Margaret Mead, Hugh Hefner, and Alfred Kinsey, were Americans. Writing from the perspective of his own country Maley states,

As America became the cultural leader of the English-speaking world, the intellectual content and practice of the sexual and cultural revolution in Australia were almost wholly derived from American models or from European originals filtered through the United States (Maley 2001, 44).

There's little doubt that much the same can be said about the source of the Sexual Revolution in English Canada: it came from the USA. The idea that homosexuality has some sort of special place in "Canadian values" simply isn't supported by either fact or history. The Sexual Revolution, and the Hollywood machine that spends much effort in exporting the Sexual Revolution around the world, was not Canadian in origin. Yet somehow the behaviours associated with an American and European inspired cultural revolution are trumpeted by the social Left in Canada as being an important component of "Canadian values." For these people, when it comes to sexual mores, "Canadian values" = "Hollywood values." How "Canadian" is that?

The Sexual Revolution was a major factor in the cultural attack on the traditional family that has been underway for the last four decades or so. It is a root cause of many of the social ills that currently plague Canada and the other Western nations: pornography, unplanned pregnancies that lead to abortion, the spread of sexually transmitted diseases including HIV/AIDS, promiscuity, the popularity of homosexuality, and other such things. The Sexual Revolution has undermined the most healthy way of life in favour of other inferior, and self-centered, lifestyles.

MARRIAGE

By the 1970s the view that marriage was particularly bad for women was gaining steam. Sociologist Jesse Bernard argued that marriage damaged the emotional and psychological health of women, while at the same time benefiting men. Marriage was good for men and bad for women. This view was widely accepted in some segments of society. And it helped to undermine marriage (Waite and Gallagher 2000, 161-162).

But the substantial amount of social science research conducted since the 1970s disproves that view. This research has been summarized by Linda Waite and Maggie Gallagher in the book *The Case for Marriage*. Men do benefit from marriage, of course. But women also benefit greatly from the institution. It's a win-win situation. Married women (and men) are happier, healthier, more satisfied, safer and better off financially than those who are single or merely cohabit. Waite and Gallagher point out that "virtually every study of happiness that has ever been done has found that married men and women are happier than singles. The happiness advantage of married people is very large and quite similar for men and women and appears in every country on which we have information" (Waite and Gallagher 2000, 168).

Waite and Gallagher summarize many of their conclusions as follows:

> Both married men and women live longer, healthier lives, but in this measure men need marriage more. Mortality rates were higher for the unmarried of both sexes, but 50 percent higher among women and 250 percent among men. The relatively unhealthy lives of single men, compared to those of single women, seem to explain the gender gap in marriage benefits here. When it comes to money, marriage makes both men and women better off. Men get larger gains in earning power than do women, who get only a small marriage premium at most. But then married men, unlike single men, share their incomes with their families, raising

the household income of their wives and children. So although both men and women gain from marriage, overall, women gain even more financially from marriage than men do. When it comes to sex and sexual satisfaction, once again both husbands and wives are better off because they dared to say, "I do." But as for sex, contrary to the popular stereotypes, women seem to benefit even more from marriage itself than men do. Single women are far less likely to have any sex at all, and far less likely to enjoy it when they do, than married women. . . And we saw ... that marriage provides some protection for women from domestic violence, at least compared to women in cohabiting relationships. Both husbands and wives are less likely to be victims of criminal violence than unmarried men and women (Waite and Gallagher 2000, 170).

Traditional marriage is beneficial for both parties. And this form of family, the traditional family, is also the best lifestyle for children as well.

EFFECTS ON CHILDREN

Over the last 30 years or more, there has been a growing body of research on the societal impact of sexual behaviour and family forms. Generally speaking, among social scientists, there have been those who have been concerned about the decline of the traditional family and those who have been optimistic about that change. These latter researchers, in fact, do not see a "decline" in the family as such. They just believe that the family is changing forms—that there is an increase in the diversity of family forms.

While there are good reasons not to place too much weight on social science research (it's certainly not precise like natural science research, for example), the accumulation of evidence over the last 3 decades has been pointing in a direction indicating the superiority of the traditional family over every other family form. Looking at the research results alone, there is little doubt that, generally speaking, children thrive to a greater degree within traditional family settings than other family settings.

The preponderance of evidence on this point is so clear that "family scholars" (academics who specialize in studying the family) have increasingly been adopting the view that the traditional family is best for children. Years earlier there was less agreement on this point. But the weight of the accumulating evidence has pushed many family scholars to reassess their previous views that did not attribute much importance to the traditional family form.

The growing awareness among family scholars of the importance of the traditional family for children's well-being has been indicated in a recent study entitled *The Shift: Scholarly Views of Family Structure Effects on Children, 1977-2002* by Norval Glenn and Thomas Sylvester. Glenn and Sylvester examined every article in the *Journal of Marriage and Family* (the most influential academic journal on family social science in the world) to identify those that discussed the effects of family structure on children. These articles were then categorized and rated based on the kind of study they represented and the conclusions they reached on the effects of family structure.

Basically, Glenn and Sylvester found that from the late 1970s to the mid-1980s, there was a shift in views from the more optimistic perspective of "family diversity" towards a more concerned view, a stance which was decidedly more conservative and reflective of the "traditional family". The research over that time had (in some cases at least) demonstrated the superiority of the traditional family over other family forms in terms of their effects upon children. Interestingly, this shift occurred despite the fact that a "large majority of family scholars are politically liberal" (Glenn and Sylvester 2006, 7). Scholars who are not ideologically predisposed to support the traditional family can nevertheless be convinced of its superiority over other family forms as a result of the accumulating social science research.

In sum, the "preponderance" of social science research currently "indicates that family structure matters, and matters to an important degree, for children" (Glenn and Sylvester 2006, 12). Not only that, but one family structure is superior to the others; "children who grow up in non-traditional families clearly do not fare as well on the average as children raised with both biological or adoptive parents" (Glenn and Sylvester 2006, 11).

Another recent study, *Family Matters: Family Structure and Child Outcomes*, summarizes much of the recent research on the issue. The unavoidable conclusion is that "recent research suggests that the effect of non-traditional family structure on children's academic and social development is negative and significant" (Schneider et at 2005, 9). Whether one looks at preschool, elementary, or secondary education, children from non-traditional families fare on average below those from traditional families. They are also more likely to engage in misbehaviour at school, more likely to smoke, more likely to use alcohol and illegal drugs, be sexually active and have trouble with the law than children from traditional families. "Research indicates that most children in non-intact families are at an educational and social disadvantage compared to children in traditional families" (Schneider et al 2005, 27).

COHABITATION

In contrast to marriage and the traditional family, cohabitation or "living together" without marriage is a significantly inferior way of life. The research on this issue has been summarized by David Popenoe and Barbara Dafoe Whitehead in a study entitled *Should We Live Together?* As they point out, women are the big losers in this kind of relationship.

> Annual rates of depression among cohabiting couples are more than three times what they are among married couples. And women in cohabiting relationships are more likely than married women to suffer physical and sexual abuse. Some research has shown that aggression is at least twice as common among cohabiters as it is among married partners. Two studies, one in Canada and the other in the United States, found that women in cohabiting relationships are about nine times more likely to be killed by their partner than are women in marital relationships (Popenoe and Whitehead 2002, 7).

Yet it is likely that children are the biggest losers in this popular new form of family arrangement.

> Children need and should have parents who are committed to staying together over the long term. Cohabiting parents break up at a much higher rate than married parents and the effects of breakup can be devastating and often long lasting. Moreover, children living in cohabiting unions with stepfathers or mother's boyfriends are at a higher risk of sexual abuse and physical violence, including lethal violence, than are children living with married biological parents (Popenoe and Whitehead 2002, 2).

Basically, the research about cohabitation can be summarized as follows:

> Living together before marriage increases the risk of breaking up after marriage.
> Living together outside of marriage increases the risk of

domestic violence for women, and the risk of physical and sexual abuse for children.

Unmarried couples have lower levels of happiness and well-being than married couples (Popenoe and Whitehead 2002, 1).

EFFECTS OF DIVORCE

Judith Wallerstein is perhaps the foremost authority on the effects of divorce in the world. She has conducted the most comprehensive study on the effects of divorce to date. When she began her study in the 1970s, she was optimistic about the children of divorce, expecting them to overcome the experience. But as she learned, such was not the case.

> Children in postdivorce families do not, on the whole, look happier, healthier, or more adjusted even if one or both parents are happier. National studies show that children from divorced and remarried families are more aggressive toward their parents and teachers. They experience more depression, have more learning difficulties, and suffer from more problems with peers than children from intact families. Children from divorced and remarried families are two to three times more likely to be referred for psychological help at school than their peers from intact families. More of them end up in mental health clinics and hospital settings. There is earlier sexual activity, more children born out of wedlock, less marriage, and more divorce. Numerous studies show that adult children of divorce have more psychological problems than those raised in intact marriages (Wallerstein et al 2000, xxix).

Children are better off with their mother and father, together. "Only the presence of their two biological parents seems to provide the stability most children need during their formative years" (Robertson 2002, 6).

EFFECTS OF DAYCARE

The widespread use of daycare as a substitute for maternal care for the last 30 years or so has provided more evidence for the superiority of the traditional family. Although the research in this area is still disputed and controversial, there is an increasing preponderance of evidence which shows that children are better off when cared for by their mothers rather than by strangers in an institutionalized context.

For one thing, children who are regularly in daycare are notably more likely to get sick. Mary Eberstadt writes that there are "three rather obvious reasons" why this is so.

> First, infants in full-time care are almost certainly not being breast-fed, or not much at any rate, so the immunological benefits of human milk are not being supplied to them. This raises the risks of their contracting ailments no matter where they are. Second, certain specific things about babies and toddlers, such as diaper-wearing and constant hand-to-mouth contact, make them germ carriers beyond compare, especially germs transmitted by saliva or feces. Third, the sheer number of children encountered every day in such institutions—which is far higher than for children at home even in large families—further and dramatically raises the likelihood of infection. It is like playing pathogen roulette with five bullets instead of two (Eberstadt 2004, 5).

Aside from the health problems, daycare is also associated with increased belligerence and aggressiveness among children. This is likely because the children are not happy. They would rather be with their mothers (Eberstadt 2004, 8, 12). "In sum, the evidence that daycare is bad for children (both long- and short-term) is massive and is growing" (Robertson 2002, 28-29).

HOMOSEXUALITY

All human beings would agree that health is a good thing, be it physical or mental health. It seems reasonable to conclude, then, that patterns of behaviour that contribute to good health are superior to patterns of behaviour that do not. As a result, we are able to make rational judgments about certain behaviours, and even label some "good" and others "bad." Since "the degree of health one enjoys in both body and soul is a consequence largely of how one lives, one may speak realistically and knowingly of a healthy way of life, one which is to that extent a good way of life, one productive of comprehensive good health" (Craig 1994, 332). Simply put, some lifestyles are good for you, and others are not.

Homosexuality is not a way of life that contributes to health and the flourishing of the human condition. Various sex acts involved in homosexuality are extremely unhealthy and contribute to high rates of sexually transmitted diseases among homosexuals. It's worth mentioning, too, that sex also becomes potentially unhealthy to sexually promiscuous heterosexuals. Nevertheless, homosexuality is inherently unhealthy and there is considerable empirical evidence to this effect.

Those who are unwilling to accept the fact that homosexuality is an unhealthy lifestyle will certainly not be convinced by the considerable evidence to that effect. But homosexuality cannot contribute to human flourishing in the way that monogamous heterosexuality can. "To present the homosexual 'lifestyle' on a par with family life is as remarkable and reprehensible as to present cigarette smoking on a par with eating vegetables, given what we know about the relation between smoking and lung cancer" (Palm 1994, 11).

Besides basic physical health, there is also evidence of high rates of mental health problems among homosexuals. Some homosexual activists claim that the mental health problems are the result of homophobia and society's unwillingness to accept homosexuality as normal. This assertion is not supported by the evidence.

> An extensive study in the Netherlands undermines the assumption that homophobia is the cause of increased psychiatric illness among gays and lesbians. The Dutch have been considerably more accepting of same-sex relationships than other Western countries—in fact, same-sex couples now have the legal right to marry in the Netherlands. So a high rate of psychiatric disease associated with homosexual behaviour in the Netherlands means that the psychiatric disease cannot so easily be attributed to social rejection and homophobia. The Dutch study, published in the Archives of General Psychiatry, did indeed find a high rate of psychiatric disease associated with same-sex sex. Compared to controls who had no homosexual experience in the 12 months prior to the interview, males who had any homosexual contact within that time period were much more likely to experience major depression, bipolar disorder, panic disorder, agoraphobia and obsessive compulsive disorder. Females with any homosexual contact within the previous 12 months were more often diagnosed with major depression, social phobia or alcohol dependence. In fact, those with a history of homosexual contact had higher rates of nearly all psychiatric pathologies measured in the study. The researchers found "that homosexuality is not only associated with mental health problems during adolescence and early adulthood, as has been suggested, but also in later life." Researchers actually fear that methodological features of "the study might underestimate the differences between homosexual and heterosexual people." (Diggs 2002, 6-7).

Despite the current cultural acceptance and even popularity of homosexuality, it is not a healthy way to live. It is a lifestyle with serious physical and psychological drawbacks. When the smoke of propaganda clears, the widespread acceptance and popularity of homosexuality will decline. It will lose its lustre.

REASONS FOR OPTIMISM

The effects of the Sexual Revolution are uniformly bad. Some people may enjoy a kind of "freedom" for a while, sowing their wild oats, but this cannot be the basis for the good life or human flourishing. Western societies are being devastated by the selfish pursuit of sexual pleasure. As Maley rightly observes,

> The promise, as with all revolutions, was emancipation from illusion and oppression in the interests of human flourishing. The test of the merits of a revolution is its fruits. For more and more children and couples the fruits of the 1960s revolution are bitter indeed (Maley 2001, 182).

Ironically, the worse this situation gets, the more likely people will be willing to look for a solution.

> It is precisely the growing realisation of the consequences for children and adults that gives hope. As the evidence of unhappiness, suffering, and wider social disorder accumulates, it becomes more and more difficult to ignore (Maley 2001, 206).

If some lifestyles are obviously unhealthy, and others obviously beneficial, over time people will likely acknowledge this situation and begin to choose the beneficial way. Reality cannot be ignored forever.

The reason for optimism is that there is a way of life that is life affirming and genuinely conducive to human flourishing, namely, the traditional family advocated by the Christian Right and others. This is the vision of two biological (or adoptive) parents committed to each other for life, raising their own children. It's also a vision that leads to more children, and this fact has demographic implications.

> [C]onservative Protestants who attend church weekly have stronger marriages and more children than the national average. Some have even suggested that we may be on the cusp of, or already engaged in, another Great Awakening, where America's reservoir of religious belief might refresh our culture again (Carlson 2007, 91-92).

In contrast to the traditional family are lifestyles that emphasize sex without pregnancy (i.e., without children), and abortion when pregnancy does result. Children are largely seen to be a burden and to be avoided. For those who do want children, often it's just one or two. And they are likely to be sent to daycare.

One side favours children and the other side largely tries to avoid children. Since "demography is destiny," there is reason for the Christian Right to be optimistic for the long-term. Those who believe in the traditional family will continue to have and raise children. Many of those who support the Sexual Revolution will have fewer progeny. It's very difficult for homosexuals to produce offspring, and feminists often see children as obstacles to their personal goals. From a demographic perspective, the lifestyle advocated by the Christian Right has a much brighter future. And the children raised by parents in traditional families also have a brighter future, as the social scientists tell us.

The life-affirming and child-affirming way of life is best for all concerned. This isn't just a conservative Christian "value judgment," it's the conclusion drawn from research by many family scholars. A kind of natural selection is at work, selecting the traditional family above the lifestyles promoted by the Sexual Revolution. Nature will run its course, favouring the traditional family and traditional morality. This is reason enough to be optimistic about the future for those in the Christian Right. It's a much better and surer hope than some sort of political success, however desirable that may be.

The future is bright. Hold the fort.

REFERENCES

Carlson, Allan. 2007. *Conjugal America: On the Public Purposes of Marriage*. New Brunswick, NJ: Transaction Publishers.

Craig, Leon Harold. 1994. *The War Lover: A Study of Plato's Republic*. Toronto: University of Toronto Press.

Diggs, John R. 2002. *The Health Risks of Gay Sex*. Scottsdale, AZ: Corporate Resource Council (a project of the Alliance Defense Fund).

Eberstadt, Mary. 2004. *Home-Alone America: The Hidden Toll of Day Care, Behavioral Drugs, and Other Parent Substitutes*. New York: Sentinel.

Glenn, Norval, and Thomas Sylvester. 2006. *The Shift: Scholarly Views of Family Structure Effects on Children, 1977-2002*. New York: Institute for American Values.

Kass, Leon R. 1985. *Toward a More Natural Science: Biology and Human Affairs*. New York: The Free Press.

Maley, Barry. 2001. *Family & Marriage in Australia*. St. Leonards, NSW: The Centre for Independent Studies.

Palm, Daniel C. 1994. *Homosexuality and Health: Some Public Health Facts That America's Children Are Not Getting*. Claremont, CA: The Claremont Institute.

Popenoe, David, and Barbara Dafoe Whitehead. 2002. *Should We Live Together? What Young Adults Need to Know about Cohabitation Before Marriage: A Comprehensive Review of Recent Research*. Piscataway, NJ: The National Marriage Project.

Robertson, Brian C. 2002. *Forced Labor: What's Wrong with Balancing Work and Family*. Dallas: Spence Publishing Company.

Schneider, Barbara, Allison Atteberry, and Ann Owens. 2005. *Family Matters: Family Structure and Child Outcomes*. Birmingham, AL: Alabama Policy Institute.

Waite, Linda J., and Maggie Gallagher. 2000. *The Case for Marriage: Why Married People Are Happier, Healthier, and Better Off Financially*. New York: Broadway Books.

Wallerstein, Judith S., Julia M. Lewis, and Sandra Blakeslee. 2000. *The Unexpected Legacy of Divorce: The 25 Year Landmark Study*. New York: Hyperion.

CHAPTER 9 | CONCLUSION

The Christian Right in Canada had its genesis in response to the Sexual Revolution of the 1960s, especially the legalization of abortion and the advance of homosexual rights. There were precursors to the Christian Right before then, especially associated with the Social Credit Party. But what is commonly thought of as the Christian Right in Canada largely began to take shape in the early 1970s. Thus, contrary to some claims in the popular press, the Christian Right did not first make its appearance in recent years – say, the late 1980's through to the time of the "gay marriage" debate. The historical record makes this an easy point to demonstrate.

The Christian Right in Canada has been, for the most part, a home-grown movement. The three people who have been most important to the movement historically, Rev. Ken Campbell, Ted Byfield, and Gwen Landolt, are all from Ontario (although Byfield made his name out West). To see the Christian Right in Canada as an American import or transplant is to entirely miss the mark. Certainly there have been occasional American influences through magazines, books, and visiting speakers, but exactly the same can be said about American influences on elements of the social Left such as the abortion rights and homosexual rights movements.

In fact, if American influence is truly a concern, it is the social Left which finds much of its inspiration from the United States. And ironically, this can be seen most clearly in the inspiration for and history of that supposed bastion of "Canadian values," the Charter of Rights and Freedoms.

For most of its history, 1867-1982, Canada had a constitution where civil rights and liberties were protected by "unwritten" constitutional conventions inherited from the United Kingdom. Although this form of rights protection was quite successful, some Canadians, especially intellectuals, found the American ideal of a constitutionally-entrenched "bill of rights" more attractive. Many people on the Left were quite taken with the liberal policy activism of the United States Supreme Court which began by the late 1950s under the leadership of Chief Justice Earl Warren.

Judicial activism of this sort was only possible through interpretations of the US Bill of Rights, and since Canada's 1960 Bill of Rights was just a piece of regular legislation rather than part of the Constitution, such activism was largely out of reach for Canadian judges. In order for Canada to have left-wing policies imposed by the courts, Canada would need a constitutionally-entrenched rights document. And it was with this hope in mind that many Canadian leftists supported the Charter of Rights and Freedoms (Cairns 1992, 22).

In adopting the Charter, Canada was shifting away from its primarily British-inspired type of Constitution, to a more American-inspired type of constitution. Seymour Martin Lipset, an internationally-renowned scholar, writes that "Perhaps the most important step that Canada has taken to Americanize itself—far greater in its implications than the signing of the free trade treaty—has been the incorporation into its constitution of a bill of rights, the Charter of Rights and Freedoms" (Lipset 1990, 225).

Similarly, University of Western Ontario law professor Robert Martin states that "The Charter is, culturally, historically, and ideologically, an American document" (Martin 1996, 11).

If people are concerned about American values being infused into Canadian policy-making, they need look no further than the Trudeau Constitution adopted in 1982. That was when so-called "Canadian values" were finally brought into Canada's constitution, direct from Washington DC, courtesy of the Canadian admirers of the US Supreme Court. In a very real sense, Canadian Christian Right activists have been fighting against the American-inspired values of Hollywood and the Sexual Revolution which have been enshrined in the Charter of Rights. These people are the true Canadian patriots.

Ultimately, the values involved on both sides of the culture war transcend national boundaries. The conflict between social conservatives and the social Left is found in all of the Western nations. It's not the "Canadian values" of the Left versus the "American values" of the Right, but traditional Western morality versus the perspective of the Sexual Revolution. It's a civilisational and cultural civil war.

This is a fight, really, over different ways of life for human beings. Which way of life is best? Is traditional morality oppressive and restrictive, holding people back from real enjoyment of their lives and true happiness? Many think so today. But as the walls of traditional morality have been broken down in favour of sexual freedom, it's becoming easier to see the price that is being paid. And it's often children paying the highest price. Clearly, the traditional family is the better way of life. And as such it is likely that people will return to this way of life at some point in the future. For these reasons – and because they serve the Lord of history – conservative Christians can and should be optimistic for the future.

REFERENCES

Cairns, Alan C. 1992. *Charter Versus Federalism: The Dilemmas of Constitutional Reform*. Kingston & Montreal: McGill-Queen's University Press.

Lipset, Seymour Martin. 1990. *Continental Divide: The Values and Institutions of the United States and Canada*. New York: Routledge.

Martin, Robert. 1996. "A Lament for British North America." In *Rethinking the Constitution: Perspectives on Canadian Constitutional Reform, Interpretation, and Theory*. Don Mills, ON: Oxford University Press.

CHAPTER 9 | AFTERWORD

The main issues that provoked the rise of the Christian Right in Canada—abortion and homosexual rights—continue to be newsworthy. As of this writing, Conservative MP Stephen Woodworth has a motion before the House of Commons which calls for the creation of a committee to study when human life begins. This motion is widely understood as being a not-so-subtle attempt to spark debate about abortion in Parliament.

Homosexual rights are now firmly entrenched in Canada. However, this issue is still in the news, often due to "anti-homophobia" initiatives in the schools. And due to sensitivity towards so-called "homophobia," some Christians have found it difficult to publicly advocate opposition to homosexuality without negative repercussions.

Despite the current dominance of pro-abortion and pro-homosexual views in the government and media, many people on the Left seem concerned about the continued viability of the Christian Right in Canada. Most concern focuses on the presence of

Christian influences in the Conservative government. The continued electoral success of the Conservative Party of Canada has undoubtedly led to a few federal policies being more socially conservative than what could be expected from a Liberal or NDP government. But it has not been any sort of triumph for the Christian Right in Canada, that's for sure. The Harper government poses no threat to current policies on abortion and homosexual rights.

Besides the Conservative government, there are a few other noteworthy developments involving the Canadian Christian Right in recent years. The growing public presence of Charles McVety and Faytene Kryskow; certain "human rights" cases; and, of course, Marci McDonald's book *The Armageddon Factor*, are all significant in this regard.

The Conservative Government

The election of Stephen Harper as Prime Minister in January, 2006, has been the cornerstone of left-wing fear-mongering about the threat to Canada posed by the Christian Right. The Liberal government of 1993-2006 under Prime Ministers Jean Chretien and Paul Martin had been strongly in favour of policies promoting homosexual rights and abortion. In the eyes of many leftists, the new Conservative government would try to repeal the various sexual and reproductive rights championed by the Liberals (and NDP, and Bloc Quebecois).

The Conservatives have implemented some social conservative policies. For example, the Liberal government's plan for a national child-care program was abandoned. Instead, a $1200 per year tax credit was implemented for each child under six years of age. The Law Commission of Canada, basically a federally-funded left-wing legal think tank, was abolished. Similarly, the

Court Challenges Program, a government-funded channel for financing left-wing court challenges, was ended. Status of Women Canada also had its budget reduced somewhat. "Although the Harper government's response fell short of disbanding Status of Women, its action left the organization significantly diminished as an agent of social change" (Warner 2010, 230).

Furthermore, the Harper government appointed conservative-leaning judges, such as David Brown who was appointed to the Ontario Superior Court in September 2006. Brown had represented social conservative groups in cases involving abortion and homosexual rights (Warner 2010, 233).

However, as will be seen below, the Harper government is clearly not carrying the ball for the Christian Right.

Charles McVety

Among Harper's Christian Right supporters has been Rev. Charles McVety, the President of Canada Christian College. McVety had been involved in attempts to get conservative Christians nominated as Conservative Party candidates for the 2006 federal election. The Conservatives appeared to want to maintain McVety's support after the election.

When federal Finance Minister Jim Flaherty presented his first budget in May 2006, McVety was his guest in the House of Commons VIP gallery. He had been drafted to help sell the government's child care policy—one that scuttled the Liberals' plan to provide a national child care program and replaced it with a tax break for families with children (Gruending 2011, 20).

McVety publicly claimed that he had a certain degree of influence in Harper's government. According to Dennis Gruending,

In April 2008, Reverend Charles McVety bragged that he had many friends among the Harper Conservatives who govern in Ottawa. During the week of April 14 of that year, he testified before the Senate banking committee in support of legislation that he said had been drafted partly as a result of his lobbying. This legislation, Bill C-10, proposed to deny tax credits to films that the government deemed offensive (Gruending 2011, 19).

Bill C-10 became too controversial for Harper and was dropped, much to McVety's chagrin.

McVety had more significant problems, though, when his television program Word TV was forced off Crossroads Television System (CTS) in 2010 by the Canadian Broadcast Standards Council (CBSC). Someone complained to the CBSC about comments McVety made on air about certain homosexual issues. McVety explains that after the complaint,

The Council held secret hearings, never notifying us to the charge. We were not given due process. They tried us without hearing from us. We were not represented in any way. We didn't even know the trial was taking place. Basic internationally recognized judicial rights were abandoned in their rush to judgment. Without notice, the CBSC sent out a press release to the media containing viscous, wrongful accusations against us on December 8th, 2010 followed by a 141 page report (McVety 2011, 8-9).

Anyway, less than two years later, in June, 2012, McVety was able to get his TV program on Vision TV under the name The Canadian Times.

Faytene Kryskow/ Grasseschi

In recent years one of the most prominent leaders of the Christian Right in Canada has been Faytene Kryskow (who would become Faytene Grasseschi in 2011 after marrying Robert John Grasseschi).

Faytene became a Christian in 1995. She relates this experience as follows:

> In 1995, when I accepted Jesus as my Lord, Redeemer, and Savior, so many things that had been out of alignment in my life straightened out in an instant. The things I had been running to for fulfillment—immoral relationships, earthly success, alcohol, and so forth—fell off of me as I received the washing of the Holy Spirit (Kryskow 2009, 117).

But it wasn't until 2005 that she took any interest in political affairs. The factor that changed her focus to politics was the debate over same-sex marriage. She was passionately opposed to same-sex marriage, so as a result, that issue triggered her desire to bring political change to Canada.

> If the truth be known, up to that point in 2005, though I had been a Christian for ten years already, in that time I had not voted in any municipal, provincial, or federal election. Even though I had a heart to change my world, I didn't realize the importance of faithfully accessing the tools of democracy right in front of me to change my nation (Kryskow 2009, 74).

With her new focus on political activism, in August, 2005, she organized a team of young adults who traveled from Vancouver to Ottawa over a ten day period, meeting with political leaders, as well as holding rallies at five provincial legislature buildings and six churches. Their activities were covered in the media. As Kryskow puts it, "The nation was taking notice, and it was exciting to see God back us up as we stepped out of our comfort zones in a big way" (Kryskow 2009, 134).

A few weeks after they arrived in Ottawa, the Liberal government fell in a vote of non-confidence. On January 23, 2006, a minority Conservative government was elected. Kryskow believed that this was very significant.

After 12 years of socially liberal rule, Canadians elected a new government made up of many Members of Parliament that held fast to socially conservative and biblical values on a variety of fronts. The leader of this party has been clear that he is a Christian. This admission was actually a really big deal. In my nation, where secular media is in the habit of demonizing anyone who professes faith in Christ, to admit such a thing would be thought of by some as political suicide (Kryskow 2009, 140-141).

In the fall of 2006, Kryskow moved to Ottawa from Vancouver to establish an office for her youth activism organization, 4MY Canada.

With the election of a Conservative government, Kryskow was hopeful that same-sex marriage could be overturned. However, when the government held a parliamentary free vote in December 2006 over whether to re-visit the same-sex marriage issue, a sizeable majority voted "no". Kryskow interpreted this event in spiritual terms: "It is my belief, that the initial legislation from the spring of 2005 opened a door in the spirit realm over our nation and gave sodomistic strongholds greater leverage and greater access over the mindsets of the citizens of Canada" (Kryskow 2009, 147).

Besides the same-sex marriage issue, Kryskow has been very concerned about abortion. She has worked to establish a way for prayer to be offered against abortion in Canada around the clock, a "24/7 prayer siege for life." Her organization was heavily involved in supporting Bill C-484, the Unborn Victims of Crime Bill. This bill, introduced as a private members bill by Conservative MP Ken Epp, would have offered legal protection for unborn children in cases where a "wanted child" was harmed or killed in the womb. Naturally, the idea of any sort of legal protection for unborn children enraged the pro-abortion crowd and also upset the Prime Minister, who ensured that the bill would fail.

Similarly, in December, 2010, Harper helped to torpedo Bill C-510. That bill, proposed by Conservative MP Rod Bruinooge, would have made it a crime to coerce a woman into getting an abortion.

Kryskow was also very interested in finding out about Canada's Christian heritage. Before much of her activism, she began to research Christian influences in Canadian history and discovered a lot of relevant material. Subsequently, she felt that the Lord would have her publish the results of her research. The resulting book, published in 2005, was entitled *Stand on Guard: A Prophetic Call and Research on the Righteous Foundations of Canada*. Copies were sent to every Canadian MP and Senator and to the Parliamentary Library.

> Within a matter of months, I was finding myself on national talk shows, addressing the nation and bringing awareness to our righteous history and foundations. It was wild. Even though we were self-distributing we sold thousands of copies. Within the year, the book was plastered all over the nation with no marketing agent other than Holy Spirit! According to the number that we have sold, had it been distributed on the main stream market, I am told it would be considered a best seller in Canada (Kryskow 2009, 181).

Undertaking the research for this book had a strong effect on Kryskow. As she puts it, "Through a series of visions, prophetic revelation, and research, I came to find that my nation had been covenanted to God at the foundation" (Kryskow 2009, 221). Canada had a distinct relationship with God that could be seen in aspects of the country's history which she had uncovered with her research.

> I had no idea of this history. These facts were not taught in our schools, and I could not remember even having ever heard a homily or sermon about this part of our nation's history. It was a hidden covenant, a buried inheritance, seemingly dormant in the history books, museums, and graveyards of our land. However, the life of God bound up in these promises was not dead. It was alive (Kryskow 2009, 222).

In the first few years of her 4MY Canada Association, Kryskow and her colleagues have been very active on Parliament hill meeting with politicians and lobbying on behalf of socially conservative legislation.

> During this time, we received audience with more Members of Parliament than any other organization in the nation—Christian or non. To date, we have had well over 300 sit-down meetings with MPs, Senators, and even the Prime Minister of Canada himself. Along with these accomplishments, we have had opportunity to speak into and influence (on a variety of levels) key legislation that will affect the moral and spiritual climate of our nation (Kryskow 2009, 206).

According to Kryskow, this degree of access is unprecedented.

> Never in the history of our nation has an organization with such a small budget—basically none—and such a low profile—we are not famous or political kids—received such favor and gained such influence in such a short period of time (Kryskow 2009, 207).

In Kryskow's view, a lot of progress has been made in advancing the Christian cause. As she puts it,

> I actually believe we are in the midst of the greatest moral turnaround that Canada, and perhaps the Western world, has ever seen. Why? I believe it is because God, in His sovereignty, has stirred His Church to begin to rise up and show up in the moral battlefields of our nation, and by His grace, we are responding to the call. Whether we call it discipling nations or something else, the truth is that we are starting to rise up and to do just that (Kryskow 2009, 258).

Kryskow's youthful and energetic appeal has attracted considerable support among the Charismatic wing of Canadian Christianity. She has quickly become one of the recognized leaders in Canada's Christian Right.

Stephen Boissoin and the Human Rights Commissions

In June, 2002, Stephen Boissoin had written a spirited letter-to-the-editor of the *Red Deer Advocate* opposing homosexual rights in Alberta. Boissoin was at that time the Central Alberta Chairman of the Concerned Christian Coalition (CCC), and identified himself as such in the letter. Dr. Darren Lund, a professor at the University of Calgary, filed a complaint against Boissoin and the CCC with the Alberta Human Rights Commission, alleging that the letter was "likely to expose a person or a class of persons to hatred or contempt," namely homosexuals, in violation of Alberta's Human Rights, Citizenship and Multiculturalism Act.

To make a long story short, Boissoin had to answer to a "human rights" Panel for his letter. The Panel consisted of one lawyer, Lori Andreachuk.

Boissoin's lawyer, Gerald Chipeur, engaged an internationally-respected political philosopher from the University of Calgary, Barry Cooper, to provide an expert opinion on the complaint against Boissoin. Cooper concluded that Boissoin's letter did not constitute an expression of hatred:

> It seems to me to be as clear as possible that Boissoin is engaged in political debate and in elaborating the grounds of his beliefs. It is also clear that, far from expressing hatred of homosexuals, he has expressed understanding and practiced compassion with respect to those whom he considers are suffering "an unwanted sexual identity crisis," and to those who are, at least metaphorically, "enslaved" to one or another kind of personal problem (Cooper 2005, 18).

Cooper's expert opinion was basically dismissed by the Human Rights Panel, i.e., Lori Andreachuk.

Andreachuk's ruling, issued on November 30, 2007, was based more on left-wing ideology than established evidence. After summarizing the testimony placed before her, she concluded as follows: "Having considered the matter in its entirety, the evidence and the case law, I find that the statements made by Mr. Boissoin and the CCC are likely to expose homosexuals to hatred and contempt due to their sexual preference" (2007 AHRC 11, 72). And, of course, this could not be allowed: "In this case, the publication's exposure of homosexuals to hatred and contempt trumps the freedom of speech afforded in the Charter" (2007 AHRC 11, 79).

A few months later, on May 30, 2008, she issued her so-called "remedy" in which she prohibited Boissoin and the CCC from ever again making "disparaging remarks" about homosexuals, as well as Lund or Lund's witnesses. Boissoin and the CCC were also ordered to make a written apology to Lund, to request the *Red Deer Advocate* to publish her Order and their apology, to pay Lund $5000 and to pay up to $2000 to one of Lund's witnesses for her expenses (2008 AHRC 6, 5-6).

Boissoin appealed Andreachuk's ruling to the Alberta Court of Queen's Bench. The Court of Queen's Bench ruling, issued on December 3, 2009, overturned Andreachuk's decision. In this ruling, Justice E.C. Wilson listed a long string of errors committed by Andreachuk that invalidated her conclusions and remedy: "In the result I am satisfied that the individual and cumulative errors committed by the Panel permit of little deference to her various findings of fact and/or application of the law to those facts. Her errors of law led her to incorrect conclusions. The panel's decision cannot stand" ([2009] ABQB 592, 26).

Furthermore, all the things that Andreachuk ordered Boissoin and the CCC to do were beyond her authority and completely invalid, even if her ruling had been correct (which it wasn't): "Accordingly, had the Panel correctly decided that the Appellant's letter violated the *Act,* all of the resultant remedies imposed were without legal foundation or beyond the authority granted by s. 32 of the *Act*. All remedies are, accordingly, set aside" ([2009] ABQB 592, 34).

In sum, Wilson's decision was a startling slap-down of Andreachuk's awful work, and a notable victory over the arbitrary powers of Alberta's Human Rights Commission. Unfortunately, Lund has appealed this decision so the danger has not yet passed.

To add context to this issue, it's interesting to note another case that the Alberta Human Rights Commission considered in 2003. A fellow named Quintin Johnson in Red Deer was looking through CDs at a local music store and came across a CD by a group called "Deicide." Deicide's album contained a song called "Kill the Christian". Part of the song basically goes like this, "Kill the Christian, kill the Christian, kill the Christian, kill the Christian, kill the Christian, kill the Christian, kill the Christian." The rest of the song contains phrases like "I will love watching you die." Anyway, this song clearly breathes hatred against Christians.

Quintin Johnson brought this matter to the Alberta's Human Rights Commission. A three-person Panel headed by Lori Andreachuk, the same person who ruled against Stephen Boissoin, looked into the matter. But in this case, Andreachuk took a very different direction: "It is the decision of this panel that there is very little likelihood of a representation to expose a person or class of persons to hatred or contempt in the context of this particular medium which is unlikely to be taken seriously or credibly by the target group" (Quintin Johnson 2003, 18). Boissoin's language was considerably milder than Deicide's, yet his was deemed to be "hate" and he was to be punished. Deicide's glorying in the murder of Christians was seen in an entirely different light, and not something the Commission needed to act upon. With this in mind it is easy to see why many Christians consider so-called "human rights" commissions to be biased against them.

Another "human rights" case was also directly relevant to the Christian Right. The Christian Heritage Party of Canada and the Skeena/Bulkley Valley Electoral District Association (EDA) of the Party reproduced on their websites a WorldNetDaily story about some scholarly articles written against homosexuality. In December, 2006, the Skeena/Bulkley Valley EDA received notice that a complaint had been filed against it with the Canadian Human Rights Commission (CHRC) for posting that article. The complaint was also filed against the Christian Heritage Party itself and the Party leader of the time, Ron Gray.

Ron Gray was willing to enter into mediation with the complainant (a homosexual activist in Edmonton), and communicated this to the CHRC. The Commission ignored Gray and declared that "both parties have refused mediation." To make a long story short, the CHRC determined that the complaints were unfounded and the matter was dropped. However, as Gray put it, the incompetence of the CHRC "cost me two and a half years and $51,000; and seriously impaired my service to the CHP during those years" (Gray 2011, 9).

Another case of potentially great significance concerns Christian activist William Whatcott. In 2001 and 2002 Whatcott had distributed anti-homosexual flyers to homes in Regina and Saskatoon. Several complaints were then filed against Whatcott with the Saskatchewan Human Rights Commission (SHRC) for engaging in speech that exposed homosexuals to hatred, ridicule, belittlement, or otherwise affronted their dignity. In 2005 the Saskatchewan Human Rights Tribunal ordered Whatcott to pay $17,500 to four complainants and also ordered him to stop distributing anti-homosexual flyers.

> Whatcott appealed the "human rights" ruling to Saskatchewan's Court of Queen's Bench which upheld the ruling in 2007. That decision was appealed to the Saskatchewan Court of Appeal which overturned the ruling in 2010. However, the SHRC then appealed the Court of Appeal decision to the Supreme Court of Canada. The case was heard before the Supreme Court on October 12, 2011. The Supreme Court's decision is expected later this year and will have a significant impact on the future of free speech in Canada (Tuns 2011, 6).

Human Rights Commissions aren't the only threats to conservative Christians who oppose homosexuality. As the culture in general has shifted into a more favourable stance towards homosexual rights, people with public profiles especially need to be careful about what they say.

On May 10, 2011, Damian Goddard, the on-air host for Rogers Sportsnet, sent out a message in support of traditional marriage on his personal Twitter account. Immediately, an avalanche of negative reactions to his tweet began. Shortly thereafter, he was fired from his job (Paddey, 2011, 18). It appears that the influence of the homosexual rights movement is now so extensive that even some private companies will not tolerate public support for traditional marriage from their employees.

Marci McDonald and *The Armageddon Factor*

From the perspective of the Christian Right, one of the most notable events in recent years was the publication of Marci McDonald's book *The Armageddon Factor: The Rise of Christian Nationalism in Canada* in May, 2010. McDonald sets out to warn Canadians that they will lose their rights and freedoms unless a rising conservative Christian political movement is exposed and halted.

> She had returned to Canada in 2002 after spending a few years in the United States and was shocked to discover that some Canadians were not in favour of gay rights. "Homegrown evangelical firebrands were emerging, spouting the same polarizing calls to the political barricades that I thought I had left behind in Washington" (McDonald 2010, 6). It would seem that in her view, support for homosexual rights leads naturally to societal harmony, whereas opposition to homosexual rights leads to polarization.

It is true, as she points out, that conservative Christians have gained influence in Ottawa since 2005, largely because the Conservative Party won the federal elections of 2006 and 2008 (not to mention 2011). There are some conservative Christian MPs in the Conservative Party, so when that party became the government it was inevitable that those Christians would gain influence. Also, some new Christian organizations have been formed since 2005, and they are having an impact. In this respect there is a grain of truth to McDonald's charge that conservative Christians are more influential now than a few years ago.

However, her thesis is grossly exaggerated. The federal government is not doing anything about the two policy areas of greatest concern to conservative Christians—abortion and homosexual rights. Indeed, Prime Minister Harper has publicly emphasized on a number of occasions his complete support for a "woman's right to choose." So, sadly, McDonald has nothing to worry about on these fronts.

Many conservative Christian activists are held up to scorn by McDonald as threats to Canadian democracy. McDonald wants to warn Canadians about a group she calls Christian nationalists, "a militant charismatic fringe with ties to Harper's Conservatives that has gained influence out of all proportion to its numerical heft" (McDonald 2010, 10). She then notes the central characteristic of this group: "What drives the growing Christian nationalist movement is its adherents' conviction that the end times foretold in the book of Revelation are at hand. Braced for an impending apocalypse, they feel impelled to ensure that Canada assumes a unique, scripturally ordained role in the final days before the Second Coming—and little else" (McDonald 2010, 11).

She has some rather nasty things to say about these Christian nationalists too. According to her, "Theirs is a dark and dangerous vision, one that brooks no dissent and requires the dismantling of key democratic institutions" (McDonald 2010, 359).

McDonald's book was heavily criticized by such notable commentators as Ezra Levant and David Frum. Much of this criticism appeared in the *National Post*. However, McDonald also received some criticism from people who were very sympathetic to her perspective.

Dennis Gruending, a one-time NDP MP, had many nice things to say about her book, but he had criticism as well. "McDonald's focus in the book," he wrote, "is both a strength and a considerable weakness." The strength is the detailed examination of numerous conservative groups. "The weakness is that McDonald spends much of her time and energy focusing on people who appear to be on the fringe, such as the custodian of the Big Valley Creation Science Museum in Alberta" (Gruending 2011, 34).

Gruending then adds the following criticism:

> The religious right is here and it is not going away. Further, it is not some alien force wholly transplanted from elsewhere, despite the significant American influence at work. We must learn to understand these people, many of them our neighbours or family members, and to engage them. On that score, unfortunately, the book comes up a bit short. One has the feeling that McDonald is examining a species that she describes well but does not really understand (Gruending 2011, 34).

Despite its shortcomings, McDonald's book is a thorough exploration of contemporary conservative Christian activism in Canada containing a considerable amount of meaningful information. Its appearance sparked widespread discussion about the Christian Right in Canada.

Other Developments

The Association for Reformed Political Action (ARPA) was founded in 2007 and hired Mark Penninga to be its Executive Director. Penninga assisted in the formation of numerous local ARPA groups in Ontario, Manitoba, Alberta and BC. ARPA has grown steadily, and in 2011 a young lawyer, André Schutten, was hired to be the Ontario Director and Legal Counsel. Also in 2011 this organization published a book entitled the *Christian Citizenship Guide: Christianity and Canadian Political Life*. ARPA's star is rising.

As mentioned earlier, Conservative MP Stephen Woodworth introduced a motion before the House of Commons which calls for the creation of a committee to study when human life begins. The official government view on this motion, as expressed by Chief Government Whip Gordon O'Connor, was adamant that no discussion of abortion should take place:

> As we know, Motion No. 312 is sponsored by a private member, not the government. I can confirm that as a member of the Conservative caucus for nearly eight years, the Prime Minister has been consistent with his position on abortion. As early as 2005 at the Montreal convention and in every federal election platform since, he has stated that the Conservative government will not support any legislation to regulate abortion (*House of Commons Debates* 2012).

Stephen Harper has held to the so-called "pro-choice" position throughout his public career, and he has never wavered on that point.

> Pro-life activists Mary Wagner and Linda Gibbons have been in-and-out of jail over the last few years. Mary Wagner's offense was entering abortuaries to dissuade women from having their babies aborted. Linda Gibbons has been protesting against abortion in locations where there are "temporary" injunctions against pro-life protests (Gosgnach and Jalsevac 2011, 8).

On a more positive note, recent years have seen an increasing presence of young women in pro-life leadership. Among the most notable of these are Andrea Mrozek, who is the Manager of Research and Communications at the Institute of Marriage and Family Canada (IMFC); Faye Sonier, legal counsel for the Evangelical Fellowship of Canada; and Stephanie Gray, the director of the Canadian Centre for Bio-ethical Reform (Newman 2011, 18-20).

Canada's National March for Life, an annual pro-life protest on Parliament Hill, has been increasing in size every year, and set a record in 2012 of about 19,500 attendants (Tuns 2012, 9). So there are some hopeful signs for those who desire to protect unborn children.

Conclusion

Like all social movements, the Christian Right in Canada changes over time as new groups and leaders emerge while others fade. Nevertheless, the issues that sparked the rise and growth of the Christian Right continue hold public attention. Despite setbacks and an immediate future that looks rather bleak, the traditional morality espoused by the Christian Right will ultimately prevail. The opposing perspective, which advocates lifestyles of impotent sexuality (homosexuality) or infertility (abortion), will not be able to sustain a society in the long-run.

REFERENCES:

Boissoin v. Lund, 2009 ABQB 592.

Cooper, Barry. 2005. "An Analysis of the Human Rights Complaint of Darren E. Lund against Stephen Boissoin." Calgary: Prepared fort Gerald Chipeur.

Gosgnach, Tony, and Steve Jalsevac. 2011. "Prosecutors seek 4-6 month jail sentence for Mary Wagner." *The Interim*. December: 8.

Gray, Ron. 2011. "The process is the punishment." *Reformed Perspective*. March: 7-10.

Gruending, Dennis. 2011. *Pulpit and Politics: Competing Religious Ideologies in Canadian Public Life*. Cochrane, AB: Kingsley Publishing.

House of Commons Debates. 2012. Volume 146, Number 111, April 26.

Kryskow, Faytene. 2005. *Stand on Guard: A Prophetic Call and Research on the Righteous Foundations of Canada*. Vancouver, BC: Credo Publishing.

Kryskow, Faytene. 2009. *Marked: A Generation of Dread Champions Rising To Shift Nations*. Shippensburg, PA: Destiny Image Publishers.

Lund v. Boissoin, 2007 AHRC 11.

Lund v. Boissoin, 2008 AHRC 6.

McDonald, Marci. 2010. *The Armageddon Factor: The Rise of Christian Nationalism in Canada*. Toronto: Random House Canada.

McVety, Charles. 2011. "Canadian Government Censors the Gospel." *Evangelical Christian*. November/December: 7-8.

Newman, Alex. 2011. "Young, Female—and Pro-Life." *Faith Today*. May/June: 18-21.

Paddey, Patricia. 2011. "Where is Free Speech Heading in Canada?" *Faith Today*. September/October: 18-22.

Quintin Johnson v. Music World Ltd., HMV Canada, and A.V.E. Entertainment (formerly known as Top forty Music), 2003 AHRC.

Tuns, Paul. 2011. "Freedom of religion, speech in hands of Supreme Court." *The Interim*. December: 6.

Tuns, Paul. 2012. "Record 19,500 at National March for Life." *The Interim*. June: 9-12.

Wagner, Michael. 2011. *Christian Citizenship Guide: Christianity and Canadian Political Life*. Lethbridge, AB: ARPA Canada.

Warner, Tom. 2010. *Losing Control: Canada's Social Conservatives in the Age of Rights*. Toronto: Between the Lines.